Robert Shipboy MacAdam (1808–95)

Dedicated with much affection and gratitude to
Mammy and Daddy from an ever-loving son.

Arthur John

Is tibhe fuil ná usice
'Blood is thicker than water'

Robert Shipboy MacAdam
(1808–95)

*His Life and Gaelic Proverb
Collection*

AJ Hughes

The Institute of Irish Studies
The Queen's University of Belfast
First published in 1998

First published in 1998
The Institute of Irish Studies
The Queen's University of Belfast

This book has received support from the Cultural Diversity
Programme of the Community Relations Council, which aims to
encourage acceptance and understanding of cultural diversity.
The views expressed do not necessarily reflect those of the
NI Community Relations Council.

British Library Cataloguing-in-Publication Data
A catalogue record for this book is available from the British Library.

ISBN 0 85389 698 4

Set in Bembo
Printed by W. & G. Baird Ltd, Antrim

Contents

Notes

Indexes

List of illustrations

We are grateful to Professor Richard Clarke, archivist at the Royal Victoria Hospital, Belfast, and Roy Yeats of the Belfast Harbour Commissioners for their help in sourcing the illustration on p 5, which is reproduced by kind permission of the Belfast Harbour Commissioners. The illustration on p 60 is reproduced by courtesy of the Deputy Keeper of the Records, the Public Record Office of Northern Ireland and L'Estrange & Brett, Belfast.

Acknowledgements

I should like to thank all those who have contributed in various ways to the production of this book. First and foremost to the Cultural Diversity Group, of the Community Relations Council for Northern Ireland for a subvention in aiding the costs of production. Thanks are also due to Ultach Trust (Iontaobhas Ultach) for its financial support in meeting some of the initial typing cost, kindly undertaken by Mrs Karen Rice. I should also like to acknowledge the staff of Special Collections, Main Library, Queen's University for their courtesy and co-operation and John Killen and the staff of the Linen Hall Library. A special word of thanks is due to Professor B Ó Buachalla whose magisterial scholarship in penning *I mBéal Feirste Cois Cuain* has been a constant source of personal knowledge and inspiration over the years.

It is also a pleasure to thank those friends and colleagues who have read and commented upon drafts of the text, especially Margaret McNulty and Catherine McColgan, both of the Institute of Irish Studies. Also Jonathan Bardon, Dr Colm Beckett, Dr John R Curran, Dr Ciarán Ó Duibhín, Micheál A Ó Murchú, Fionnuala Williams and Fiachra Mac Gabhann. For advice on languages other than Irish and English I should like to record the help received from the following staff from Queen's University: Dr Estelle Sheehan, Latin; Dr Isabel Torres, Hispanic Studies; and Ms Lynne Press, Department of Italian Language and Literature. For references and discussion I thank Professor Brian Walker, Director of the Institute of Irish Studies, the Queen's University Belfast and my colleagues there Dr Peter Collins, and Patrick McWilliams and Angélique Day of the Ordnance Survey Memoirs Project.

Any shortcomings or errors in this book must, of course, remain my sole responsibility.

AJ Hughes
Institute of Irish Studies, the Queen's University of Belfast, and
The Centre for Irish and Celtic Studies, University of Ulster at Coleraine

Preface

Robert Shipboy MacAdam (1808–95) was one of Belfast's most distinguished citizens. A successful Belfast industrialist, at a time when the city was undergoing its remarkable nineteenth-century expansion, he also contributed immeasurably to the arts, literature and intellectual pursuits in his native Ulster, and in Ireland as a whole through his involvement in organisations such as the Belfast Library and Society for Promoting Knowledge (now the Linen Hall Library), the Literary Society, the Belfast Natural History and Philosophical Society and his founding, in 1853, of the *Ulster Journal of Archaeology*.

He was a man of many interests and talents but one of his greatest passions was the Irish language and he championed its study and preservation with distinction and enthusiasm. In his early 20s he was secretary of the Ulster Gaelic Society, formed in 1830, and went on to become one of the leading collectors of Irish-language manuscripts, folklore, songs and proverbs. MacAdam was also a prime mover in the inclusion of a question on the Irish language in the 1851 census.

Following the decline of his business interests, from the mid 1860s onwards, and the death of many of his friends and contemporaries, MacAdam spent his later years in relative obscurity. It is only in recent decades that his achievements are beginning to be fully recognised and exposed.

As a teacher of Gaelic Studies (on one of the courses included on the part-time degree programme at the Institute of Continuing Education, Queen's University Belfast, and at Armagh) I have become aware of the limited amount of published material in English which is presently available on the role of individuals such as MacAdam, a Presbyterian, who had a deep involvement in the cultural life of Belfast during the late eighteenth and early nineteenth century. Irish readers will have benefited from Professor Breandán Ó Buachalla's seminal 1968 work *I mBéal Feirste Cois Cuain* 'Belfast by the Harbour', while those who can not read Irish will be served by recent works such as Pádraig Ó Snodaigh's *Hidden Ulster: Protestants and the*

Irish Language or Roger Blaney's recent work on *Presbyterians and the Irish Language*. These last two books fill the gap left by Ó Casaide's meritorius 1930 account, *The Irish Language in Belfast and County Down A.D. 1601–1850*, a source no longer in print.

The idea of this book, then, is twofold: first, to outline the part MacAdam, and others of his class and background, played in fostering Gaelic language, literature, folklore and music in late eighteenth and nineteenth-century Belfast; and second, to include a modern unified edition of MacAdam's *Six Hundred Gaelic Proverbs Collected in Ulster*. These proverbs first appeared in print between 1858 and 1862 in the *Ulster Journal of Archaeology* which was under his editorship at that time. A faithful reprint of this collection shows the extent of Robert MacAdam's scholarship and linguistic flair while, more importantly, it also allows the reader direct access to MacAdam's personal thoughts and opinions on the nature of language and society in the Ireland of his day.

Robert MacAdam (1808–95).

The Life and Times of Robert Shipboy MacAdam, 1808–95

Belfast: the emerging city

Robert MacAdam was born in Belfast in 1808 when, with a population of 20,000, it had yet to witness the remarkable expansion of population which occurred before the end of his life, when this prosperous and tidy town had become a large industrialised city. Although small by today's standards, the early nineteenth-century town had already evolved considerably from the urban centre,[1] which had been very much in the shade of Carrickfergus from the twelfth to the seventeenth centuries.[2]

In the medieval period Belfast was noted only for its small castle at a ford which marked the crossing point between the counties of Antrim and Down.[3] It developed slowly as a plantation town under the ownership of the Chichester family and by the seventeenth century Belfast had acquired a charter as a town. The surname MacAdam featured among the arrivals to the town during that period; the nineteenth-century historian, Benn, includes an account by a 'Captain John MacAdam' of the capture of Belfast by the Scotch in 1641.[4]

By the middle of the eighteenth century many of the townspeople of Belfast were complaining about the rundown nature of the town, which they felt was a result of the short leases and tenacies issued by the Chichester family (now the Earls of Donegall), whereby no obligation to carry out improvements was required. Around this time the Fifth Earl of Donegall granted new 99-year leases which, twinned with the eventual demise of the property holdings of the Chichester family, paved the way for the more rapid rise in population and industry in Belfast. Nevertheless, the conditions of some of the later leases granted by the Fifth Earl, which were considered as overbearing and excessive by some of his tenants, precipitated disturbances in Belfast and the surrounding rural hinterland by the 'Hearts of Steel', a movement of agrarian protesters. The assertion of rights by the Presbyterian middle classes, who challenged the monopolising stranglehold of the old Ascendancy, meant that 'Belfast had the reputation of being the most radical and seditious centre in Ireland'.[5] The new lease conditions and the consequent upsurge in industry saw Belfast's population expand from 8,500 in 1757 and 13,000 in 1782. Although, in a marginal note in the manuscript of his Irish dictionary, Robert MacAdam commented 'Belfast is not equal to Limerick in size',[6] the reputation of Belfast had been spreading as the nineteenth century wore on. One commentator wrote in 1833 in the *Dublin Penny Journal*: 'Of the other towns in Ireland, Cork is spirited and contains an intelligent and reading population; and the same remark applies to Limerick. But neither Limerick or Cork or Waterford can compare with Belfast'.[7]

The MacAdam family business: the Soho Foundry

Robert MacAdam was born into the enterprising and commercially successful middle-class Presbyterian community of Belfast, which was poised on the brink of phenomenal expansion. His father James MacAdam (1755–1821) was a hardware merchant who had a shop in Belfast and the young Robert Shipboy MacAdam bore the maiden surname of his mother Jane Shipboy (1774–1827), a native of Coleraine in Co Derry. An obituary published in the year of his death, 1895, stated that:

> Robert Shipboy MacAdam was born in Belfast in 1808, at his father's residence in High St., two doors from Bridge St., on the Castle Place side. He was educated at the Royal Academical Institution, and early in life entered his father's hardware business.[8]

On the death of James MacAdam Senior, his sons James (1801–61) and Robert continued and developed the family's commercial interests.[9] Thanks to the MacAdam brothers' joint endeavours business improved briskly.

By 1833 they were able to move from High Street[10] to a private residence in what was steadily becoming a more select area of town, 18 College Square East. Around 1834 they established the Soho Foundry with other business associates.[11] It eventually employed more than 250 workers producing a variety of iron products and turbine engines. The MacAdam brothers were to

James MacAdam (1801–61).

the fore in recognising a niche for such a foundry to supply the
needs of emerging industries:

> The textile trade brought in its wake a need for iron-foundries
> primarily to supply textile machinery. The first opened in 1792;
> a number of others over the next few years. Macadam's Soho
> Foundry, opened in Townsend Street about 1834, is still partly
> standing; the street front is another of the vernacular classical
> style. It has a simple monumental brick façade, designed to
> impress with the strength and solidity of the manufacture. The
> lower windows to the street are blank, the upper ones heavily
> pedimented, all admirably proportioned. The gateway is flanked
> by enormous (and very practical) iron bollards. Later on this fac-
> tory participated in the boom in prefabricated ironwork; and in
> 1849 exported to Cairo a set of large cast-iron windows for the
> palace of an Egyptian prince.[12]

Colm Beckett notes that the turbo engines produced in the
Soho Foundry won prizes at trade shows and were much talked
of in engineering circles. One of these engines, manufactured in
the Soho Foundry continued to operate in the Cogry Flax and
Spinning Company, in Doagh, Co Antrim until 1974, while
another functioned until the late 1960s in Spicer's paper mill in
Cattleshall, Surrey. This latter turbine is now preserved as an
exhibit in a museum run by the Surrey Archaeological Society.[13]

Dr James MacDonnell (1763–1845)

One of the most influential figures in Robert MacAdam's life
was Dr James MacDonnell, who also happened to be one of the
most prominent individuals involved in the provision of schools,
libraries, hospitals and learned and literary societies in mid nineteenth-century Belfast. A native of the Glens of Antrim, and son
of a Catholic father and a Presbyterian mother, MacDonnell was
educated in a hedge school in one of the caves at Red Bay quite
near to his family home.[14] Later on, he was sent to the David
Manson school in Clugston's Entry, Belfast where he was a class-
mate of Mary Ann and Frank McCracken (siblings of Henry Joy
McCracken).[15] James MacDonnell then went to Edinburgh to
study medicine and on his return to Belfast in 1784 he set up
practice in Donegall Place where he was to earn himself a reputation as a first-rate physician. His social conscience and

Dr James MacDonnell (1763–1845).

Christian charity, however, were reflected in his untiring efforts
for the less fortunate people of Belfast, and among his great
achievments was his involvement in the setting-up of the Belfast
Dispensary in 1792, the Belfast Fever Hospital in 1797 and the
General Hospital in 1801, which later became the Royal
Victoria Hospital. Indeed Sir William Whitla attributed to him
the foundation of the Belfast Medical School (which ultimately
became the Faculty of Medicine at Queen's University, Belfast):
'If any one name is to be singled out from the founders of the
Belfast Medical School . . . it must be that of MacDonnell'.[16]

In addition to his medical career MacDonnell was also a leading member of the literary and cultural circles of his day. He was
one of the founding members of the Belfast Library and Society
for Promoting Knowledge and he was also to feature promi-
nently in the Literary Society and other similar Belfast-based
societies of the period. An Irish speaker from an early age
MacDonnell was also deeply interested in Gaelic language, literature and music, particularly the harp.

The Belfast Harp Festival 1792

James MacDonnell, and his two brothers Randal and Alexander,
had, for a period of two years, the services of a blind Tyrone
harper called Art O'Neill (c. 1734–1815) in their father's house
in the Glens of Antrim. Randal seemed more interested in sport
than in music practice, and James' gift was for academic study
rather than the harp (which he nonetheless played moderately
well). It appears that the third MacDonnell brother, Alexander,
'played quite handsomely'. However, on the death of their father
Michael MacDonnell in 1780, Art O'Neill had to leave his relatively comfortable position in the MacDonnell household
where, as Dr James later recalled in a letter to Edward Bunting:
'During two years he lived . . . he was treated as a poor
Gentleman – had a servant . . .'[17]

When one considers this formative musical training which
the MacDonnell children received in their early youth from Art
O'Neill, it is not surprising to learn that Dr James MacDonnell
was the author of the following circular issued in 1791:

> Some inhabitants of Belfast, feeling themselves interested in
> everything which relates to the Honor, as well as to the

Prosperity of their country; propose to open a subscription which they intend to apply in attempting to revive and perpetuate THE ANCIENT MUSIC AND POETRY OF IRELAND. They are solicitous to preserve from oblivion the few fragments, which have been *permitted* to remain as Monuments to the refined taste and Genius of their Ancestors.

In order to carry this project into execution, it must appear obvious to those acquainted with the situation of this Country, that it will be necessary to assemble the Harpers, almost exclusively possessed of all the remains of the MUSIC, POETRY and ORAL TRADITIONS of Ireland.

It is proposed, that the Harpers should be induced to assemble in Belfast (suppose on the 1st of July next) by the distribution of such prizes as may seem adequate to the subscribers: And that a person well versed in the Language and Antiquities of the Nation, should attend, with a skillful musician to transcribe and arrange the most beautiful and interesting parts of their knowledge.

An undertaking of this nature, will undoubtedly meet the approbation of Men of Refinement and Erudition in every country: And when it is considered how ultimately the SPIRIT and CHARACTER of a people are connected with their NATIONAL POETRY and MUSIC it is presumed that the Irish Patriot and Politician, will not deem it an object unworthy of his patronage and Protection.[18]

An account of the opening concert of this festival which took place in Belfast on Wednesday 11 July 1792 describes the excitement of this important event. The performers, each normally playing three tunes, were: Dennis Dempsey [Hempson] (aged 68, blind) Co Derry, Arthur O'Neill (55 blind) Co Tyrone, Charles Fanning (56) Co Cavan – winner of first prize, Daniel Black (75 blind) Co Derry, Charles Byrne (80) Co Leitrim, Hugh Higgins (55 blind) Co Mayo, Paddy Quin (70 blind) Co Armagh, William Carr (15) Co Armagh (only one tune), Rose Mooney (blind) Co Meath, and James Duncan (45) Co Down.[19]

Edward Bunting (1773–1843)

The task of transcribing the melodies played by the various harpists at The Belfast Harp Festival fell to a young Co Armagh man, Edward Bunting, the son of an English engineer. As a musical child prodigy he came to Belfast at the age of 11 as assistant

organist at St Anne's Parish Church[20] and as his reputation grew
he was known throughout Belfast as a Professor of Music. He
lived in the inn run by the McCracken family in Rosemary
Lane for almost 30 years. Here Edward Bunting grew up in the
company of the McCracken children John, Mary Ann, William,
Frank and Henry Joy who was later to become a leader of the
United Irishmen. He was also part of a circle of celebrated
habitués of the McCracken establishment such as Wolfe Tone,[21]
Thomas Russell ('The Man from God Knows Where')[22] and Dr
James MacDonnell. It would appear that the young Bunting
enjoyed, if not revelled in, the status of an *enfant gâté*:

> He became a professor on his own account and abilities as a per-
> former had become developed, his company was courted by the
> higher class of Belfast citizens, as well as by the gentry of its
> neighbourhood and in short the boy prodigy became an idol
> among them . . . courted, caressed, flattered and humoured as he
> was . . . wayward and pettish he remained through life, and, for a
> long period at least, occasionally idle and we fear dissipated for
> hard drinking was the habit of the Belfastians in those days.[23]

Bunting's fondness for the high life, did not inhibit him from
producing the important three-volume work, *A General
Collection of Irish Music*, the first volume of which appeared in
1796, the second in 1809 and the third in 1840. Here, however,
one can detect the steadying hand of Dr James MacDonnell
who, along with the McCracken family, advised and encouraged
Bunting in the period before his marriage and subsequent move
to Dublin in 1819. Following the publication of the first volume
of *A General Collection of Irish Music* in 1796, Bunting went to the
countryside to collect more tunes throughout Ulster and
Connaught and as far south as Co Tipperary. As he did not have
an accurate knowledge of written Irish, (although it would seem
inconceivable that he did not possess a reasonable amount of
conversational Irish) the Co Down schoolteacher Patrick Lynch
(Pádraig Ó Loingsigh) was financed by the McCracken family
to go into Connaught and transcribe the Irish words of the song
tunes recorded by Bunting.

   Lynch was the same scholar employed to teach the Irish language in the Belfast Academy. One of his pupils in Belfast was
Thomas Russell, then librarian in the Linen Hall Library. Lynch
also produced a Gaelic magazine, *Bolg an tSolair*, which was

printed in Belfast by the *Northern Star* in 1795.[24] Employment was also forthcoming for Lynch from the senior churchman and Trinity College academic, Whitley Stokes who commissioned an Irish translation, in a script adapted for those more familiar with English orthography, of the Gospel according to St Luke and the Acts of the Apostles: *An Soisgeal Do réir Lucais, Agus Gniovarha na Neasbol* (Dublin 1799).[25] We also learn that Samuel Coulter of Dundalk paid Lynch 13 pence per page for copying manuscripts relating to Ulster Gaelic poets Peadar Ó Doirnín (c. 1700–69)[26] and Pádraig Ó Prontaigh (the original family name of the Brontë sisters).[27]

Lynch has left some animated accounts of his wanderings through Connaught in search of Irish songs, which survive as part of his correspondance with the McCracken family of Belfast, his patrons for these expeditions:

> I made good progress in Castlebar. I got forty seven songs in it, having stayed ten days, it cost me just two guineas . . . I walked the town not knowing whom to apply to and and passing by a brogue-maker's shop I heard him singing an Irish song. I stepped in and asked him if he would take a pot of beer. He came with me to the house of John McAvilly, a jolly publican, who sang well, and was acquainted with all good singers in town. Under Tuesday I found out a hairdresser, a shoemaker, a mason and a fiddler – all good singers . . . I send you here a list of 150 songs with the names of the persons and places where I got them for Mr Bunting's use . . . I heard of a blind piper Billy O'Maily, who had the greatest variety of Irish songs . . . Paid my bill *2s 2d*, and went to the house were I had seen Blind Billy yesterday, sent for him, gave him a shilling and grog, took down six good songs, cost me *2s. 8½d*. My money is near gone . . . I have made good progress – 177 songs . . . My dear Miss Mary I have been very attentive, very zealous, and very diligent in this business. I have near 200 songs. I have done all I could yet I am detained for want of travelling charges.[28]

The Bryson family: James, Andrew and Samuel

In 1774 James Bryson, a 44-year-old Presbyterian minister from Holywood, Co Down, was appointed as third minister in succession of the Second Presbyterian Church (Rosemary Street) in Belfast and in 1778 he became the first minister of the Donegall

Street congregation. James Bryson was to become a committee and honorary member of the Linen Hall Library[29] and was highly respected in the Belfast of his day. Although a member of the Masons, he was also active in the United Irishmen[30] and presided, as chairman, when a motion was passed in the Linen Hall Library on 17 January 1792 on the 'propriety of their publicly declaring their sentiments on the great important question of admitting the Roman Catholics to a full and immediate participation of the rights enjoyed by their fellow-citizens and countrymen'.[31]

One of James' sons Andrew was a Presbyterian minister in Dundalk where he more often than not preached in Irish.[32] Another son was Samuel (1778–1853) who trained in the medical profession and was listed as Assistant Surgeon in the 32nd Regiment and also recorded as 'apothecary and surgeon' of both 96 High St and Ballymacarret.[33] This same Samuel Bryson, under the Gaelic form of his name Somhairle Mac Brise, produced careful copies of eight Irish-language manuscripts which contained many of the essentials of early Irish literature such as: The Cattle Raid of Cooley (*Táin Bó Cuailnge*), The Children of Lir (*Oidhe Chloinne Lir*), The Tale of Deirdre and the Slaughter of the Sons of Uisneach (*Imtheacht Dheirdre agus Oidhe Chloinne Uisnigh*),[34] The Life of St Patrick (*Beatha Phádraig*), etc.[35] Indeed Aodh Mac Domhnaill (Hugh McDonnell), the Co Meath scribe employed by Robert MacAdam to copy Irish manuscripts also composed a six-verse poem in the Irish language singing the praises of Samuel Bryson's skills as a physician after he had treated him successfully.[36]

Rev William Neilson (1774–1821)

Another Presbyterian very much to the fore in Irish language circles in Belfast at this time was the Rev William Neilson, the son of Dr Moses Neilson of Rademon in Co Down. Moses Neilson opened an academy in Rademon which, in addition to educating the sons of members of his own congregation, also 'prepared young men intended for the Catholic priesthood in Latin and Greek'.[37] Fr Luke Walsh, from the same area, set out in his 1844 work, *The Home Mission Unmasked*, to expose, what he viewed as: 'the frauds, deceptions and falsehoods practised by the agents of the Home Mission of the General Assembly of the Presbyterian Church in Ireland', could only but applaud the generosity and unwavering uprightness of William's father: 'I was educated myself by a Presbyterian Clergyman, a man of as great moral worth and sterling integrity as Ireland could boast of – the Dr. Moses Neilson of Rademon in the County Down.'[38]

In summing up William Neilson's career, Breandán Ó Buachalla, concludes that William inherited many of the virtues of his father Moses.[39] It is not clear whether or not William was a native Irish speaker although his excellent command of the language would suggest that he was. Ciarán Ó Duibhín points out that his father Moses Neilson was an Irish speaker[40] who used Irish in his sermons at Rademon, and Ó Duibhín goes on to cite a late eighteenth-century source which implied that Irish was the language of both communities in this part of Co Down at the time: 'The Dissenters and Papists of this parish mostly speak in that language [Irish], and his [Rev Moses Neilson's] prayers and discourses are made in it.'[41]

At any rate, William Neilson's attendance at the hedge school run by the Ó Loingsigh (Lynch) family of Loughinisland, Co Down, where Patrick Lynch – future teacher of Irish at the Belfast Academy – was to be his tutor, would have ensured a solid grounding in Irish at an early age. This was certainly an important prerequisite for the successor of the Rev Andrew Bryson at The Dundalk Presbyterian Church where 'it was considered that the minister of this congregation should be able to speak Irish'.[42] It is hardly surprising, therefore, that William Neilson should have slotted so admirably into this vacant position in 1795. Indeed the Rev William Neilson's oratory skills in Irish were not confined to Dundalk, as the *Belfast Newsletter* reported, on 9 July 1805, how he preached sermons in Irish in Belfast 'to a numerous and respectable audience', while the *Hibernian Magazine* September 1805 refers to the fact that he was on a tour throughout Ulster 'preaching in Irish'.

As a scholar and linguist William Neilson demonstrated outstanding ability. In his student years he wrote an English grammar which became a standard text-book in many Ulster schools. He built a fine reputation as a classical scholar, due to publications such as his *Greek Exercises in Syntax, Ellipsis, Dialects Prosody and Metaphrasis* (Dundalk 1804), which went into eight editions

Rev William Neilson (1774–1821).

by 1842; *Greek Idioms* (Dublin 1810); and *Elementa Linguae Graecae* in 1820. He was elected to the Chair of Greek in the University of Glasgow in 1821 but died before taking up the post.[43] He was also a Hebrew scholar.

In 1808 he published *An Introduction to the Irish Language in three parts: I An original and comprehensive grammar; II familiar phrases and dialogues; III extracts from Irish books manuscripts, in the original character with copious tables of the contractions.*[44] This work may well have contributed to Rev Neilson's election as a member of the Royal Irish Academy in Dublin and it would also have assisted his appointment to future teaching posts. He also had valuable teaching experience from his days as a minister in Dundalk where he helped set up a school which was 'attended by all denominations and from it has sent students for TCD, Maynooth and the Scotch Universities'.[45] In his *Introduction to the Irish Language* Neilson was quick to point out not merely the importance of Irish from a philological and historical perspective but also its worth and beauty as a spoken language in the Ireland of his day:

That the Irish is the best preserved dialect of the ancient and extensive Celtic language, is allowed by the most liberal and enlightened antiquarians. To the general scholar, therefore, a knowledge of it is of great importance; as it will enable him to trace the origin of names and customs, which he would seek in vain in any other tongue. To the inhabitant of Ireland it is doubly interesting. In this language are preserved the venerable annals of our country, with as much fidelity, as is usually found in the primitive records of any nation; while the poetic and romantic compositions, with which the Irish manuscripts abound, afford the finest specimens, of elegant taste and luxuriant imagination. But it is, particularly, from the *absolute necessity* of understanding this language, in order to converse with the natives of a great part of Ireland, that the study of it is indispensable. If Irish be no longer the language of the court, or the senate, yet the bar and the pulpit require the use of it; and he that would communicate moral instruction, or investigate the claims of justice, must be versed in the native tongue if he expects to be generally understood, or to succeed in his researches. In travelling, and the common occurrences of agriculture and rural traffic, a knowledge of Irish is also absolutely necessary . . . it is surely reasonable and desirable, that every person should be able to hold converse with his country men; as well as to taste and admire the beauties of one of the most expressive, philosophically accurate, and polished languages that has ever existed.[46]

In 1818 William Neilson was elected to the Belfast Academical Institution as 'Head-master of the Classical school' where he was Professor of Irish, Greek, Latin, Hebrew and Oriental languages – a position he maintained until his death three years later. Irish was already taught in the Belfast Academy by Patrick Lynch and with people such as Dr James MacDonnell among the founders of the Belfast Academical Institution, it is hardly surprising that the authorities at the Institution proved similarly receptive to the inclusion of Irish on the school's curriculum. Campbell, in his treatment of the role of the Belfast Academical Institution, sums up its aims and functions as follows:

> This school was planned to serve the needs of Belfast's expand-
> ing business and professional classes. It also had the function of
> educating potential Presbyterian ministers. It was predominantly
> Nonconformist in enrolment but also took some episcopalian
> and Catholic pupils. It was an unusual organisation in so far that
> it was both a school and a college. In contrast to the universities
> of England and Scotland it imposed no religious test on its
> entrants.[47]

Considering the role which this institution had in the prepara-tion of candidates for the Presbyterian ministry, and the need for a command of the Irish language which the Synod felt to be necessary for ministers in Ulster at this period, an accomplished grammarian such as Neilson, was eminently suitable as an Irish teacher.

The Belfast Academy and the Belfast Academical Institution

While industrial Belfast began to prosper at the end of the eigh-teenth century, similar progress was made in the provision of institutions for education, literature and the arts. Both of the MacAdam brothers had received their education at the Belfast Academical Institution and they, in their turn, would come to the forefront in such activities. The aims of the Institution, as set out at its establishment, serve to underline the liberal and toler-ant quality of the Presbyterian ethos in Belfast, at this time:

The object of the Academical Institution was and is, shortly and simply this – to diffuse as widely as possible throughout the province and population of Ulster the benefits of education both useful and liberal and by that the means to prevent the hard and disgraceful necessity, in such a great and prosperous community, in sending their children to seek in other countries, with much risk to their health and morals, for that instruction and those literary qualifications and honours which might equally be obtained at home . . . Of nothing are the Boards more desirous than that pupils of all religious denominations should communicate by frequent and friendly intercourse in the common business of education, by which means a new turn must be given to the national character and habits, and all the children of Ireland should know and love each other.[48]

Known today as the Royal Belfast Academical Institution and still occupying its original site in the city centre, the Belfast Academical Institution was established in 1810, to cope with the increased demand for education in Belfast.[49] It was preceded by the Belfast Academy, founded in 1785, and is still in existence to this day as the Belfast Royal Academy – now on the Cliftonville Road in North Belfast – although Academy Street near St Anne's Cathedral bears witness to its original site in the city centre.[50] In both these schools the Irish language and its literature were regarded as important and actively promoted. Pádraig Ó Loinsigh (Patrick Lynch), the Irish scholar from Loughinisland in Co Down, offered his services in the *Northern Star*, on 16–20 April 1794:

Irish Language
An attempt to revive the grammatical and critical knowledge of the Irish language in this town is generously made by Mr Lynch: he teaches publically in the Academy and privately in several families. This language recommends itself to us, by the advantages it affords the students of Irish and Eastern Antiquities, especially to those who wish to acquire the knowledge of Druidical Theology and worship, as sketched by Cæsar and Tacitus.

It is particularly interesting to all who wish for the improvement and Union of this neglected and divided Kingdom. By our understanding and speaking it we could more easily and effectually communicate our sentiments and instructions to all our Countrymen; and thus mutually improve and conciliate each other's affections.

The Linen Hall Library (top) and the Belfast Academical Institution in the early 1800s.

The merchant and artist would reap great benefit from the knowldege of it. They would then be qualified for carrying on Trade and Manufactures in every part of their native country.

Such knowledge, we understand, could easily be acquired in three or four months by the assistance of Mr Lynch.[51]

The Academy was by no means the only institution in Belfast promoting the Irish language and Gaelic literature and music in the late eighteenth century. By 1788, The Belfast Reading Society had been established from which sprang The Belfast Library and Society for Promoting Knowledge (now known as The Linen Hall Library).[52] In 1798 a full list of members included 'Jas M'Adam'[53] (the father of Robert Shipboy and James) and he was also listed as a member of the committee in 1803 and 1810.[54] It was unsurprising therefore, that his sons James and Robert served as committee members in later years.

In the *Belfast Newsletter* 22 May 1818 the following appeared:

The Irish Language.
Doctor Neilson proposes to open a class for teaching Irish in the Belfast Academical Institution on Monday next 25th inst., at seven o'clock in the evening. The class will meet every Monday, Wednesday and Friday. Terms: One Guinea per Quarter.

The MacAdam brothers at the Belfast Academical Institution

Ó Buachalla gives the roll of names of those attending Neilson's Irish class in May 1819, found in the personal copy of Neilson's *An Introduction to the Irish Language* which belonged to RJ Tennent, an old boy of the Belfast Academical Institution and former Belfast MP between 1847 to 1852: 'Irish Class List, May 1819: R. Carlisle, J. Mac Adam, R. Tennent, Wm. Simms, R. Vance, Jas. Gibson, Francis Ward, Sam. Coulter, Edmund Hayes, R.J. Tennent'.[55]

The 'J. MacAdam' in question was probably James, elder brother of Robert. Born in 1801 he received his education at the Belfast Academical Institution before going on to Trinity College Dublin. James' main pursuits were of a scientific nature. He took advantage of the opportunities afforded by the construction of the Irish railway system to study the geology of the

country and was elected a Fellow of the Royal Geological
Society and amassed quite a collection of exhibits in his home.[56]
He was appointed as first Librarian to the Queen's College in
1849 although he relinquished this post after one year as it
apparently hindered his other activities.[57] While he had the joint
responsibility of running the Soho Foundry, James, like his
younger brother and partner Robert, wished to indulge his academic pursuits: 'This is by no means the life that I should wish
to lead but I am bound to assist my brother with a hope of occasionally getting away on scientific matters'.[58] James MacAdam's
contribution to learning has been summed up as follows:

> The librarian James MacAdam, an alumnus of the Institution
> [Belfast Academical Institution] and of Trinity College, Dublin,
> was an excellent example of a Belfast type in which the pursuit
> of business and devotion to learning were successfully combined.
> He was one of the founders of the Botanic Gardens and an ama-
> teur geologist of some distinction. He had been assistant secretary
> of the Institution and in that capacity had been responsible for
> the management of its library; and he had been a candidate for
> the chair of mineralogy and geology in the new college.[59]

Robert MacAdam's first involvement with the Irish language

Although there is no roll extant which confirms that Robert
MacAdam attended the classes of the Rev William Neilson at
the Belfast Academical Institution, it seems a reasonable assump-
tion that he did. Robert would have been 13 years old when
Rev Neilson died – a hypothesis supported by the fact that the
name of Robert MacAdam appears in the register of the
Academical Institution in the year 1818,[60] the same year of
William Neilson's appointment. That the MacAdam brothers
should have gone to the Belfast Academical Institution to be
educated was a logical progression given the establishment's
proximity to their home and the fact that their father James was
also a founder member of the Institution.[61] What is more debat-
able, however, is whether or not the Belfast Academical
Institution would have been young Robert's first exposure to
the Irish language.

Ó Buachalla points out that there was a Robert MacAdam
Senior living in Belfast in the late eighteenth and early nine-

teenth century who was a collector of Gaelic songs, some of which have turned up in the manuscripts which were in the possession of Robert Shipboy MacAdam. For example, on page 40 of Belfast Public Library Irish MS XXXI Robert Shipboy states that the foregoing poems and songs 'were collected by R. Mac Adam Sen.'[62] Robert Senior was also a committee member of the Linen Hall Library in 1813[63] and was earlier listed on the music committee of the Irish Harp Society, a body established by Dr James MacDonnell and Edward Bunting in Belfast in 1808 'primarily to provide blind boys and girls with the means of earning a living by teaching them the harp; secondarily to promote the study of the Irish language, history and antiquities'. In the light of this family connection with Irish music, Robert MacAdam's first exposure to the Gaelic language may not have been through the classroom, it is likely that young Robert's tuition by the Rev William Neilson at the Belfast Academical Institution would have contributed greatly to his enthusiasm for the Irish language and laid the foundations for his later expertise in the subject. In the foreword to the first volume of the *Ulster Journal of Archaeology*, which Robert launched and edited in 1853, he paid homage to Rev Neilson's work in the sphere of the Irish language, placing his name among the leading luminaries of his age: 'nor must we omit that of our townsman, Dr Neilson, to whose exertions, at a critical moment, we are perhaps, indebted for a renewed interest in the ancient language of Ireland'.

There is no doubt that Robert MacAdam would have been attracted to the cultural, literary and artistic aspects of the language, but Irish was also still very much a functional language in widespread daily use at this point. As the Rev Neilson said in outlining his reasons for introducing Irish into the curriculum of the Belfast Academical Institution (pp 13–14):

> . . . it is surely reasonable and desirable, that every person should be able to hold converse with his country men; as well as to taste and admire the beauties of one of the most expressive, philosophically accurate, and polished languages that has ever existed.

Aside from its aesthetic qualities, then, there were practical reasons for learning the Irish language which would have been spoken quite extensively in rural Ulster at this time, and would have

been heard in the streets of Belfast at market or in the taverns
where visitors or recent arrivals to town would have gathered.

Irish as a spoken language in rural Ulster in the early nineteenth century

When Swiss-born scholar Heinrich Wagner began his four-
volume *Linguistic Atlas and Survey of Irish Dialects* in the 1950s,
most of his Ulster material was collected from Co Donegal –
where Gaeltacht areas still exist – although he did manage to
locate native speakers of Irish in counties Cavan, Tyrone and
Rathlin Island, Co Antrim,[64] in addition to Omeath, Co Louth.[65]

Between the beginning of the twentieth century and the time
of Wagner's fieldwork of the 1950s, native speakers of Irish were
also found in the Glens of Antrim, and in counties of Derry,
Monaghan and Armagh.[66] GB Adams, in his in-depth analysis of
the returns to the question on the use of the Irish language for
the six northern counties from the 1911 *Census of Ireland*, concluded that while the overall figure represented 2.3 per cent of
the total population, some areas of the six counties had returned
figures of 20–30 per cent Irish-speaking.[67]

If one goes back further to pre-Famine rural Ulster in which
Robert MacAdam grew up, one finds that the numbers of Irish
speakers increase dramatically. We know, for example, that when
the Kilkenny-born Irish-language scholar John O'Donovan
(1806–61) began fieldwork for the first Ordnance Survey of
Ireland in the 1830s he was to encounter Irish speakers in virtu-
ally all of the counties in Ireland. O'Donovan's official task was to
standardise the anglicised spellings of, in the main, the c. 65,000
townlands of Ireland, although in the *Ordnance Survey Name Books*
he often entered what he considered to be the original Irish forms
of the name in question.[68] In many instances O'Donovan
recorded the Irish names of the townlands from speakers of Irish
in the locality. For example in Downpatrick he recorded the Irish
name for Saul (a parish in the Barony of Lecale, Co Down) as
Sabhall Phádraig, from an old local man, Luke Killen. *Sabhall* is an
Irish word for 'barn' which is borrowed from Latin *staballum* (as in
the English *stable*). The form *Sabhall Phádraig*, preserved by Killen,
can be traced back as far as the text of the Tripartite Life of St
Patrick, compiled nearly 1000 years earlier in c. 900 AD.[69]

A significant part of the colossal Ordnance Survey of Ireland at six inches to the mile in the first half of the nineteenth century, in its early stages, included an accompanying set of memoirs. It was unfortunate that this aspect of the project had to be abandoned after Ulster was surveyed, as the extant material on the northern counties constitutes an invaluable detailed portrait of Irish parish life before the Great Famine.[70] From this source it is clear that Irish speakers were to be found throughout the length and breadth of Ulster, although some areas contained many more than others. The mountainous districts and those removed from the main towns proved particularly disposed to the preservation of Irish. Although O'Donovan was able to find Irish speakers among the older generation in Lecale, Co Down, his contemporary on the survey, Lieutenant TH Rimmington observed, in January 1835, of the parish of Ardglass: 'the English language is entirely spoken, the Irish having quite fallen into disuse'.[71] Similarly, in letters written during the course of the Ordnance Survey in the Newry area, O'Donovan records his difficulty in locating a local informant who spoke Irish, before being led by the Rev Mr Glenny to the octogenarian 'Old MacGilvoy'.[72] Of course, the central area for Irish-speaking in Co. Down at this period was around Castlewellan, an area which Mícheál Ó Mainnín suggests 'seems to have included the [civil] parishes of Clonduff, Drumgath, Drumballyroney, Drumgooland, Kilcoo, Maghera, Kilmegan, Loughinisland and Down'.[73] The reference to Loughinisland, of course, reminds one of the Irish-language school which was run there, and the presence of scholars such as the family of Pádraig Ó Loingsigh (Patrick Lynch, the Irish-language teacher in the Belfast Academy in the late eighteenth century), and Revs Moses and William Neilson.

In addition to the accounts by John O'Donovan, and by other personnel involved in the Ordnance Survey, one can find further corroboratory accounts of other contemporary commentators. Abraham Hume, compiling a report for the British Association in 1874, pronounced that 'as late as 1820 . . . the Irish language was spoken along with English from Ballynahinch to near Newry'; while Christopher Anderson in his *Historical Sketches of the Native Irish* estimated that 93,000 out of a total population of 325,410 for Co Down were Irish speakers.[74]

There were several surveys of the level of Irish spoken in Co Tyrone in the eighteenth century. One estimate put the figure at two-thirds of the population while a 50 per cent figure was cited in a tract published by Dr Whitley Stokes of Trinity College Dublin in 1806 'on the prevailing language in most counties of Ireland'.[75] Stokes' figure was more or less confirmed by the slightly later investigation conducted, in the late 1820s, by Christopher Anderson in his *Historical Sketches of the Native Irish* which estimated that around 140,000 out of the total of 261, 865 inhabitants of that county, returned for the 1821 census, spoke Irish.[76] It is also of note that an Irish-language devotional work was published in Dublin in 1849 entitled *The Story of the Life and Passion of Our Lord and Saviour Jesus Christ* which was aimed specifically for 'the use of Ulster folk in Derry and Tyrone in their own provincial language'.[77] This work was signed 'R Ua C' which Ó Tuathail has successfully identified as Ristéard Ó Cionga, or the Rev Richard King.

Richard King (1815–1900), a native of Cork, was educated at Trinity College Dublin and ordained a Church of Ireland minister in 1841. Between the years 1851 and 1858 he was curate at Armagh before moving on to Ballymena Diocesan School where he served as principal until the year of his death. Rev King was a prolific scholar and his books included many devotional works in English, a catechism and a life of Christ, plus a three-volume *History of the Church of Ireland* and a *Memoir of the Primacy of Armagh*. Kate Newmann notes that the Rev Robert King 'was a devoted scholar of the Irish language, and published an Irish translation of the Book of Common Prayer'.[78]

Nearer Belfast, in rural Co Antrim, the Irish language would also have been heard in many areas. Thomas Fagan, in his fair sheets for the Ordnance Survey Memoir of the Parish of Aghagallon, in south-west Co Antrim on the shores of Lough Neagh, wrote that 'The Irish language too prevailed to a great extent throughout the period about 40 years back, particularly in the Montiaghs. A few settlers from other districts still speak Irish fluently but none of the natives of the parish'.[79] Further north in County Antrim, Lieutenant J Greatorex in his Statistical Account of the Parish of Loughguile, September 1833, remarked of the '6,889 souls' in the parish:

> They are a mixture of the Scotch and English emigrants, with the primitive inhabitants. The pure race of the latter are to be found

in the mountainous range of the parish, and the Irish language made use of to this day, but very partially.[80]

The Glens remained a bastion of Irish language and lore and was explored by Robert MacAdam in the 1830s for the purposes of recording Gaelic songs, and folk stories.

The Irish language in trade and communication in nineteenth-century Ulster

In the advertisement for Irish classes to be given by Patrick Lynch, placed in the *Northern Star* 16–20 April 1794, pains were taken to point out that one of the incentives listed for learning Irish was that the 'merchant and artist would reap great benefit from the knowledge of it. They would then be qualified for carrying on Trade and Manufactures in every part of their native country'. The Rev William Neilson made a similar point in his outline of the various reasons why Irish was going to be offered as a subject on the curriculum of the Belfast Academical Institution:

> But it is, particularly, from the *absolute necessity* of understanding this language, in order to converse with the natives of a great part of Ireland, that the study of it is indispensable. If Irish be no longer the language of the court, or the senate, yet the bar and the pulpit require the use of it; and he that would communicate moral instruction, or investigate the claims of justice, must be versed in the native tongue if he expects to be generally understood, or to succeed in his researches. In travelling, and the common occurrences of agriculture and rural traffic, a knowledge of Irish is also absolutely necessary.[81]

As an example of the need that would have been felt by English-speaking settlers in nineteenth-century Ulster to acquire a knowledge of Irish for commercial purposes, one can cite the account by J Stokes in the Ordnance Survey Memoirs for the parish of Drumachose in Co Derry:

> The parishioners are very anxious to obtain books from the Irish Bible Society.[82] They have also a wish for some acquaintance with the Irish language, as they feel their ignorance of it highly inconvenient, not only in their intercourse with some parts of the county, but also on visiting other counties to purchase goods. In the markets where Irish is spoken those unacquainted with the

language are regarded as foreigners, and to cheat them is considered a praiseworthy deed. This wish to acquire the language prevails in all the surrounding parishes.[83]

In Counties Down and Armagh one can adduce an identical use of Irish at fair and market, as WH Patterson received the following information from a correspondent 'from the mountainous district in the South of Down' in 1880:

> There are a good many Irish-speaking people in the neighbourhood of Hilltown, but I think nearly all of them can speak English; when, however, they frequent fairs in the upper parts of the Co. Armagh for instance at Newtownhamilton or Crossmaglen, they meet numbers of people who speak English very imperfectly, and with these people the Down men converse altogether in Irish.[84]

It is worthwhile recalling that, in addition to trade with Britain and further afield, the MacAdam family business at home (an ironworks and saddlers) relied on local trade with both the Ulster town and countryside. The evidence of Robert MacAdam's correspondence clearly shows that travel throughout the rural areas formed a central part of the family business commitments and would, therefore, have been a commercial advantage in having a command of Irish, at that time, in order to facilitate and successfully carry out such trade.

Robert MacAdam's early involvement with language and literary societies

While a knowledge of Irish was commercially useful for conducting business in some parts of rural Ulster, the language was clearly not seen by Robert as a mere vehicle for conducting transactions. For him, the language was much more – it was a mode of expression which he sought to use and propagate at any available opportunity. Indeed one may well assume that as much, if not more, of his energies and talents were spent in promoting and fostering the arts and amassing his Irish-language collection in Belfast than in furthering his business enterprises, although he pursued both with a great deal of success from the 1830s to the 1860s.

The literary historian, Breandán Ó Buachalla draws our attention to the fact that Samuel Bryson was a neighbour of the

MacAdam family in High Street and the Bryson boys would have been contemporaries of Robert MacAdam at school and, presumably, play. Nearby was McCracken's inn in Rosemary Lane, for so long Edward Bunting's lodgings, and a focal point in the heart of the town for social and cultural intercourse. Dr James MacDonnell's house in Donegall Place was also in the immediate vicinity, and it is noteworthy that in 1828 both the senior Dr MacDonnell and the young 18-year-old Robert MacAdam appeared as lecturers on the same evening of a meeting of the Natural History Society.

Dr MacDonnell was a highly respected figure in the MacAdam household. Publically, he was renowned for his Herculean work in Belfast health provision and his organisation of the Harp Festival in 1792, but he was also a close acquaintance of Robert Shipboy's father. Both the Doctor and James MacAdam Senior were founder members of the Belfast Academical Institution (1810) and both served on the Board of the Linen Hall Library – two institutions which would each become the future *alma mater*, and place of leisure reading and learning for RS MacAdam and his older brother James.

Robert Shipboy MacAdam, then, was a product of the era of great liberal and intellectual development in Belfast, coming a generation after solid foundations had been laid by the likes of James MacDonnell, Mary Ann McCracken, his own father and others. Through time Robert himself was to play a pivotal role in continuing to support the cultural and intellectual well-being of Belfast, and in facing up to the responsibility of ensuring that these same institutions and societies could be sustained and therefore enjoyed by, and of benefit to, future generations in the emerging city. From an early age he became actively involved at committee level in the societies which had been established in his native city in the decades leading up to and following his birth. In later years MacAdam was to become President of the Belfast Literary Society for two terms of office, the first in 1846–47 and the second from 1856–57.[85]

Robert MacAdam formed a close friendship with Dr MacDonnell which remained constant from the time of Robert's début on the social and intellectual scene in Belfast as a young man in the late 1820s until James MacDonnell's death in 1845.

During the 1790s, Dr James MacDonnell was a regular visitor to McCracken's tavern in Rosemary Lane, or at least up until the period following the aftermath of the hanging of Henry Joy McCracken in 1798, when the doctor refused a request from Mary Ann McCracken to come and try to revive the body of her dead brother. James MacDonnell was later pressured into adding his signature to a document, in 1803, which sought the arrest of United Irishman Thomas Russell. In a later letter the MacDonnell conceded 'I had not done it an hour until I wished of all things it was undone'.[86] His marginal involvement with Russell's arrest and subsequent execution at Downpatrick gaol was sufficient to ensure that Mary Ann McCracken would not speak to her childhood friend for the next 20 years, while well-known botanist and founding member of the Belfast Academical Institution John Templeton (1766–1825)[87] withdrew his membership of the Literary Society 'to avoid his former friend McDonnell', although a reconciliation between the two appears to have been brokered in later years by Mary Ann McCracken.[88] Similarly, Belfast luminary, and founder member of both the United Irishmen and the Belfast Academical Institution, Dr William Drennan (1754–1820) described James MacDonnell as a 'Contemptible cold-blooded Judas' and 'the Brutus of Belfast'.[89]

However, the rapport between the senior doctor and the MacAdam did not suffer from the events of surrounding 1798 as they had, after all, transpired five years before MacAdam's birth, and the bond of friendship between them strengthened after their joint lecture evening in 1828. One common interest shared by both men was their fluency in Irish and their keeness to promote the language. It was significant that Dr MacDonnell employed Irish-speaking nurses to look after his children in Belfast.[90] As a logical extension, then, of their linguistic interests and aspirations Dr MacDonnell and the young MacAdam, in collaboration with Dr Reuben J Bryce, were to set the seeds for *Cuideacht Gaedhilge Uladh*, or the Ulster Gaelic Society.

Cuideacht Gaedhilge Uladh: The Ulster Gaelic Society

The publication of Christopher Anderson's *Historical Sketches of the Native Irish* was to act as a catalyst in the founding of the

Ulster Gaelic Society in 1830. Anderson assessed the contemporary state of the Irish language and its literature, and as part of his treatment of this subject, the author urged that the language should not be left to perish without anything being done to preserve it. Instead, Anderson went on to suggest how the Irish-speaking population could be educated in their native tongue. *Historical Sketches of the Native Irish* had an immediate impact on Lord Downshire, the Fourth Marquis of Down, a wealthy landlord who possessed holdings of over 100,000 acres of estate in King's County (modern Offaly), Wicklow, Antrim and Down. His father, the Third Marquis, had acted as patron of the Harp Festival in 1792, while the Fourth Marquis himself was welcomed with *Céad Míle Fáilte* ('A Hundred Thousand Welcomes') by his tenants in his Hillsborough estate in 1833. The Fourth Marquis' brother, Lord George Hill was a fluent speaker of the language and a collector of Irish manuscripts.[91]

On reading a substantial portion of Anderson's 1829 book, Lord Downshire, sent a copy to Dr James MacDonnell urging him that some action be taken:

> ... I have not yet read the book through, but I have been led to think from the portion which I have perused, that 'The Ancient Irish Literature' ought no longer to remain in the obscurity in which it has laid for so many centuries. I should wish to see this object treated as a foundation for further enquiry and proceedings ... Such an undertaking would be serviceable in many ways and tend to drive men's minds from speculative discussions and political disputations from which this country has suffered so much to a subject well worthy of attention and well calculated to replace Ireland in the station she formerly held among Nations as a nursery of learning and the resort of pious and learned men.[92]

James MacDonnell duly responded, (28 January 1830) thanking Lord Downshire for lending him Anderson's *Sketches of the Native Irish*,[93] and confided:

> [what Anderson] proposes to do is what several people *here* have been wishing for and attempting to do altho' none of us have seen it in so clear and comprehensive a manner. We have a small society and a subscription for keeping up a class of Irish Scholars ...[94]

As early as 1828 we have evidence of MacAdam sending a native Irish-speaking scholar, Tomás Ó Fiannachta (Thomas Feenachty) to Ballinascreen in Co Derry with a view to setting up Irish schools in the district.[95] This scheme identifies MacAdam as a forward-thinking theorist in educational practice for his time, ahead even of the insightful Scottish Presbyterian commentator Christopher Anderson:'He [MacAdam] was a personal friend of several hedge-schoolmasters and, in contradiction to the trend towards teaching English in schools, he favoured the teaching of Irish to children in those areas where the language was widely spoken.'[96]

In his response to Lord Downshire Dr MacDonnell's letter also included a printed 'Statement of the objects of the Belfast Gaelic Society' for the former's perusal. On 7 February 1830 Downshire concluded his response to Dr MacDonnell in encouraging and enthusiastic terms:

> I like the plan of the Society as explained in the 'Statement' referred to and I will thank you to let me know who the sub- scribers to the Society are besides yourself and what contribu- tions are required. I imagine the Irish Celtic Society in Dublin is founded upon the same principles and for the same object and I hope one day to see the funds so enlarged as to enable the two societies to rescue the ancient Literature and History of Ireland from the obscurity in which it has too long remained. At the time of my writing to you the letter to which you have replied I was not aware that a Society had already been formed in Belfast. The object is worthy of the generous feelings which so usefully animate the minds of many respectable and learned individuals like yourself and I request that you will lay my first letter before the Society.
> I remain, Dear Sir,
> Your faithful and obedient servant.
> Downshire.[97]

This offer of support and encouragement from Lord Downshire was a timely one for MacDonnell and his junior collaborators MacAdam and Reuben Bryce. In the same year the Ulster Gaelic Society came into being, with Lord Downshire as presi- dent, Dr MacDonnell as chairman and MacAdam and Bryce as co-secretaries. Rev RJ Bryce (1797–1888), a professor of math- ematics and eventual principal at the Belfast Academy, was yet another of the leading Presbyterian figures in Belfast at this time. Like MacDonnell he was a member of the board of the Linen Hall Library, and Anderson relates that the Rev RJ Bryce LLD was 'Principal of the Belfast Academy, and Minister of the United Presbyterian Congregation, York Street; also author of several valuable books'.[98]

Reuben Bryce was also a personal friend of English-born Anglo-Irish novelist Maria Edgeworth (1767–1849) whose *Castle Rackrent* won her universal acclaim in 1800. The first publication of the Ulster Gaelic Society was an Irish translation by Tomás Ó Fiannachta in 1833, of Maria Edgeworth's works *Forgive and Forget*, and *Rosanna*. The book was dedicated to Lord Downshire and in their foreword (written in Irish) the secretaries stated how they hoped that the publication would facilitate the reader to learn Irish, and also expressed a desire that its contents would be of moral sustenance to the reader:

> We hope that many who shall read this short book will follow the fine example of hard-working farmer Rosanna, so that they might lead a life of happiness and fulfilment. It is also our hope that all malice and evil intention which has beleaguered and disgraced our country can be banished; and that the reader will follow, on every occasion, the adage of Morris, i.e. 'Forgive and Forget'.
> We remain, Esteemed Reader
> Your humble and ever-faithful servants
>
> R. Æ Brise
> R.S. Mac Adaimh Secretaries of the Society.[99]

In the same year Irish was reintroduced in the Royal Belfast Academical Institution, under the recommendation of the Board which was chaired by Dr MacDonnell and had as secretary Robert MacAdam's older brother James. Irish scholar Tomás Ó Fiannachta was appointed professor of Irish, and as Ó Buachalla points out, the main interest in reopening this post was to aid candidates preparing for the Presbyterian ministry: 'The Synod of Ulster have passed a law making the study of Irish *imperative* for holy orders. They will not now ordain without that qualification'.

At the same time as these Belfast developments, Philip Barron was coming to the fore as a language revivalist in Co Waterford, where he founded an Irish-language college in Bonmahon, Co Waterford in 1835.[100] He launched a magazine, *Ancient Ireland*, which ran from January to May of that year: 'a weekly magazine established for the purpose of reviving and the cultivation of the

Irish language'. This magazine was to sell over 30,000 copies but
it did not last more than a year and the apparently disheartened
Barron subsequently left the country – although we have evidence of MacAdam entering into correspondence with him in
1836 (see page 31). Nevertheless, during the short existence of
Ancient Ireland many contributions were submitted to it from
members of the Ulster Gaelic Society. The president, Lord
Downshire, wrote to Barron congratulating him on his achievement and aims:

> I enter very fully into your views respecting ancient Irish litera-
> ture. I am not myself the possessor of any Irish manuscripts but
> my brother Lord George Hill, has paid attention to the subject
> and desires me to say that he will be very happy to promote your
> views – and that whenever you should happen to be in Dublin if
> you will call upon him at the castle, he will show you some man-
> uscripts which he has, and which are rather curious.[101]

Downshire continued, drawing Barron's attention to the fact
that there 'is an Irish Society in Belfast, to which my brother and
I subscribe – Dr McDonnell and Dr Bryce are at the head of it
– and I shall submit your letter to Dr McDonnell'.

In a separate submission to *Ancient Ireland*, Thomas Feenachty
bemoaned the shortage of textbooks in Irish as an acute prob-
lem: 'The Irish Professorship in the Belfast College, is, as yet, but
an experiment. In the article of class-books, a great want exists.
The chief obstacle to reviving the cultivation of the Irish language is the want of elementary books'.[102] It was obvious that
Feenachty himself was taking practical measures to rectify this
situation, for in addition to his translation of *Forgive and Forget*
(*Maith agus Dearmad*), both he and Robert MacAdam combined
to produce: *An Introduction to the Irish Language intended for the
Use of the Irish Classes in the Royal Belfast Academical Institution.*[103]
As further evidence of the urgency felt concerning the provision
of suitable textbooks, MacAdam (writing to Barron, 20 June
1836, in relation to printing and character sets), reiterated sentiments similar to those expressed by Feenachty: 'the outcry for
"Books, Books" is very great indeed and let us not allow the
enthusiasm to evaporate lest in might be difficult to revive'.[104]

In addition to his unstinting efforts on behalf of the Ulster
Gaelic Society, Robert MacAdam was particularly active in
another of the great cultural institutions of the day, the Belfast

Natural History and Philosophical Society, founded in 1821.[105]
MacAdam served as secretary for the years 1832–33, 1834–35,
1837–38; treasurer 1867–71; vice-president 1851–56, 1871–73,
1881–86. While in office, MacAdam would doubtless have
enjoyed the support and encouragement of Dr MacDonnell in
his early years in the BNHPS as the Glensman was among the
founders of that society. MacAdam rightfully regarded Dr James
MacDonnell as 'an intellectual giant of his day' and when he died
in 1845 MacAdam paid respectful homage to his social mentor's
achievements:

> For half a century he [Dr MacDonnell] was the centre of literary
> and scientific matters in Belfast. He was a medical man of exten-
> sive practise but his taste collected round him all those who cul-
> tivated science or literature in the Province. He had a great library
> and collection of Irish antiquities and was uniformly the person
> to whom all travellers of distinction were introduced when com-
> ing to Belfast. I have met many foreigners at his home.[106]

Members of the committee of the Ulster Gaelic Society felt free
to draw each other's attention to any visiting scholars or luminaries who happened to be in town, and to arrange for social visits and introductions. For example, MacAdam in sending a
subscription to Phillip Barron (20 June 1836) asked: 'Are there
any subscriptions which I can receive for you here [Belfast]? I
wish to send you Dr McDonnell's and my own'.

When the redoubtable John O'Donovan, visited Belfast during the course of the Ordnance Survey in the mid 1830s, he
records: 'I was introduced by McAdam to Dr MacDonnell and
Dr Bryce'. O'Donovan wrote glowingly of Dr MacDonnell and
the welcome he received at his home, but it would appear that
O'Donovan did not take as kindly to Robert MacAdam, ini-
tially, at any rate. O'Donovan found MacAdam somewhat possessive of his manuscripts, although O'Donovan himself does not
seem to have treated MacAdam with due courtesy on this occasion:

> I can never forget the kindness with which he [Dr MacDonnell]
> received me, and the trouble he took to direct me in my object . . .
> I breakfasted this morning with Doctor McDonnell in whose
> possession the original manuscript is. It is well written and I find
> that in McAdam's copy several mistakes have been committed in

lengthening out the contractions ... When I told McAdam that
Mr Petrie had taken a copy of it he did not seem altogether satisfied ... I have thought it better to get the thing thus managed
than be under a compliment to McAdam who is very jealous of
his manuscripts'.[107]

Robert MacAdam: the international perspective

Intellectual activities aside, the MacAdams had a business to run
and promote. It would appear that most of the international
travel for the Soho Foundry, as far afield as Egypt, fell to Robert.
His reported knowledge of around 13 languages would seem to
be borne out not only by his citation of Latin, Greek, Italian,
Spanish, French, Italian and Scottish Gaelic proverbs in his
printed collection which appeared in the *Ulster Journal of
Archaeology*,[108] but also by his wide travels. In fact, Ó Buachalla
draws attention to the fact that, while Robert and his wealthy
Egyptian client and close friend Ibrahim Pasha normally com-
municated with each other in French, Robert had picked up
sufficient Arabic to pen a short account of his friend Ibrahim in
the margin of one of his manuscripts.

While business may have been a principal reason for Robert
MacAdam embarking on such visits abroad, he seemed to take
advantage of the opportunity to widen his knowledge of the history, culture and language of the countries he visited. If one
looks at the titles of the lectures which he gave between the years
1829 and 1857 to The Belfast Natural History and Philosophical
Society and The Belfast Literary Society, a picture emerges of his
wide-ranging reading, travels and tastes, both at home and
abroad:

Robert MacAdam: talks to The Belfast Natural History and Philosophical Society

29/7/1829:   'An Excursion to the West of Ireland'
12/1/1831:   'The Natural Magic of the Ancients'
15/5/1833:   'The Potato'
24/9/1834:   'Physical Geography of France'
9/11/1834:   'Statistic and Natural History of Switzerland'
10/5/1837:   'Notes on a Tour in Belgium and France'

Robert MacAdam: talks to The Belfast Literary Society

6/11/1836:	'Translation of Count A. de Bylandt's *Geological Tour in Bohemia*'
13/2/1837:	'Account of a Tour in Belgium'
12/2/1841:	'Statistics of Belgium'
6/2/1842:	'Notes of a Tour by Himself in 1834 thro' parts of Switzerland, Savoy, and the South of France'
4/3/1844:	'Tour in Switzerland'
12/4/1847:	'State of Society in Sweden from Laing's *Travels*'
5/4/1852:	'The Trace of the Scandinavian in Ireland'
2/2/1857:	'On the Changes now in Progress in the English Language'.[109]

MacAdam as a collector of Irish manuscripts and folklore

So far, we have a picture of Robert MacAdam emerging from a successful Belfast Presbyterian commercial class which was equally concerned with the provision of a liberal education and health-care for all classes and creeds. Preoccupation with intellectual pursuits and the arts was also an integral part of their everyday lives.

The family business passed from James MacAdam (†1821) to his sons James and Robert Shipboy who developed the foundry which traded in Ireland, Britain, Europe and beyond. Success in business did not absorb all their energies, and each, in their own individual way, continued to build on the education they had received at the Belfast Academical Institution. Similarly both became involved with the cultural societies of the era and made major contributions to the quality of life and ambience of their native town which William Thackeray, following his visit to Belfast in 1842, declared to be 'as neat, prosperous, and handsome a city as need be seen. It looked hearty thriving and prosperous as if it had money in its pocket and roast beef for dinner'.[110]

The MacAdam brothers, in their new abode in the fashionable College Square East, were part and parcel of the Belfast described by Thackeray. Even so, Robert also ventured deep into the Ulster countryside whenever it was possible. On these visits he delighted in speaking Irish and he recorded folklore and sayings, and bought, or arranged to have copied, any Irish manuscripts he might come across. Time and time again, we find references to him corresponding about these with local people. One typical example of his mixing of business and pleasure is his letter to one of the Liffin brothers, of Inishowen in Co Donegal, which contains an apology for not being able to visit them as business matters called him back to Belfast from Derry:

> Derry
> 7th September 1833
> Sir,
> When I came from Belfast about a week ago I fully intended to have paid a visit to Carn and Clonmany and to have done myself the pleasure of calling on you and your brother; but on my arrival here to-day I found letters waiting for me which recall me home sooner than I expected. I am thus disappointed of the gratification I had hoped for and of the information I was sure of receiving from you on different matters relating to Irish Literature. I must therefore defer my visit for some time longer and in the meantime you will be good enough to accept from me the accompanying little publication in Irish, being the first book printed by the Ulster Gaelic Society to which I belong.[111] If you would not think it too much trouble I would feel greatly obliged by your writing to me some time during the next month or two and letting me know whether you think Irish schools would be encouraged in Innishowen, or whether anything of the kind is already established. You were good enough in a former letter to mention that some old people in your neighbourhood were able to repeat old poems and Fenian tales. I am particularly desirous to see these preserved and published and shall willingly take an opportunity of going down to Innishowen for the purpose of writing them down with you and your brother's assistance. During last week I was several days engaged in that manner in the Glens of County Antrim and succeeded in writing a good number from the old people there.
>
> When you see your brother, Mr. Con Liffin you will please remember me to him. Tell him that I am taking ever care of the Irish books he lent me and that some of them are partly copied. If he would have no objection to part with them and would put a value on them I would be glad if you would mention it in your letter.
> Hoping to hear from you,
> I am Sir,
> Your obedient Servant,
> Robt. S. McAdam.[112]

We are also made aware in this letter that Robert MacAdam visited the Glens of Antrim to record lore from old local Gaelic story-tellers. In May 1835 James Boyle, an employee engaged on Ordnance Survey Memoir work passed comment not only on the predominance of Irish in the parish of Layd but also on the fact that, as one of its sons, Dr James MacDonnell was given pride of place with regard to the collection of local traditions or the acquisition of manuscripts:

> Many of the lower orders in the Glens neither speak nor under-stand a word of English, and most of their stories are recited in Irish; to these the people are very fond of listening. Many of the old people who used to tell them are now dead. There are not now any old manuscripts in the Glens; they used to abound but Dr McDonnell of Belfast (whose connections live in this parish) has collected them all, and to no-one else would the people give them.[113]

MacAdam's friendship with Dr MacDonnell may have helped to open doors in the Glens. It also emerges from Boyle's memoir for the same parish that MacAdam would have found plenty of Gaelic lore in the Glens:

> There are many old persons who do little but recite tales and sto-ries about ghosts, fairies, enchantments and the wonderful doings of Ossian, Fin McCoul and a great many other giants who made Lurigethan hill the scene of their fabled exploits. The people are also very superstitious, having a firm belief in all manner of charms, goblins etc. There are not now any clan marches, but many beautiful Irish airs are sung in both the English and Irish language, particularly in Glenariff.

This strong Gaelic tradition continued on into the current cen-tury as Glensman and renowned international folklorist James Hamilton Delargy or Séamus Ó Duilearga (1899–1980)[114] recorded Irish-language material from local *seanchaí* Barney Bhriain MacAulay of Glenariff in the 1920s.[115]

MacAdam's excursions were not confined to Inishowen or the Glens of Antrim. Even in Belfast, we have evidence of him taking down folklore and songs from individuals who were reared in Gaelic-speaking areas but who had come into the town in search of work. One prime example of such collection was his acquaintance with a blacksmith from Co Louth:

This story was taken verbatim from a blacksmith in Belfast about the year 1830. He had been a rebel in '98, made prisoner at Tara and according to the humanity of the officer on guard was suffered to run away while exhibiting an action of great muscular strength.[116]

In 1833 a 'James Maguire of Ballinamore, County Leitrim' wrote to MacAdam from Enniskillen seeking a pound for two boards of 'backgammon (or the playing tables) or in Irish *tamhlisc*'. In the course of the letter it emerges that books, or manuscripts had previously changed hands between Maguire and MacAdam as the former makes reference to 'the reign of Cairbre Lifeachair a gabrael of the Liffey. He reigned 37 years and that is 38 generations from me. You will find this King's reign in the last book I gave you'.[117] As late as 1854 we see MacAdam continually on the lookout for an opportunity to combine a business trip with the chance to extend his Irish collection. As he wrote to Corkman John Windele, a similarly-minded antiquarian and language revivalist who also employed scribes and collected manuscripts:[118]

> I find that I have a number of duplicate Irish manuscripts and it occurs to me that if you have any such we might make exchanges and thus benefit both collections. If you have, let me know and as I shall be in Cork once or twice in Spring on business I would bring my duplicate manuscripts along with me to show you.[119]

In the same letter MacAdam informs Windele:

> I was in London for a few weeks lately and spent a good many agreeable days in the Library of the British Museum. Among the Irish manuscripts I observed a copy of the Moy Tuireadh. I shall be there soon again and if there is any passage you wish copied I will do it for you.

The Home Mission and the 'Bible War' in the Glens of Antrim 1842–4

Of the various religious bodies to emerge in the nineteenth century to provide religious instruction for Ireland's poor, it has been argued that 'The Irish Society had a greater emphasis on the Irish language, and was therefore more involved with Roman Catholic areas of Ireland'.[120] As part of its plan to widen the availability of Irish-language versions of the scriptures in Ireland, The Irish Society, under the direction of the Presbyterian Synod of Ulster, set up an organisation entitled the Home Mission in 1836. This latter educational body set up schools to provide schoolchildren with a grounding in the bible and by 1844 Henry Joseph Monck Mason, in *History of the Origin and Progress of the Irish Society*, declared: 'more interesting scenes I have never witnessed than the triumphs of the Irish Bible in the dark mountains of Ulster'.

In 1841 George Field (under an Irish form of his name which he rendered Seorsa Ó Mhachaire)[121] issued a book intended as 'a footway' to the Irish language:

Casán na Gaedhilge, An Introduction to the Irish Language; compiled at the request of the Irish Teachers; under the patronage of the General Assembly of Ireland, And Dedicated to them as a tribute of their esteem for their zeal in preserving and extending their Mother-tongue, By their friend and countryman, S. ÓM.

Field, who lived in Castle Place, Belfast, had written to Robert MacAdam, in Irish, giving him the words of a song, *Feadag an Iolaire* 'The Eagle's Whistle'.[122] In addition to stating in the preface, that his grammar 'has been compiled for the use of the Native Irish and for those who wish to acquire a knowledge of our sweet and venerable mother tongue', Field also acknowledged the contribution to his work by the authors of past grammars – such as those of Rev William Neilson (1808) and Thomas Feenachty (1835) – and continued: 'I have likewise to acknowledge the assistance and instruction afforded by Michael McNulty, Hugh Gordon, Hugh McDonnell, Michael Branagan and other native Irishmen'.

These Irish speakers were all teachers: Michael McNulty taught in Co Leitrim and Hugh Gordon in Loughinisland, Co Down during 1824–27 before going on to become an Irish scripture reader in Kerry 1843.[123] In a letter to Robert MacAdam, dated 8 May 1844, Brian MacGucian requested work for his own son and for a 'Mícheál A Bhrangan'.[124] Hugh McDonnell, the third party mentioned by Field – and a future close companion to Robert MacAdam – was to play a significant part in the controversy surrounding the Home Mission in the Glens of Antrim which erupted in long-running, vitriolic correspondences in the Catholic periodical the *Vindicator* and a Protestant publication of the period *Banner of Ulster.*[125]

The issues of contention centred on accusations of prose- lytism and around whether or not the schools in question had actually been established or whether the roll books had been fal- sified in order 'to take the money which the Synod gave us for doing nothing', as four teachers were to write in the *Vindicator* in 1842. The teachers and inspectors (salaried by the Home Mission) contradicted both each other and even themselves in a series of published letters and statements, although a glimpse of the probable reality emerged when Fr Luke Walsh, PP of Culfeightrin, using testimony which he had obtained from Hugh McDonnell,[126] seemed to soften and admit that there were schools of this nature for a short time but after their clo- sure, the teachers continued to claim payment for bogus instruc- tion. The curate also stated that any monies received fraudulently from this programme had been returned to him. For their roles as inspectors, Hugh McDonnell and his predecessor, Mr Moloney, came in for cutting criticism from the Culfeightrin PP, who described them as 'renegade' and as being prepared to sell the birthright 'for a mess of potage'.

Accusation upon counter-accusation followed. At one point Fr Walsh demanded to see the text of a letter from McDonnell in order to verify the handwriting, and furiously proclaimed:

> When I had satisfied myself that proselytism was the object of your mission and not teaching the vernacular, from a love of the Irish language, I first suspended them – that is I suppressed your schools, and when I found out that those teachers were hum- bugging you, and taking your money for *doing nothing*, and prac- tising a fraud, I then suspended them – that is to say I denied them Christian rites until they would desist and promise to give to the poor of God the wages of their sin.

This latter, rather coded reference to a donation 'to the poor of God' seems to partly, but most indirectly, answer the question as to what Fr Walsh did with the money he recovered from the repentant teachers. The financial arrangements for the teachers were '1 shilling each for every person they taught to read the primer; 1s 6d. each for teaching the Gospel; and 2s for teaching to read the epistles'.[127]

Rev Robert Allen (1789–1865) the director of the Home

Mission, still resisted, arguing that some of the teachers 'have been tempted to deny to the priest that they were teaching for fear of his displeasure and the persecution that would thence arise'.[128] Fr Walsh returned to the fray with a letter to the *Banner of Ulster*, three to the Directory of the Home Mission and an open letter to 'The Presbyterians of Ireland' which he sent to the Presbyterian Moderator Dr Stewart. Very much forced onto the defensive, Rev Allen tried to appeal to logic by asking if these schools did not exist:

> Then I ask why is the good man [Fr Walsh] so uneasy – why waste so much time, and trouble, and paper, and virtuous wrath about a non-entity? Can a thing that is merely fictitious – that has no existence – do him or others any harm?

In terrier-like fashion Fr Walsh embarked upon a total review of all the matters involved and in a seeming *coup de grâce* he published a letter from Hugh McDonnell, which declared that he had given false returns in order to keep his position and satisfy his employers and implying that the superintendent was aware of the situation.

As a sting in the tail of the 'Bible War' saga, Charles McLoughlin, a miller by trade but erstwhile teacher for the Home Mission, won £70.00 compensation as damages for loss of earnings in a legal action he took against Fr Luke Walsh.

The work of the Home Mission, the controversy surrounding it and resistance to proselytism, was to have a significant role in creating suspicion against the involvement of outsiders in the preservation of the Gaelic language.

MacAdam's Irish scribe, Aodh Mac Domhnaill or Hugh McDonnell of Co Meath

The Hugh MacDonnell at the centre of the Glens of Antrim 'Bible War' was a native Irish speaker, Aodh Mac Domhnaill, who was born in the townland of Lower Drumgill, near Dromcondra in north-east Co Meath. On 7 February 1827, there is a record of his marriage to Bridget Roe in Ardee, Co Louth. Breandán Ó Buachalla is of the opinion that he remained in Co Meath until the death of his wife Bridget, aged 34, in 1836,[129] and Colm Beckett surmises that he was the 'Hugh McDaniel, Carrickleck' whose name appears among the subscribers to M Clarke's *Man's Final End* and who was also attached to the Irish Society for Promoting the Education of the native Irish through the Medium of their Own Language under the auspices of the Church of Ireland.[130] Beckett also points out that a teacher named Owen McDaniel (possibly a relation of Hugh's) was teaching in Carrickleck for the Kildare Place Society in 1823 but was later killed as a result of disturbances in 1830, in relation to the bible teaching, which erupted in 1830. Following Hugh McDonnell's removal to Co Antrim first as teacher and then as an inspector for the Home Mission and the subsequent termination of his three-year period in the latter post from 1839–42, we find that he has secured employment in a much more convivial environment and in more private and less contentious circumstances with Robert MacAdam.

Beckett suggests that Robert MacAdam may first have come into contact with the McDonnell family of Co Meath through Hugh's father James, as MacAdam, in a marginal note in manuscript XXXI in the Belfast Public Library, records the phrase 'Repeated to me by Old McDonal 1831'.[131] Leaving aside any judgement of Hugh MacDonnell's worth as an inspector from the sorry saga of his Home Mission years, where Fr Luke Walsh had castigated him as a member of the 'set of abandoned and unprincipalled swindlers', Hugh's reputation as an Irish scholar was fairly solid. His credentials, would have been enhanced, by George Field's acknowledgement in his 1841 book *Casán na Gaedhilge: An Introduction to the Irish Language*. In any case, when the unemployed Hugh McDonnell came to Belfast in search of work, following his sojourn as a Home Mission inspector in the Glens of Antrim, Robert MacAdam was to come to his aid. From the years 1842–56 his services as an Irish scribe, folklore collector and manuscript copyist were secured on a full-time basis by Robert MacAdam in Belfast. In return for these services Hugh was provided with lodgings and a salary, and according to Beckett Hugh McDonnell lived at 88 Millfield, five minutes walk from MacAdam's home in College Square.[132]

One of Hugh McDonnell's initial duties was to go out into the rural areas of Counties Louth, Armagh and Donegal to collect songs, folkore, manuscripts and other Irish language materials. On his travels McDonnell would explain that he came on behalf of Robert MacAdam of Belfast, and Ó Buachalla quotes from letters MacAdam received from a variety of Irish scholars scattered throughout the countryside: Michael Levins of Drogheda, offered a manuscript of Keating's seventeenth-century *History of Ireland* and 'three Ogham's with instructions for reading them'; P McGahan, from Dongooly, Co Louth, sent in stories; while Patrick McGeough of Lurgankeel (whose forwarding address was c/o Michael Coburn, Publican, Dundalk) expressed doubts as to the *bona fide* nature of McDonnell's mission:

> I beg leave to state that in the month of December last I was visited by a man of the name of Hugh McDonald who stated to me that he was by your order and direction collecting Irish manuscripts for the purposes of publishing them in print. Some of them he was purchasing for ready money and some for love of returning them . . . I lent him a valuable Irish manuscript sow I request that you'l have the kindness to let me know by letter whether these promises may prove effective or not that myself and others may be satisfied by your favourite reply, or that we may understand was he an impostor.[133]

Many correspondents appeared to have had designs on the role which McDonnell was undertaking. For example Brian McGucian proposed the services of both his own son and those of Mícheál Ó Brannagáin (a former Home Mission teacher); while Bernard Tumalty recommended the services of Co Louth scholar Nicholas Ó Cearnaigh (c. 1802–65)[134] and criticised the scholarship of Peter Gallegan.[135]

Despite these advances it would appear that Robert MacAdam was satisfied with McDonnell's services as he continued to employ him for over a decade and a half.

Peadar Ó Gealacáin or Peter Gallegan (1792–1860)

When a second scribe was required, MacAdam turned to Peter Gallegan (Peadar Ó Gealacáin). Born in Monnterconaught, Co Cavan, Peter Gallegan had been a long friend of Hugh McDonnell's and composed an Irish lament on the death of Hugh's wife Bridget in 1836. He had been a hedge-school master and took up a teaching post for a while with the Irish Society in Co Meath where he described the resulting tension between the Catholic and Presbyterian churches, similar to that witnessed in Co Antrim, only that the depth of feeling in the Meath case was dramatically illustrated by the tragic murder of one of the teachers, Owen McDaniel, in 1830.

As a scribe, Peadar was a prolific copyist with a neat and accurate hand. Furthermore, he was evidently filled with a deep love for his subject: 'O Heavens! was there ever anything half so sweet or to be compared to our dear but neglected Irish language'.[136] In 1844 Peter Gallegan began his first Irish manuscript for Robert MacAdam, a text containing the life of St Maodhóg, with a second following shortly after, 300 pages on the works of blind Co Louth poet Séamus Mac Cuarta (c.1647–1729).[137] Peter Gallegan was to describe Robert MacAdam (Máighistir Roibeart Mhac Adhaimh) as the 'defender of the Old Irish tongue' (*cosantóir na Sean-Ghaoidheilge*), and their relations remained on a solid footing until just before Peter's death in 1860. In 1851 Peter wrote to MacAdam:

> Sir
> I have taken a little turn at the harvest here just in order to save a trifle to buy some linen as I was totally run out of shirts last summer which often grieved me that I could not save one half-crown the whole time in Belfast after spending near four months there. I received a note from Hugh McDonnell in which he stated that he had some conversation with you previous to that and that you remarked to him that you had two years work for me in the writing business. I suppose now, Sir, at the very lowest calculation I think that about five shillings a week would not be unreasonable for me to get in order to pay for my lodging and to live as frugal as possible.
>
> As I began your books, of course, I should wish to finish them and other things which I remarked to you in your office.
>
> I was lately requested by a schoolmaster who holds a National school to take on as usher which would bring me five shillings a week but I would rather go to you at the same rate of payment. I have a great many Irish scraps and poems that you never met with as yet. There are also some old men in this neighbourhood who have some songs which I could not meet with in your collections but on hearing that I was on the mission of providing Irish songs and poems I could not get anything from them unless I made them some little remuneration and it very often happens that my little earning was too scanty for myself much less to graze their hand with a fool's token which they required of me and scarce as my cash was I bribed some for their songs.[138]

From the reference to 'your office' we know that Gallegan – who usually transcribed from his home in Co Meath – had visited Belfast and the Soho Foundry. A lively account of Peter Gallegan's month-long stay in Belfast survives in an Irish-language poem which recounts the exploits of a country-loving small farmer in the big city, describing his virtual petrification on beholding the mechanised engine-filled busy shopfloor of the foundry which he likened to an inferno where the workers' faces were smeared with oil as black as the berry on the sloe, wheels turning and a clamour which drained his limbs of all courage.[139] The folklorist and collector Henry Morris, who translated portions of this long poem into English, comments that Gallegan 'was quite bewildered by a visit to MacAdam's ironworks – the Soho Foundry, in Townsend Street, Belfast; and he describes the workers as a lot of black demons under the command of arch-demon, Joe English, the foreman'. While Henry Morris attributed the poem to Gallegan himself, Colm Beckett prefers to interpret it as a composition of Hugh McDonnell's.

The poem alludes to the warm generosity of MacAdam and to his unstinting support for the Gaelic cause:

> For a manly man is MacAdam, who highly esteems the Gaelic,
> And who is friendly to, and beloved by all its bards and poets.
> 'Tis our hope that the High-King will shower luck on him in this world,
> And, after death, elevate him to the skies.
> And as regards the famed fount of the muses,
> By my conscience, methinks he has drained it dry.
> For in the language of authors and a study of their verses
> I should not compare with him any other man whether of Ulster or Leinster.[140]

Daunting as the floor of the Soho Foundry proved for Gallegan himself, it was later to provide a means of living for his son, also christened Peter. In a letter to Robert MacAdam, dated 12 April 1854 and signed 'Peter Gallegan Senr.', he sent MacAdam a catalogue of books and manuscripts for his perusal. As a postscript he added:

> I am anxious to know whether my son Peter (who works in the Foundry) will go to America at present as I gave him the preference to go on my pass and that I would remain till sent for as it is not safe to remain in Belfast there being so many cases of Cholera.[141]

Art MacBionaid or Arthur Bennett (1793–1879)

One of MacAdam's other correspondents at this time was Bryan Sharkey, of Rothbody, who wrote to MacAdam in May 1845 to arrange to send material about Art Mac Cumhaigh (c. 1715–73), a poet of the parish of Creggan (Counties Armagh and Louth): 'I was very busy heretofore with agriculture and I had no time to write until now and I will send you by degrees all that I have'.[142] Another was Patrick Higgins, a police sergeant, stationed in Ballyshannon, Co Donegal, who MacAdam had visited on his tour throughout Ulster. In September 1845 Higgins wrote to MacAdam:

> I send you *Cáineadh Whaley* [ie 'Whaley's Complaint'] and a few other short verses. I am very glad to hear that you succeeded so well on your Northern excursion and that you arrived safe at home ... I cannot omit stating that I never met any man so fit to spell the language and lay it down on paper so correctly as yourself upon which I congratulate you.[143]

Another Irish scholar, Arthur Bennett, or Art MacBionaid lived in the townland of Ballykeel, near Forkill in South Armagh. His father, John Bennett (b 1760), was an Irish teacher. Although Art was a stonemason by trade, he was also well-versed in Irish language, history and related matters. He began sending Robert MacAdam songs and poems to Belfast in 1844, but by October of the same year a degree of tension was discernible. Art acknowledged the receipt of an order for 9/6d, the price MacAdam deemed reasonable for material that had been obtained for him in the south Armagh area by Bennett, but Art added bluntly in his letter to MacAdam: 'The proprietor of that money felt deeply indignant at you and me'. Further on in the same letter Art also added a self-composed verse in Irish complaining of a lack of ink, paper, snuff, or candles and entreating MacAdam to win his favour by sending him the required items.[144]

After an interlude in Art's communication to Belfast, Robert MacAdam asked Hugh McDonnell to write a poem in Irish appealing to Art to resume as before and on receipt of McDonnell's verses MacAdam duly sent them off to Ballykeel. Although MacAdam and McDonnell imagined this poem would be well received, nothing could have been further from the truth. In reply, Art returned a stinging Irish-language satire lambasting McDonnell for such audacity: 'Reflections upon Hugh MacDonnell's conduct for assuming the name of a poet'.[145] Many more exchanges were to follow before Art mellowed. In the meantime Art had managed to secure patronage as a scribe from south Armagh priest and Gaelic scholar Fr Patrick Lamb (1790–1860), although Fr Lamb warned John O'Daly – his colleague in a project to publish the life and work of Ulster Gaelic poet Peadar Ó Doirnín (c. 1704–68) – that Bennett 'is of very singular and odd disposition. I consider he is very fond of his own opinion and would withdraw both from you and me his contribution if we once displeased him'.[146]

A reconciliation was eventually achieved between Bennett and the Belfast-based duo, MacAdam and McDonnell – at the fourth attempt. Relations settled down, for a time at least, so that in years to come Bennett would describe Hugh McDonnell as 'a sharp-edged, erudite poet' (*file faobhrach focalcheart*). However, in 1850 when Bennett proposed to MacAdam the compilation of an extended history of Ireland, Art wanted to write this in English while Robert MacAdam was quite insistent that it be undertaken in Irish. Bennett remained equally intransigent: 'As for the compiling of the Elizabethan Wars etc. in Irish, I would not undertake it upon any consideration'.

Despite the heated language of this letter, the postscript which Bennett appended affords an insight into how MacAdam conducted his meetings with these rural Irish-language scholars whose main sources of livelihood were a variety of more mundane occupations and trades. These included: Sergeant Higgins, of Ballyshannon; farm labourer Peter Gallegan taking 'a little turn at the harvest'; and farmer Bryan Sharkey. On this occasion, Art Bennett invited MacAdam, if he was passing by Newry on business, to come and interrupt him at his work as a stonemason so that both could discuss matters of Irish antiquity:

> P.S. As I am cribbing a footpath on the new road round by the Poorhouse of Newry since Decr. last, and will till April next, should you come to Newry at any time you could see me every dry day, but I come home at night. I am very glad that poor Hugh McDonnell is cleverly recovered from his illness'.[147]

Eventually MacAdam's hard-headed resolution, as potential

patron of the work, held sway and Art began his proposed history in Irish and forwarded an initial excerpt to Belfast.
MacAdam, however, did not find the first sample of the work to
his liking, and when he responded in early March, with a token
remuneration, the South Armagh scribe was incensed and
promptly returned a letter to Belfast, dated 20 March 1850,
which began:

> I acknowledge the receipt of your letter inclosing a few sheets of
> paper and *2s 6d*. I can't say (altogether) that you made little of my
> proposed work. It was as much as the Redeemer of the World was
> sold for. I anticipated the result.[148]

Unsurprisingly, communications between the two soon ground
to a halt and Art Bennett would eventually find an alternative
patron in the form of Newry stationer Edward Augustus
Maginnis (1822–77). It seems ironically fortunate that Art would
see his way to penning this project in Irish despite his earlier
assertions to MacAdam that this would not be undertaken 'upon
any consideration', Unfortunately, however, Art Bennett's substantial history would not appear in book form until well over a
century following his death, although the full printed Irish text
of Bennett's 'History of the Gael with the Foreigner' has been
recently published under the editorship of Monsignor
Réamonn Ó Muirí.[149]

Plans for a Gaelic newspaper and MacAdam's English–Irish dictionary

Robert MacAdam's Irish-language interest was not confined to
Ulster and he corresponded on several issues with the Cork
Irish-language publisher Thomas Swanton. In 1845 MacAdam
wrote to Swanton requesting 'an improved Irish *current handwriting* fit for business and the like', but, as was his wont, the
Belfastman also took the opportunity to enquire in the same letter, as to the salient linguistic features of the dialect of Irish spoken in Munster. Later on, in 1851, we find MacAdam airing the
idea of a weekly national newspaper in Irish with his friend
Swanton:

> *Shaoil me go minic da m-beidheadh páipear-nuaidheacht Gaoidheilg
> ag dul thart na tíre gach seachtmhain, mur ata na páipeair Béurla, go*

d-tuigeadh muintir na h-Éirinn go h-uile é faoi bheagan aimsire, ge b'é
air bith cóigeadh da'r beathuigheadh iad . . .

. . . *Da mbeidheadh na h-aimsireadha beagán níos fearr, agus an*
ghorta as cuimhne na n-daoine, saoilim go m'b'éidir linn páipear
Gaoidheilg fhaghail suas uair 'sa t-seachdmhain. Cuingbhigh so ann do
mheabhair . . .

I have often thought that if there were an Irish-language newspaper circulating the entire country on a weekly basis, after the
fashion of English-language papers, that the entire population of
Ireland, no matter what province they may be from, could understand it in a short space of time . . .

. . . If times were to improve somewhat and the memory of the
famine[150] were erased from people's memory, I think we could
establish an Irish-language weekly. Please bear this in mind . . .[151]

In the meantime, we have evidence that MacAdam was taking
very practical steps to improve the position of the language in his
attempt to compile a substantial English-Irish dictionary.
Unfortunately, the dictionary has not, of yet, been published but
the manuscript survives in the Main Library, Queen's University
Belfast as MS1/153, Hibernica ('Henry') Collection, where it is
described as 'Collection of materials for an English-Irish
Dictionary of Ulster Irish 23 portfolios, wanting letter F,
c. 1830'. Colm Beckett dates the compilation of the work to the
years 1842–56 on the basis of internal evidence such as half a
dozen references to Daniel O'Connell and the mentioning of
the railway which, as Beckett points out, was completed between
Belfast and Lurgan in 1841, Portadown 1842, Armagh 1848,
Dublin 1853.[152]

The surviving manuscript consists of 1,145 pages (11.5 x 14.5
inches) with three columns of 1 and 13/16 inches and a fourth
wide column of 4 and 2/10 inches. In addition to the loss of volume F, the beginning of G is also missing, as is the introduction
(*Díonbhrollach*) although we are fortunate in that, rather mysteri-
ously, a microfilm copy survives of the latter. The introduction,
in Irish, is in the hand of Hugh McDonnell,[153] although Beckett
suspects that this may have been taken down from Robert
MacAdam's dictation. Beckett also interprets the word-order in
the dictionary as resembling the text of Samuel Johnston's
English dictionary which was reprinted in Dublin in 1798. From

the outset, MacAdam gives a clear indication of his motives for undertaking this mammoth work: 'I assure you it is a measure of the extent of my fondness for my native land and for my glowing love of the language . . .'[154] However, he also outlined reasons why his dictionary was based on the language of the ordinary people, and these included the fact that the language of many of the Irish dictionaries previously published tended towards the erudite and were removed from common speech.[155] He did not refrain from controversy in reminding his potential readers that 'the Catholic church does not preach in Irish despite that fact that the Irish language has been the guardian of the faith this past three centuries. But what can I say here!'[156] It is obvious that the welfare of the Irish language was MacAdam's chief concern:

> And as a result of these past hardships we see day by day that her indignant uncertain children are forsaking her [the Irish language], with the result that she now resembles a terminally ill patient whose condition has only been worsened by any prescribed medicine or cure.

It is quite clear that MacAdam's main collaborator in the compilation of the English-Irish dictionary was his Meath scribe Hugh McDonnell. MacAdam was evidently sensitive to any potential accusation that might be levelled against himself personally for undertaking such a task – as he was not a native speaker of the language – and in anticipation of such criticism he declared:

> The scripture says that a man must not wage war or build a house without first reckoning his household and counting his money, I have done likewise, I did not begin this work until I secured for myself a trusty assistant, namely Hugh McDonnell, a native speaker of Irish from his youth who has comprehensively studied Gaelic authors and as well as being a poet in his own right he is esteemed by one and all throughout Ireland on account of his expertise in the native language.[157]

The following, then, are some examples I have selected randomly from fascicule A of MacAdam's English-Irish dictionary to give an example of its layout and its potential as a source for Irish lexicography:

Abolish		*do dheanamh air shiubhal le, do sgrios, do chur air neimhnidh, do chur a g-crich, do chur ar g-cúl.*	He abolished the law altogether. *Rinn se air siubhal leis an dlíghe go huile.* They abolished the privileges of the clergy. *Rinn siad air siubhal le ceart na h-eaglaise.*
Abuse v.a.	to make an ill use of	*baoith-chaitheamh, droch-úsaid a dheánadh, droch-bhail a thabhairt air.*	He abused his property. *Thug sé droch-bhail air a mhaoin.* He abuses the talents that God has given him. *Ghnidh se droch-úsaid de na tíodhlaca a thug Dia dó.*
	to deceive		He abused your good nature by asking you too often for money. *Ghlac se buntaiste air do nádur mhaith ag íarraidh airgid ro-mhinic ort.*
	to reproach rudely	*do sgolladh, do mhasladh, droch-chaint a thabhairt, do dhíbliughadh, do dhi-moladh.*	She stood and abused me for half an hour. *Sheas si do mo sgolladh air feadh leath-uaire.* He abused me like a pick-pocket. *Sgoll se me mur bheidheadh fear piocadh pócaidh.*
	to beat brutally to maltreat	*do bhualadh, droch-úsaid a thabhairt*	He abused his horse dreadfully. *Thug se droch-úsaid an-mheasardha do n-a ghearran.*
Accede v.a.		*do theacht le, do thabhairt isteach.*	Afer some conversation they acceded to my terms. *Tar éis beagan comhráidh thug siad a steach do m 'fhuráil.* Do you think he will accede to your terms? *Measann tu a d-tiocaidh se air aon inntin leat?* or *Measann tu a d-tiobhraidh se a steach ann san nidh a ta tu íarraidh?*
Accumulate	to collect to assemble to heap up	*do chnuasadh, do chruinniughadh, do bhaliughadh, do charnadh, do chruachadh.*	accumulated *'n-a charthaidh* The snow is accumulated in the valley. *Ta an sneachta na charthaidh (na charnán) sa n-gleann*
Accurate	exact precise	*fíor-cheart, lán-cheart, beacht, dearbhtha.*	
Assistance		*cuidiughadh congnadh (or cúngnadh) furtachd fóir*	He gave me assistance. *Thug se cuidiughadh damh.* He called out for assistance. *Sgairt se a mach air chuidiughadh.* We all went to his assistance. *Chuaidh sinn uile ann a chonganta (thartháil).* Patrick came to my assistance like a man. *Thainig Pádraig ann cúnganta liom mur bheidheadh fear ann.*
Atone hard.		*sasadh thabhairt, cúitiughadh thabhairt.*	He atoned for his bad conduct by working *Thug se sasadh ann a dhroch-ghníomhaibh le h-obair chruaidh.*
Attach		*do chur le (chéile), do chur an aice.*	They attached a string to the end of it. *Ghreamuigh siad sriongan do n-a chionn.* He attached it to the wood with glue. *Ghreamuigh se don adhmad é le gliú.*

		His friends are all greatly attached to him. *Tá a cháirde uile docra ceangailte dhó.* The Irish are greatly attached to their country. *Tá speis mhór aige na h-Eirionnaigh ann a dtír féin.*
Audible	*so-chloiste*	Your voice is hardly audible. *Cha mhó ná go g-cluintear do ghlór (Ní mó ná go g-cluintear do ghlór).*
August adj	*uasal, onórach, ard-fhuilteach.*	
Awhile	*tamull; air feadh tamuill, seall, sealad.*	Wait a while *Fuirigh* (and *Fuirigh go fóill*).

British Association Exhibition, Belfast 1852 and the *Ulster Journal of Archaeology*

In the midst of this frenetic activity on the cultivation of the Irish language in the 1840s, the Soho Foundry was also in need of constant attention. MacAdam wrote to Cork Irish-language and manuscript collector John Windele (1801–86):

> I have been so busy a man for some time looking after the grosser matters of this life that I could not get a moment to open my mind's eyes. I always go on hoping that I will some time have leisure but like the Repeal I see no immediate prospect of it.[158]

The Soho Foundry had a workforce of somewhere between 200 and 250 full-time staff, and among the manuscripts, now preserved in the Library of Queen's University Belfast, there are two receipt books in Robert MacAdam's hand containing details of transactions with customers in Leeds, London, Liverpool and places further afield such as Paris and Cairo.[159]

As if his business and Irish-language pursuits were not sufficient, Robert MacAdam also undertook the vice-presidency of the Belfast Natural History and Philosophical Society in 1852. In the same year his brother James and he were invited to organise a major exhibition in Belfast for the British Association for the Advancement of Science, and in a letter dated 31 August 1852, James explains how Robert and he were too preoccupied preparing for the exhibition (to be staged during the arrival in Belfast of the British Association for the Advancement of Science in 1852) to attend the opening ceremony in the presence of the Lord Lieutenant on 1 September: 'I and my brother were invited but did not go, being too busy at the Museum, I at the minerals and he at the antiquities'.[160]

PROSPECTUS.

The Ulster Journal of Archæology.

THE remarkable Exhibition of Northern Irish Antiquities and Historical Reliques, at Belfast, on the occasion of the Meeting, in that town, of the British Association for the advancement of Science, has opened up a new and fertile field of Archæology. The province of Ulster was already historically remarkable, as being the last part of Ireland which held out against the English sway, retaining its ancient customs to a comparatively recent period ; and for the extraordinary changes of population afterwards superinduced by a new and extensive colonisation. It was also, at an earlier period, known to have been the battle-field of the native Irish Chieftains and the Scandinavian Sea-kings. Other distinct races of men, from time to time, are recorded to have effected settlements in the district, whose lineal descendants yet remain.—But, until the present Exhibition, it was not suspected that all these varied events had left vivid and unmistakeable traces throughout the whole Province. The correspondence elicited by the Exhibition, and the objects themselves which were exhibited, have proved that almost every townland in Ulster retains memorials of its singularly chequered history. The mountains still preserve their ancient Cairns and Cromlechs of pre-historic times ; the vallies their earthen tumuli, covering the sepulchres of heroes. The peat-bogs daily give up their ancient treasures, of gold, silver, and bronze. Even the modern innovations, the railway and canal, assist in revealing the singular relics of a former age. Finally, the descendants of the ancient families still retain in their possession many authentic and interesting records and local traditions. The whole Province, in fact, at this moment teems with the most varied and remarkable memorials of successive phases of society, still accessible, and still capable of complete elucidation. The tangled web of Northern Irish History can yet be unravelled by existing aids ;—but in twenty years more the case will be different. The men who are now the depositories of family and local history will be no more, or will have become the denizens of another land ; the manuscripts will be lost ; the bronzes, the gold and silver, will be consigned to the melting-pot ; and thus a chasm will occur in our historical annals, never again to be filled.

It is therefore believed, that the present is a fitting opportunity for endeavouring to rescue from oblivion what remains of the History of Ulster ; and accordingly, a number of gentlemen in Belfast and the neighbourhood, interested in Irish Archæology, propose to establish a Journal for this especial purpose, and now announce their intention.

The Ulster Journal of Archæology will appear Quarterly, and will be devoted principally (but not exclusively) to the elucidation of the Antiquities and ancient History of Ulster. Each number, be sides being a record of interesting and authentic facts, will be open to the discussion of all disputed subjects in Irish Archæology ; and will be illustrated with Lithographs of curious ancient objects.

TO BE PUBLISHED FOR SUBSCRIBERS ONLY.

ANNUAL SUBSCRIPTION TWELVE SHILLINGS.

NAMES OF SUBSCRIBERS RECEIVED BY { MESSRS. ARCHER & SONS, CASTLE-PLACE, BELFAST ;— J. RUSSELL SMITH, ESQ., SOHO-SQUARE, LONDON ;—AND ROBERT MACADAM, ESQ., 18, COLLEGE-SQUARE, BELFAST.

Belfast, September, 1852.

This exhibition took up so much of Robert MacAdam's time that his momentary silence somewhat perplexed his Cork friends Thomas Swanton and John Windele who wondered what had become of him. Swanton in particular had been writing urging MacAdam to set up a 'monthly Iberno-Celtic magazine' and reproached his Belfast fellow revivalist commenting:

> I am sorry you do not give yourself more leisure for Gaelic subjects. Hibernia in her present state demands the public services of all her efficient sons ... I shall be happy to see you and discuss and consider your plan for printing Irish in English types and a spelling which will be as simple as can be required.

Swanton then resorted to writing to Windele: 'Have you heard of or from Robert MacAdam? I wrote twice or thrice and have not a line – he was the only man in Ireland who could do much for our ancient tongue in its modern form'.[161]

Through time, MacAdam was to write to Windele to thank him for the Ogham stones which he had sent to Belfast for the exhibition: 'The Oghams which you sent have caused much wonder here and there is an anxiety to know more on the subject. We have nothing of this kind in the North'. If one examines the distribution of the available corpus of Ogham stones in Ireland it can be seen that MacAdam was certainly justified in his comment as, three-fifths of these are concentrated in south-west Munster (Counties Cork and Kerry) with only a handful in the north.[162] MacAdam also explained in this same letter how business commitments and the effort required to organise the British Association exhibition had been absorbing his time:

> Until the affairs connected with the Exhibition are over I shall be a bad correspondent. The average number of letters I have to write daily in the way of business is very large and when I attend to the concerns of 200 workmen and do all the talking as is required I assure you even in ordinary times I cannot find a great deal of leisure for lighter work. Then when in addition to this the whole labour of getting up an extensive exhibition which of itself causes a pretty considerable amount of letter writing devolves on me you will pause for a moment before you set me down as a hopeless correspondent.[163]

In his *Descriptive Catalogue of the Collection Antiquities* accompanying the 1852 Exhibition it was clearly stated that a central aim

was to 'enable strangers from other countries to judge for themselves of the nature and extent of our ancient civilization', with
an aspiration that an upshot of the whole would be 'an impulse
given to the study of Archaeology and the preservation of antiquities in Ireland'. This promotion of the Gaelic element of Irish
culture, old and modern, was in keeping with Robert
MacAdam's mottoes for the visit of Queen Victoria to Belfast
three years earlier in 1849, when she was welcomed in Irish:

> *Do mhíle fáilte a Bhanríoghain Éire*
> *Go cathraigh éigseach chríche Uladh.*
> *Mas fuar síon ar mhullaigh a sliabh*
> *Is grádhach díolos croidhe a bunadh.*

> 1000 welcomes Oh Queen of Ireland
> to the poetic city of the land of Ulster.
> If cold be the wind on its mountain-tops,
> its people's hearts are warm and loyal.[164]

Among the items on display at the exhibition were Irish manuscripts belonging to Samuel Bryson, Lord George Hill of
Gweedore, Co Donegal, and a large selection of Robert
MacAdam's personal collection. There were also harps belonging to O'Kelly, O'Neill and Hempson; two bells, one from
Bangor monastery, the other associated with St Muran: 'A most
remarkable object; it is incased in silver, elaborately ornamented
and set with precious stones. Found in the hut of a poor fisherman in Innishowen, Co. Donegal in 1850'. Further exhibits
incuded: leather sandals recovered from bogs; flint arrowheads,
bronze swords and rings, a Tara brooch, pikes, bagpipes, rectan-
gular *methers,* or wooden drinking vessels; an old wooden cup
'said to be that of Con O'Neil'; 'Turlough O'Neill's silver seal
with the "bloody hand of Ulster" attached'; and perhaps the
most bizzare item of all the 'Skull of Carolan, the celebrated
Irish bard'.

Judging by the mood of MacAdam's letter, sent to Windele in
Cork, the exhibition proved well worthy of his time and efforts:

> We have got the bustle of the Association work over and are now
> opening our Exhibition of Antiquities to the general public. It
> has been a most successful experiment as every visitor assures us.
> Never before in Ireland was such a collection of antiquities
> brought together. If at all possible you ought to take a run down

and see it – I enclose you an exhibitor's ticket hoping you may
really come. The antiquarian spirit seems to be roused among us
and finding so many persons in the Country taking an interest
in such matters we have decided on trying a 'Journal of
Archaeology' to appear quarterly . . .[165]

Industrious as ever, MacAdam kept to his promise and the following year witnessed the appearance of the the first volume of
the *Ulster Journal of Archaeology* with himself as editor. This journal survives until the present day, although it has experienced
lacunae in its publication during its existence over practically the
last 150 years. Currently, the journal is in its third series although
the issues of the *Ulster Journal of Archaeology* in this latter series
have been much more strictly achaeological in content – in the
more narrow sense of the modern discipline. In MacAdam's
reign as editor, from 1853 to 1862, the journal was much more
wide-ranging and interdisciplinary, and sometimes, anecdotal in
nature:

> The Study of Archaeology is daily becoming more attractive to
> all persons of education and taste. Combining as it now does, a
> wide range of subjects connected with literature and art, it
> affords materials for the exercise of almost every kind of talent.
> Not merely the historian, and professed antiquary, but also the
> geographer, the painter, the architect, the linguist and all the
> numberous class of explorers in the nooks and crannies of knowl-
> edge, may be each of them in this way, votaries of Archaeology.[166]

This period around the mid nineteenth century could be
regarded as a zenith in Robert MacAdam's achievements. The
Ulster Journal of Archaeology, attracted contributions from many
of the leading and most eminent scholars in the country, and
beyond.

John O'Donovan, Professor of Celtic Studies at Queen's College Belfast

In 1849 a chair of Celtic Studies was created at Queen's College
Belfast which had itself been recently established in 1845. The
first appointee to the Chair of Celtic, on a salary of £100 per
annum, was John O'Donovan:

> Another self-taught scholar was a pioneer, whose work has
> proved of permanent value, was the Professor of Celtic languages,

John O'Donovan (aged 40). As an official in the historical department of the ordnance survey of Ireland he had acquired an unrivalled knowledge of Irish topography, both through research in ancient Irish manuscripts and through field-work; and he had a large share in fixing the forms of Irish place-names that were incorporated in the first ordnance-survey maps. He had published a *Grammar of the Irish Language* (1845), and his authoritative editions of important historical texts in Irish had culminated in his monumental work on the Annals of the Four Masters, of which three volumes had appeared in 1848. The closing-down of the historical department of the ordnance survey in 1842 had left O'Donovan with no regular source of income, so that his appointment to the chair at Belfast of which the teaching duties were certain to be slight came as a timely relief for a harassed scholar.[167]

Not having any full-time students, O'Donovan's principal teaching duties in Belfast consisted of six lectures during the summer term on a variety of subjects relating to early Irish language, literature and history.[168] Among those attending O'Donovan's summer lecture courses was Robert MacAdam, and on 8 May 1851 he wrote to his Cork correspondent Thomas Swanton. The letter, written in Irish, expressed delight that Cork had appointed a Professor of Irish[169] and then went on to deal mostly with details of O'Donovan's activities in Belfast:

Our Professor, O'Donovan, arrived here a day or two ago and plans to address us, twice a week in the College, on the origins of the Irish language and its relationship to other languages. When he has done that I shall send you an account. I am glad to see that these sages are coming to life somewhat as I was beginning to think that they had either passed away or fallen asleep! O'Donovan tells me that he knows you from letters he has received from you but that he has not met you in person.

I have been trying to encourage him to start up an Irish-language monthly along the lines of *Chamber's Journal,* but he is extremely occupied with other matters and is not enthusiastic to risk becoming involved with such an undertaking. He works a great deal on ancient sources preserved in Dublin and publishes them under the patronage of the *Irish Archaeological Society.* He is a most accomplished scholar in this regard and I doubt if there is another scholar alive who can decipher these old manuscripts as comprehensively as he. He tells me there is an antiquaries society in Kilkenny and that it can boast of two or three Irish scholars

among its members.[170] Perhaps you are aware of these people, I
should certainly like to make contact . . .[171]

While it would appear that no ideological meeting of minds
occurred between O'Donovan and MacAdam – at least regard-
ing the propagation of the spoken language, where O'Donovan
seemed markedly less enthusiastic than MacAdam – it is likely
that their relationship remained fairly cordial as MacAdam was
to publish articles by the recently appointed Professor of Celtic
in the *Ulster Journal of Archaeology*. Indeed Patricia Boyne points
out that when O'Donovan began his summer lectures in the
Spring of 1850:

> He was dissatisfied with the coverage of his lectures in the Belfast
> papers, and decided to give copies of the lectures to the *Ulster
> Journal of Archaeology,* which proved a good friend and published
> twelve features from his pen during the years 1857 to 1861.[172]

MacAdam's later more reclusive years:
Oisín i ndéidh na Féinne

Boundless and indefatigable as Robert MacAdam's energy may
have appeared, the combined pressures of business at the Soho
Foundry, mounting the 1852 British Association Exhibition in
Belfast, and the publication of the first issue of the *Ulster Journal
of Archaeology* in spring 1853, took a temporary toll on his health,
resulting in a suspension of his commercial duties. He spent
some time in Scotland recuperating, and later rested near
Holywood, Co Down. On 29 December 1853 James MacAdam
wrote:

> My brother's state of health has been a great source of anxiety to
> me. He had always been a hard worker but he has overexerted
> himself in getting up the exhibition of Irish antiquities at the
> meeting of the British Association here last year and he had no
> relaxation afterwards. His health became very bad in Summer,
> however he is now nearly recovered. As the most important parts
> of the business devolve upon him I was greatly annoyed by his
> unavoidable absence.[173]

Despite this lapse in Robert's health, he was to continue with his
duties as editor of the *Ulster Journal of Archaeology* for a further ten
years. Nevertheless, by the time the first series of the *Ulster*

Journal of Archaeology had come to an end in 1863, he was quite
a solitary figure. As a confirmed bachelor he had devoted his life
to business, his Irish language pursuits and his antiquarian and
literary societies. He had been involved in scholarly and cultural
pursuits from an early age and so he was now beginning to out-
live many of his former friends and mentors.

Dr James MacDonnell passed away on 8 April 1845, fittingly
lamented in a moving elegy composed, in Irish, by MacAdam's
scribe Hugh McDonnell.[174] His funeral was one of the largest
attended at the time with the city' s rich and poor lining the
streets in their thousands to pay farewell to him as his funeral
cortège left Belfast for his native Cushendall.[175] James
MacDonnell's efforts over the previous half a century meant that
the town of Belfast was now equipped with schools, libraries and
societies which supported the Irish language and its associated
culture and interests. In many ways MacAdam could be regarded
as a successor to MacDonnell, as it was he who was to become
the central figure in Belfast literary and antiquarian circles following MacDonnell's death.

For 15 years MacAdam donned this mantle of leadership,
gathering around him a body of scribes and scholars who were
at the forefront of work on the Irish language, literature and
antiquities. Through time, however, casualties were sustained
such as the loss, in 1853, of surgeon and Irish manuscript com-
piler Samuel Bryson – and we have already seen how the strain
of managing the Irish antiquities section of the British
Association Exhibtion, almost single-handedly, had proved detri-
mental to MacAdam's physical state of health in the same year.
One of MacAdam's copyists, Peter Gallegan, appears to have
produced little for him after 1854,[176] while another loyal
scribe and Irish-language advisor of 16 years' standing, Hugh
McDonnell, left Belfast in 1856 to take up residence with his
daughter near Bunbeg in Co Donegal, where he found employment, through the offices of his son-in-law, as a teacher
with the Island and Coast Society schools. Hugh was never to
return to Belfast and remained in Donegal until his death in
1867.[177]

1861 brought personal sadness for Robert MacAdam with the
death of his brother James. Writing afterwards, to Windele in
Cork, Robert put a brave face on things explaining:

> I found so many matters pressing on my attention after my
> brother's death that I considered it more judicious to lay aside all
> less important things for a year. I am gradually getting things into
> satisfactory order and intend resuming publication of the *Journal*
> in May . . . I hope I am not lost to Archaeology yet . . . I am glad
> to tell you that that I have the *Journal* underway once more.

In spite of this positive attitude, MacAdam did take stock of what
had happened in Irish scholarly circles, as 1861 was also the year
John O'Donovan died, while Eugene O'Curry, O'Donovan's
brother-in-law, died in 1862. These two men were widely recognised as among the most brilliant authorities on ancient Irish
sources:

> But what losses we have experienced even since I published the
> last no. of the *Journal!* I really do not see how we shall ever fill the
> places of O'Donovan and O'Curry. Several archaeological
> friends, too, in the North have gone, who assisted me with their
> pen and their kind encouragement. However I shall go a while
> longer.[178]

Clare-born O'Curry (1794–1862) was also self-educated before
taking up a post in the historical department of the Ordnance
Survey alongside O'Donovan and was a scholar of similar ability and expertise as O'Donovan. One of his many great works,
Manuscript Materials of Ancient Irish History, had just been published in 1861 and was to prove a seminal work in Irish literary
history.[179] In saluting the work of O'Donovan[180] and Eugene
O'Curry, MacAdam showed an insightful appreciation of two
great scholars of the age, later echoed by Lady Gregory in the
early twentieth century:

> Through all those years we had thought so barren, a group of
> scholars had gone on with their work, the translation of the old
> Irish manuscripts. O'Curry in his *Manners and Customs of Ancient
> Ireland* had given fine pages of history and romance. O'Donovan
> and O'Daly did the same.[181]

Try as he might, the valiant MacAdam could only sustain the
expensively produced *Ulster Journal of Archaeology* (of which he
was both editor and proprietor) through its ninth issue during
1861–62, and, on his return from a trip abroad in 1863 he found
it impossible to produce a tenth volume. By 1865 he was to
receive his last letter from his constant correspondent John

Windele from Cork[182] and he was gradually becoming an Oisín-like figure, lamenting the passing of his colleagues of yester-year, the *Fianna*. He nevertheless persevered as best as he could and in 1888, the year of his eightieth birthday, he accepted the office of President of the Belfast Natural History and Philosophical Society, and was still on the committee of the Linen Hall Library.

In the meantime, business at the Soho Foundry, had declined in the years following the death of his brother James. The work-force dropped to 190 in 1866, with 40 fewer in 1870. Financial difficulties saw the gradual closure of the foundry in 1894, while in the same year he was forced to witness what must have been for him a most demoralising spectacle, the auction of his books. Five years earlier, in 1889, he had undergone a similar ordeal, the break-up his extensive manuscript collection. When the collection was nearing its height around the 1850s, Oscar Wilde's father, Sir William, made the following comments on the medical portion of the MacAdam holdings: 'Robert Mac Adam of Belfast possesses the largest private collection of Irish medical MSS in the country'.[183] As the century drew to a close, however, some 50 of his manuscripts, so painstakingly amassed over a 60-year period, were bought by Church of Ireland bishop and historian Rev Dr William Reeves,[184] while others were bestowed upon the Belfast Natural History and Philosophical Society.[185]

By the end of his life, MacAdam was an isolated, solitary, almost pitiable figure. Following his death at his home in College Square East on 3 January 1895, the *Belfast Newsletter* said of him, in its obituary column, six days later:

> Of late years he was seen little in public. He had outlived all his intimate friends and most of his contemporaries so that there are now but few remaining who could recall the variety and charm of his conversation and his apparent inexhaustible store of information.

Robert MacAdam: his legacy and achievements

When Robert MacAdam was laid to rest in Knockbreda Churchyard,[186] Belfast lost one of the great Irish-language and antiquarian figures of the nineteenth century. Born into a devel-

18 College Square East

14 Dec 1893

L'Estrange & Brett

Recd 15 DEC. 93

~~Dear Sir~~

You are probably aware that I have been confined to the house for a considerable time. Might I ask you to call here at your earliest convenience to advise me as to a matter of consequence to me The Belfast Bank Directors have advised me to apply to you at once

Yours truly

Robert McAdam

Charles Brett Esq

Letter to solicitors L'Estrange & Brett from Robert MacAdam, 1893.

oping and bustling town of the early nineteenth century, (where commercial and cultural life was dominated by an enlightened, imaginative and liberal Presbyterian class, and where level-headed business pursuits and patronage of the arts and music went hand in hand) Robert MacAdam finished his days in a fully industrialised city which had increased its population tenfold, from the time of his birth, and where sectarian divisions had become noticeably more marked.[187] Many factors contributed to this regrettable state of affairs but, whatever the exact causes, the period from the 1860s onwards appears to mark a turning point. Before this date many Presbyterians would have found it equally fashionable to have been a member of the Ulster Gaelic Society, the Harp Society, the Literary Society, or the Belfast Natural History and Philosophical Society. From this time onwards, however, Irish-language and related activities began to be regarded with circumspection. In 1875, for example, Samuel Ferguson complained that he was being thwarted in his attempts to have a Chair of Celtic restored at Queen's (having lain empty since O'Donovan's time some 15 years earlier):

> We have done our endeavour to found such a chair here but all things Celtic are regarded by our educated classes as of questionable *ton* and an idea exists that it is inexpedient to encourage anything tending to foster Irish sentiment.[188]

The careers and pursuits of Robert Mac Adam and Samuel Ferguson merit a comparison. Born in Belfast two years after MacAdam, Samuel Ferguson was also educated at the Belfast Academical Institution (and the Belfast Academy) before progressing to Trinity College Dublin. While Robert MacAdam, and his brother James, were establishing their successful business at the Soho Foundry, Samuel Ferguson was embarking upon a highly distinguished legal career, being called to the Bar in 1839, made Queen's Counsel in 1859, and Doctor of Laws in 1864. Like so many Belfast Academical Institution old boys of their day, both MacAdam and Ferguson demonstrated a keen interest in Irish language, history and antiquities. MacAdam, as we have seen, not merely amassed manuscripts and took an interest in Irish archaeology but was also a cosmopolitan and widely travelled man. In similar vein, one can note how, in the mid 1840s, Ferguson likewise travelled in Europe sketching many cathedrals

and churches dedicated to Irish saints.[189] Reminiscent of
MacAdam's situation in Belfast, Ferguson's home in Dublin was
very much a meeting place for those interested in Irish literature,
indeed Sir Samuel's book *Lays of the Western Gael* (1865) and his
epic poem *Congal* (1872) were works which did a great deal to
pre-empt and inspire much of the flavour of the later
Anglo-Irish revival of Yeat's time. While it could be argued that
Sir Samuel Ferguson rose to become a more central figure in
Irish life than Robert MacAdam, becoming Deputy Keeper of
the Public Records in Ireland (1867) and later President of the
Royal Irish Academy,[190] both men's interests and tastes were
quite similar. The similarity in tastes and interests between
MacAdam and Ferguson is to be expected, especially when
one considers their well-rounded schooling at the Belfast
Academical Institution, and the fact that they both emerged
from such a liberal and enlightened Presbyterian background in
early nineteenth-century Belfast. Furthermore, it should come
as no great surprise to learn that both men were personal
friends, considering their proximity in age. Indeed, they often
discussed matters of language and antiquities together as may be
seen from the following passage from a letter written by
MacAdam to John Windele, in Cork in 1854:

> I have two Manuscript Genealogies of the MacDonnells [of Co.
> Antrim], one dated 1618, the other 1744. I send you a translation
> comprising both ... I think I shall not be able to procure you any-
> thing more about Colla Ciotach,[191] but I saw Mr. Samuel
> Ferguson, the barrister, I yesterday and he said he would send you
> something.[192]

The final years of both MacAdam (†1895) and Ferguson
(†1896) overlapped, albeit slightly, with the emergence of the
Gaelic League in the late nineteenth century but there was no
sizeable northern Protestant participation in this organisation
comparable with that within the Ulster Gaelic Society of the
1830s. The Dublin-based Gaelic League was set up in 1893 by
Douglas Hyde (1860–1949), the son of a Co Roscommon
Church of Ireland clergyman.[193] Although its constitution made
it an apolitical and non-sectarian organisation, the adoption by
the Gaelic League at its annual congress in 1915 of a motion,
proposed by Piaras Béaslaí, supporting a Gaelic and free Ireland

was to precipitate Hyde's resignation. In addition to this, many Gaelic League figures would also become associated with Irish nationalist movements, among them Eoin Mac Néill[194] and Patrick Pearse,[195] leading figures behind the Easter Rising of 1916.

The first branch of The Gaelic League to be established in Belfast was in 1895, the year of Robert MacAdam's death, but the organisation's membership contrasted rather markedly to that of the Ulster Gaelic Society two generations earlier. Cathal O'Byrne has highlighted the tensions experienced by the arrival of the Gaelic League in Belfast:

> With the advent of the Gaelic League ... the language in Belfast came, at least partly, into its own.[196] But the League was never considered quite 'respectable' – that awful Belfast word ... To be a Gaelic Leaguer was to be suspected always. The League might shout at its loudest and longest that it was non-political and non-sectarian. The slogan did not impress Belfast. With the League's membership at ninety-nine per cent Catholic what could one expect? 'Scratch a Gaelic Leaguer and you will find a Fenian' was the formula in the old days.[197]

The crucial political developments of late nineteenth- and early twentieth-century Ireland (with an accompanying set of sectarian implications) have tended to overshadow the achievements of the Presbyterian-led Irish language revival of the late eighteenth to mid nineteenth century. Jonathan Bardon quotes from the *Belfast Newsletter,* 12 July 1867, which described Orangemen disembarking at Bangor and walking out towards Newtownards 'without interruption save the *cead mile failthes* of hosts of sympathisers'.[198]

Chris McGimpsey draws attention to the close of the era of substantial Belfast Unionist public involvement and association with Gaelic symbols:

> Equally significant was the depiction of Erin's Harp above the phrase *Erin Go Bragh* [ie 'Ireland Forever'] in large letters outside the Ulster Unionist Convention of June 1892. It was this meeting, held in a specially constructed pavilion in the Botanic Park and attended by 11,879 delegates, which saw the birth of modern unionism. As late as the turn of the century unionists were not unhappy with reference to the native tongue.[199]

It seems regrettable, in the extreme, that the activities and cultural legacy of liberal Presbyterian Belfast in the late eighteenth and early nineteenth century should be so diminished and erased from the general consciousness of our own times. By focusing on MacAdam's life and that of his associates some of the major achievements of this era have been highlighted: Dr James MacDonnell and Edward Bunting; the Harp Festival, and the *Ancient Music of Ireland;* the work of the Bryson family in Belfast; Rev William Neilson in the Belfast Academical Institution; and the work of the Ulster Gaelic Society formed, with MacAdam as co-secretary, in 1830. All in all, then, a lively and impressive scene with Irish language, literature and music lying at its core. MacAdam deserves to be remembered for his monumental accomplishments, not merely as an industrialist and businessman, as an archaeologist and antiquarian, but also as a champion of the cultivation of the Gaelic language and its broader culture, old and modern. In many ways it would be appropriate to translate what Breandán Ó Buachalla has to say of MacAdam's legacy, as it is Ó Buachalla above all other modern scholars who has been responsible for unearthing the story of the life of this remarkable, modest and most honourable of men:

> It was MacAdam who first had the idea of collecting folklore from the mouths of the common folk, although it is an honour still to be accorded to him; it was he who first had the idea of 'reviving the language' although he has yet to receive credit for this – he truly was 'the First Gaelic Leaguer'. He was a hero and a giant of a man – but a hero and giant who has been forgotten and lost in oblivion.[200]

Robert MacAdam's philosophy and achievements may best be summed up by proverb number 188 from his *Six Hundred Gaelic Proverbs Collected in Ulster,* and his own interpretation of it:
'*Sì an dìas is truime is ìsle chromas a cionn*
– the heaviest ear of corn is the one that lowliest bends its head'.

This is a beautiful metaphor, implying that the man who has most knowledge is always the most modest.

The Proverb Collection of Robert MacAdam

AJ Hughes

As a labour of love, *Six Hundred Gaelic Proverbs Collected in Ulster,* speaks volumes for Robert MacAdam's intuitive understanding of the poetry of the language and also illustrates his fondness for witticisms. The collection also gives us an insight into the extent of MacAdam's knowledge. In addition to the accolades he merits for his work as a pioneer of the Irish-language revival, MacAdam also has the honour of being an early example of a 'good European', for, in addition to his Irish and Scottish material, he also included French, Italian and Spanish proverbs – not forgetting examples in Latin and Greek.[1]

These proverbs first appeared in print under MacAdam's editorship in the first series of his *Ulster Journal of Archaeology* which ran from 1853–63. The following are the page references to the proverbs as they occur in the original articles:

Introduction by R MacAdam *UJA* vol 6 (1858) pp 172–7
Proverb numbers 1–96 *UJA* vol 6 (1858) pp 177–83
Proverb numbers 97–332 *UJA* vol 6 (1858) pp 250–67
Proverb numbers 333–457 *UJA* vol 7 (1859) pp 278–87
Proverb numbers 458–600 *UJA* vol 9 (1861-2) pp 223–36

A short collection of 31 items of local English phrases was published by an author signing himself as 'H' in an earlier volume of the *Ulster Journal of Archaeology*, 'Rustic Proverbs Current in Ulster',[2] and typical examples from this source are as follows:

8. 'Niver powr watther on a drownded mouse.' (Ulster)
(Do not injure those who are already oppressed.)
'Pour not water on a drowned mouse.' (English)

10. 'Let ivvery her'n hing by its own tail.' (Ulster) (Let every man depend upon himself. In the cottages dried herrings are suspended by a rod passed through their tails.) 'Every herring must hang by its own gill.'(English) 'Let ilka herrin hing by its ain head.' (Scottish)

The format of these examples from 'Rustic Proverbs Current in Ulster' (ie proverb plus an explanation and/or an example of when or how it might be used in conversation), seems clearly to have shaped MacAdam's layout for *Six Hundred Gaelic Proverbs* as he himself points out in his own introduction:

> Half the wit and point of a proverb consists in its apt application; and the Irish, as might be expected, are often peculiarly happy in this. I have occasionally given examples such as I have myself met with; but these are not to be taken as by any means the best; for many of the proverbs (especially those expressed in a figurative manner) are capable of an endless variety of applications, both directly and ironically; and there is no mode more frequently employed propensity to fun and humour, than the witty application of a proverb.[3]

Although it seems evident that MacAdam's mode of presentation was influenced by 'Rustic Proverbs Current in Ulster', it appears that the impetus to collect Irish proverbs in the first place may owe something to the short collections in the works of earlier and contemporary Irish scholars such as the work of MacAdam's acquaintance John O'Donovan who had previously published a short collection of Irish-language proverbs in the *Dublin Penny Journal*.[4] Whatever the major influences on MacAdam were which stimulated his initial decision to collection, it would appear that *Six Hundred Gaelic Proverbs* represents the first sustained localised collection of printed proverbs in the field.[5] Another later collector and authority on Ulster Gaelic proverbs Henry Morris would also write favourably of MacAdam's work:

> He seems to have attained to a good literary knowledge of the language. Unlike Bryson,[6] he cultivated the more modern Gaelic literature found amongst the people and in the manuscripts of the preceeding two centuries. Aided by others he made a collection of 600 Ulster Irish proverbs, and published them in the 'Ulster Journal' during the years 1858–62. O'Donovan had published a collection somewhat earlier in 'The Dublin Penny Journal' but MacAdam's remained the best and largest single collection of Irish proverbs until the publication of 'Sean-Fhocla Uladh' in 1907.[7] And they are noted down and printed with a faithfulness and accuracy which does great credit to himself and his assistants in the work.[8]

Henry Morris (1874–1945) was born in Co Monaghan and was

a prominent member of the Gaelic League in his native county where he founded a local branch in Lisdoonan, and he was also co-founder of the *Louth Archaeological Society* in 1903. A schoolteacher and inspector by profession, Henry also gained prominence as a collector of Irish songs and proverbs, publishing under the Irish form of his name, Énrí O Muirgheasa. He held a series of teaching posts throughout Ireland: Dundalk, Co Louth (1901–7), Strabane, Co Tyrone 1907, Derry City 1912 before moving on to positions elsewhere in the inspectorate in Skerries and Sligo.[9] Morris can be seen as a successor to MacAdam as he, above all others, was to carry on the collection of Ulster Gaelic proverbs in the twentieth century. Ó Muirgheasa stated that Irish-language collector Seosamh Laoide (Joseph Lloyd) advised him to begin a collection of proverbs in the barony of Farney, Co Monaghan, Ó Muirgheasa's native district and a Gaeltacht area until the beginning of this century.[10] In 1898 Ó Muirgheasa published his first modest collection of 76 proverbs in an Irish-language publication *The Gaelic Magazine*.[11] Thankfully Ó Muirgheasa continued to add prolifically to his own private collection and in 1907 he published his celebrated work on Ulster Gaelic proverbs *Sean-Fhocla Uladh*.[12]

In this first edition of *Sean-Fhocla Uladh* Ó Muirgheasa's intention appears to have been to include the entire corpus of MacAdam's *Six Hundred Gaelic Proverbs Collected in Ulster* from the *Ulster Journal of Archaeology*[13] and to these Ó Muirgheasa added over 1,000 which he himself had collected. In incorporating the text of *Six Hundred Gaelic Proverbs Collected in Ulster* into *Sean-Fhocla Uladh,* however, Ó Muirgheasa made some quite fundamental changes and omissions to MacAdam's work as it had first appeared. He also changed some of MacAdam's spellings to bring them into line with the orthography which was more commonly employed in the *Gaelic League* at that time.[14] On a more serious note, however, Ó Muirgheasa omitted all the examples of proverbs which MacAdam had cited from other languages. In addition, some of MacAdam's English-language notes were added to in the 1907 version, while MacAdam's English translation and notes were omitted in subsequent editions of Ó Muirgheasa's work.[15] Later, Ó hUrmoltaigh, in his publication of the third edition of Ó Muigheasa's work,[16] revised the entire spelling system of both

Ó Muirgheasa's and MacAdam's examples bringing them, more or less, into line with the orthography of the Official Standard *(An Caighdeán Oifigiúil),* a system adopted in most Irish-language circles from the mid twentieth century onwards.

Editorial method

Considering, the many changes and omissions which have been imposed on *Six Hundred Gaelic Proverbs Collected in Ulster* since MacAdam's own day, it was decided here, to prepare a fresh edition which reproduces the work as closely as possible to the manner in which MacAdam himself sent it to the press. In addition to proving a fitting monument to Robert MacAdam's ability as a proverb collector and comparativist (for such an early period in the subject), a second edition of his original collection also allows us an intimate insight into his personality and keen sense of humour and observation – a personality perhaps nowhere more clearly visible than in the valuable notes and comments he appended to many of the proverbs.

In preparing the current text of *Six Hundred Gaelic Proverbs Collected in Ulster* I have maintained MacAdam's original Irish spellings throughout.[17] At the same time, however, I have tried to cater for those readers and learners of the Irish language who are only familiar with the modern revised orthography of Irish. To accommodate this latter group I have supplied forms in a spelling more in keeping with current-day Irish. In providing these modern forms I have not stuck rigidly or dogmatically to a prescribed standard form, as many of the proverbs contain features which, while not standard, are nevertheless acceptable variants in the new system.[18] Features in this latter category consist of items such as the negative particle *cha/chan, char,* as opposed to *ní, níor;* relative forms of the verb in the present in future in *-(e)as;*[19] old independent *-aidh* in the present tense as opposed to *-(e)ann,*[20] traditional Ulster forms of the irregular verbs such as *ghní* 'does', *t(h)ig* 'comes', *théid* 'goes', *bheir* 'gives', etc.[21]

The reader should note, then, that the forms which occur in modern Irish orthography in this edition of *Six Hundred Gaelic Proverbs Collected in Ulster* have been undertaken by AJ Hughes, ie all those found at the end of each proverb between square brackets [ ]. Other cases where additions to the original text have been made are in the English translations for French, Italian, and Latin examples, as proverbs for these latter languages were usually cited untranslated by MacAdam in his original edition. Again, all such additions occur between brackets [ ]. Any notes indicated by an asterisk ★ in the text of the proverbs (dealt with on pp 181–4) have likewise been added by Hughes, as have the Irish and English indices to the entire Irish corpus, plus the index of proverbs from other languages (pp 181–4).

MacAdam's sources

In his Introduction to *Six Hundred Gaelic Proverbs Collected in Ulster,* MacAdam informs us that he amassed his collection during fieldwork:

> The present collection of Irish proverbs, (amounting of six hundred) though confined to the northern province, is the largest which has yet been published in Ireland, and still by no means comprises the whole of those extant in Ulster. They were written down by myself from the mouths of people, during a series of years, when opportunities brought me sometimes into contact with the Gaelic-speaking population of various localities in the north. These opportunities have been more rare of late, or I am persuaded I could have extended the collection to several hundreds more.[22]

There can be little doubt that these proverbs were obtained from living speech, as many of them have been recorded by subsequent scholars in other collections. One may note, for example, that no. 591 in MacAdam's work was also heard later in Co Monaghan by Ó Muirgheasa,[23] while further collections obtained elsewhere in Ireland (such as Co Donegal, Co Mayo, Co Clare, and Co Cork, etc) have produced a form resembling the following:

> Ní truimide don loch an lach
> Ní truimide don each a shrian
> Ní truimide don chaora a holainn
> Ní truimide don cholainn ciall.[24]

Similarly, many other examples are widely attested throughout the entire Gaelic-speaking area as a whole. For instance, proverb number 285 'The natural disposition of a cat bursts out through its eyes' was recorded by Wagner in Kerry;[25] while number 559 'When the old hag is hard pressed she must run' was heard in a story by Holger Pedersen at the turn of the century on the Aran Islands,[26] and number 494 is commonplace throughout Gaelic Scotland.[27] The Ulster origin of the proverbs in MacAdam's work need not be doubted but few clues are given as to an exact location within the province, apart from rare exceptions such as number 503 which refers to Gweedore, Co Donegal, number 506 which was 'a common saying in Louth and Meath',[28] or number 510 which refers to the Drake family of Co Meath, while the same county is referred to in numbers 341 and 498. The Meath examples may well have come from MacAdam's scribe Hugh McDonnell, or even Peter Gallegan, people who Morris (1921) counted among MacAdam's aides in preparing the work. Indeed some examples of the proverbs can be traced to usage in Hugh McDonnell's *Philosophy*[29] and his poetry.[30] While number 232 'Cows far from home have long horns' was cited in a letter from South Armagh scribe Art Bennett to MacAdam, 3 April 1850, *bíonn adharca móra ar na ba 'bhfad ó bhaile,*[31] it does nevertheless differ from the printed version, and it also appears that a few other proverbs cited by Bennett did not find their way into Six *Hundred Gaelic Proverbs.*[32]

In the absence of a specific location within Ulster it may difficult to connect the majority of these proverbs to a given area and many are ubiquitous as can be seen from number 430 'A man cannot whistle and chaw meal' which has been recorded in Tory Island,[33] or number 381 'There is hope from the mouth of the sea, but not from the mouth of the grave' the Rannafast version of which inspired the title of Donegal Gaelic writer Seosamh Mac Grianna's short story *Bíonn súil le muir ach ní bhíonn súil le huaigh.*[34] One method of checking the common occurrence of MacAdam's collection would be to examine an edition of Ó Muirgheasa's *Seanfhocla Uladh.* In this work Ó Muirgheasa has appended (U) Ulster to all of MacAdam's collection and, for example, versions of MacAdam number 217 'It is on her own account the cat purrs' have been recorded in Counties Monaghan, Armagh and Donegal.[35] Further useful sources in this regard may be found in various, smaller, local collections such as Ó Tuathail for Tyrone, Hamilton for Tory, Quiggin for Glenties, etc.

Such comparisons between the proverbs of one area and another must await the publication of a comprehensive dictionary of Irish-language proverbs and the systematic collation of all available sources. In current scholarship the three most widely known works in Irish paremiology are the Ulster collection of Énrí Ó Muirgheasa,[36] the Munster collection of Pádraig Ó Siochfhradha (1883–1964), both of which contain over 2,000 proverbs each,[37] and the two-volume Connaught collection of Ó Máille (1948 and 1952) which contains over 5,000. These three works constitute solid contributions to the study of the Irish-language proverb, but one should not understate the achievement of Robert MacAdam as his was the first major printed miscellany of provincial proverbs in the modern era.[38] Indeed as Williams points out, despite Ó Muirgheasa's extensive campaign of proverb collecting in Ulster, more than half of the proverbs in MacAdam's collection (365 in total)[39] were never heard of again, underlining, once more, our debt to MacAdam for preserving so many of our Ulster proverbs which might otherwise have remained unknown.

Six Hundred Gaelic Proverbs Collected in Ulster[1]

Robert MacAdam

We have in Ireland, at the present moment, two distinct races of inhibitants, who differ totally from each other in language, and whose early thoughts have been trained in two very different schools. The remains of the old native clans, who still habitually employ the Irish tongue amongst themselves, are only able to hold an imperfect intercourse with their Anglicised neighbours, in a language which they speak with difficulty. The native Irishman is obliged to address his landlord, or to sell his cow to his customer, in English (such as it is); but these persons have at present no interest in learning to understand his mother-tongue. Hence numberless instances occur daily in many parts of the country, in which it is found impossible to carry on a lengthened conversation between individuals of the two races. According to the last Government Census, the number of persons returned as still using the Irish language in this country was 1,524,286, or nearly one-fourth of the whole population; but even this large figure by no means indicates with accuracy the entire number of persons who understand it, or who have learned it in their infancy. It is well known that in various districts where the two languages co-exist, but where the English now largely pre-dominates, numbers of individuals returned themselves as igno-rant of the Irish language, either from a sort of false shame, or from a secret dread that the Government, in making this inquiry (for the first time), had some concealed motive, which could not be for their good. Their native shrewdness, therefore, dictated to them that their safest policy was to appear ignorant of the unfashionable language. For this reason, we may add very con-siderably to the number given by the Census.[2]

Now all these individuals have obtained whatever intellectual cultivation they possess, and most of the rules which regulate their conduct and morality, through the medium of a tongue which is now proscribed, and which (even if they could avail themselves of it) possesses no published literature. Hence the early knowledge they have acquired from their mothers, their nurses, or their companions, has all been of a traditional kind; and we may feel assured that the old sayings of their forefathers have formed a large portion of their education. We, whose earliest years are associated with books and schools, cannot readily realise the condition of persons who have obtained all their education without them; and yet such is the case with the existing Gaelic-speaking population of Ireland. The children of the last ten years, indeed, in a great majority of districts, are reaping the advantages of our new English national schools; and in the localities where the English language far preponderates over the Irish, the change will be immediate, and we may expect the young scholars to grow up with ideas like ourselves. But in those sections of the country where the Irish tongue still obstinately holds its ground (and they are many and large), this change will not take place in one generation; and in some places it would be hard to predict at what period the language will be extinct.

At all events, we have the great fact before us, that between a million-and-a-half and two millions of persons living amongst us now (a greater number, for instance, than the entire population of Norway,) speak a language of which we are most of us totally ignorant, have spoken it from their infancy, and have had no other medium for receiving their early instruction. Is it not worth while, then, to ascertain something of their manner of thinking, which must undoubtedly differ considerably from ours? One method of doing so will certainly be an examination of the popular sayings which, to a great extent, serve them as substitutes for books and literature. It will at least be curious to see in what forms the lessons of experience and common sense have embodied themselves among a race long secluded (intellectually) from the rest of the world, and confined to their own unaided genius.

The present collection of Irish proverbs, (amounting of six hundred,) though confined to the northern province, is the largest which has yet been published in Ireland, and still by no means comprises the whole of those extant in Ulster. They were written down by myself from the mouths of people, during a series of years, when opportunities brought me sometimes into contact with the Gaelic-speaking population of various localities in the north. These opportunities have been more rare of late, or I am persuaded I could have extended the collection to several hundreds more. It will be seen, on comparison, that, with a very few exceptions, the proverbs in the present list differ entirely from all those already printed, and which may be found in Hardiman's *Irish Minstrelry*,[3] *The Dublin Penny Journal*,[4] and Bourke's *Irish Grammar*.[5] In most of the cases where they agree in substance, various shades of difference will be noticed, occasioned by difference of dialect, or variety of figurative expression. Some proverbs seem to be special favourites, and are found in all parts of Ireland, familiar to everybody. Many are confined to certain localities, and contain local allusions which would not be understood elsewhere: of this kind, however, few are admitted into the present list. Some indicate a sentiment or an advice plainly; others in a figurative or an elliptical style, which is occasionally difficult to comprehend. Many present idiomatic expressions, or archaic forms, which are now uncommon in daily speech. Others, again, contain allusions to remote historical events or characters now nearly forgotten, or to customs now quite obsolete; and not a few embody traditional superstitions evidently handed down from Pagan times. Some of the specimens of these last classes which I possess are not published at present, because I have not yet satisfactorily traced out their exact meaning.

The subject, therefore, is properly an archaeological one. Old proverbs are as much the fragmentary relics of the days gone by, as the ruined walls of our castles, or the moss-grown stones of our cromlechs; and it is as well worth while to record obsolete words or phrases in our old national language, as to preserve descriptions or representations of material objects of antiquity still existing among us. We occasionally meet with words embalmed in proverbs which are only to be found in old manuscripts. To the archaeologist these popular sayings have an additional value. It is among the lower classes of a community that we must look for traces of old customs; and frequently, when these customs themselves have ceased to exist, the vestiges of them are to be found retained in popular expressions which, in the course of time, have been turned into proverbs.

Nor is the subject one that can be considered as mere literary trifling. Proverbs in many countries (perhaps in all) are in such constant use among the masses of the people, particularly the uneducated, and so interwoven with their daily speech, that they

may be looked upon as very correct indexes of the national
mode of thought and tone of morality. Lord Bacon long ago
observed that 'the genius, wit, and spirit of a nation are discovered by their proverbs'. 'I am convinced', says another writer,
'that we may learn, from the proverbs current among a people,
what is nearest and dearest to their hearts, how honour and dis-
honour are distributed among them, what is of good, what of
evil report in their eyes, with very much more which it can
never be unprofitable to know'.[26] The difference between the
English and French people, for instance, could scarcely be better
expressed (certainly not more briefly) than by two of their very
familiar proverbs, both recommending courteous behaviour, but
each for a reason peculiarly national:

> English: Civility costs no money
> French: *On attrape plus de mouches avec du miel qu' avec du
> vinaigre*
> ('One catches more flies with honey than with vinegar').

The present collection may therefore serve to throw some light
on the character of the native Irish population of Ulster, com-
prising, as it does, their favourite sayings on a great variety of
subjects.

Every civilised language possesses a large store of proverbs, the
accumulated gatherings of the wit and homely wisdom of many
generations. Numbers of these are identical, or nearly so, in all
countries, seeming, as it were, to be citizens of the world. Many
are of extreme antiquity, and appear to possess a perennial existence; being evidently so true to human nature that they are as
applicable, at the present time, to human conduct and feelings, as
on the first day they were uttered. But many are also of modern
date; and the crop has not ceased to grow even yet. The poets
have furnished not a few; and we almost forget already that it is
to Young we owe 'Procrastination is the thief of time', and to
Pope 'A little learning is a dangerous thing'. The same has been
the case at all periods, and in all countries where poetry exists;
and where does it not? Horace and Juvenal have contributed
many a pointed adage to the common stock, and so, no doubt,
have our own Irish bards. Indeed, the qualities necessary to produce a good poet – imagination and force of expression – are
often superlatively observable in proverbs; and it is by no means

unlikely that a large proportion of them have at one time formed parts of poetic compositions.

The topics treated of in these popular sayings are of such various kinds that it is not easy to define correctly what a proverb actually is. It was Lord John Russell (I think) who said that a proverb is 'the wisdom of many, and the wit of one'; a comprehensive enough definition, which will embrace most of the species. But there are many such popular phrases in all languages, which contain neither wisdom nor wit (so far as we can now see); and therefore we must content ourselves with a less brilliant definition. Proverbs (at least Irish proverbs) treat of the most miscellaneous subjects, in fact, *de omnibus rebus*; and perhaps, on the whole, the best name we can apply to them is the one given to them by the Irish themselves, namely, *Sean-Ràite*, 'Old Sayings'.[7]

The four provinces of Ireland seem, from a very early period, to have been distinguished from each other by peculiarities of dialect. This was naturally to be expected in a country in which masses of population were separated from one another, in many places, by tracts of dense forest and impassable bog, and their intercourse impeded elsewhere by the want of roads. This separation was still further perpetuated by the manner in which the invading colonists, Norman and English, distributed themselves over the island; occupying the level and fertile grounds which compose the centre of Ireland, and thus cutting off the communication between the natives on all sides. Hence it is, that in each important division of the Irish-speaking population we not only observe marked differences of pronuncation and accent, but find whole sets of words and of grammatical forms preserved in one district which are unknown or forgotten in another. One very remarkable example of this is the *negative* – a part of speech so important and so constantly in use that, of all others, it would seem the most likely to remain uniform in every dialect of a language. It is nearly so in all the Scandinavian and Teutonic dialects (Danish, Swedish, Dutch, German, English, &c.), and in the Latin and its modern descendants, the French, Italian, and Spanish. But, strange to say, in the Gaelic of Ireland we find two totally distinct negatives; the one (*Ní*) employed by the natives of the three provinces, Leinster, Munster, and Connaught; the other (*Cha*)[b8] used exclusively in Ulster, and likewise in the Highlands of Scotland and the Isle of Man, whose population have always been intimately connected with it. The geographical boundary of the northern negative in Ireland extends rather farther south than the limit of the present province of Ulster, embracing portions of the counties of Louth and Meath; in fact, bounded by the frontier of the old English 'Pale':[9] but westward the boundary almost precisely coincides with the modern limit of the province; for, on passing a distance of only a single mile from the county of Donegal into that of Leitrim, we find every person using the negative *ní*.[c10] It is a curious coincidence that, in the earlier period of the history of France, we find the North and South of that country distinguished by the word employed for yes, which in the former was *Oui*, in the late *Oc*; the two dialects being hence named the *Langue d'Oui* and the *Langue d'Oc*. The first of these appellations has long sunk into oblivion, as the northern dialect, being the language of the dominant race and of their metropolis, Paris, took the name of *La Langue Française*; but the other old designation still remains in the name of a southern province of France, Languedoc.[11] In a similar manner, we might separate Gaelic Ireland into two great divisions, characterised by 'the Language of *Cha*' and 'the Language of *Ní*'.

The origin of the northern negative has not yet been satisfactorily traced, though some have supposed it to be the remains of a very ancient form, *Nocha*. But, be this as it may, the universal and exclusive use of this old negative in Ulster, and its frequent recurrence in speech, give a character to the northern dialect which is very strange and puzzling to a southern or western Irishman. It will be found a very marked feature in the collection of Ulster proverbs now given to the public; because I have thought it right to print these popular phrases precisely in the form in which they are spoken by the native Irish of this province, and not to substitute a word which, though now recognised as the more classic by our grammarians, is practically unknown in this part of Ireland. The negative *Cha* is employed exclusively, however, in all books printed in the Scottish Gaelic, though not hitherto to be met with in any Gaelic books printed in Ireland. It is necessary to add that the word takes the several forms, *cha*, *chan*, and *char*, according to certain grammatical rules, which need not be specified here, as they are familiar to all Gaelic scholars.[12]

Some other peculiarities will be remarked by those familiar

with the ordinary Irish of our printed books; though, as a whole, the language will be found perfectly intelligible to any one acquainted with the dialects of the other provinces. It will also be readily understood by a Scottish Highlander, although to him presenting some grammatical differences more striking. The language of Ulster, in fact, forms a connecting link between the two extreme divisions of the Gaelic, and possesses an interest from retaining some forms of words lost in both. As my present object, however, is not to enter into any examination of the dialects, I will pursue the subject no further here.[13]

In order to facilitate future reference to the proverbs contained in the present collection, they are numbered consecutively; and, for further convenience, I have endeavoured to arrange a number of them under heads, where the subjects were similar; though many more, of course, admit of no kind of arrangement. It is interesting to compare together the proverbs of different nations, and to note the different modes in which similar ideas are expressed in various languages. Without attempting to institute anything like a general comparison of this kind, I have occasionally illustrated an Irish proverb by some similar one employed in another country. Various other examples will occur to any reader familiar with the subject. I have also thought it desirable to add, to many of these phrases, notes explanatory of their origin, or of the allusions they contain, which are frequently not quite obvious at first sight, as they refer to local or national customs and events. Half the wit and point of a proverb consists in its apt application; and the Irish, as might be expected, are often peculiarly happy in this. I have occasionally given examples such as I have myself met with; but these are not to be taken as by any means the best; for many of the proverbs (especially those expressed in a figurative manner) are capable of an endless variety of applications, both directly and ironically; and there is no mode more frequently employed by an Irishman for displaying his well-known propensity to fun and humour, than the witty application of a proverb. In this peculiarity he resembles the Spaniard, perhaps, more than any other. I have only further to remark that a number of these proverbs are in verse; the rhyme being indicated by the agreement of vowels, as in usual in all Irish poetry, and not by that of consonants.

Paréceme, Sancho, que no hay refrán que no sea verdadero, porque todos son sentencias sacadas de la misma experiencia, madre de las ciencias todas.

('I am of opinion, Sancho, that there is no Proverb which is not true, because they are all sentences drawn from experience itself, the Mother of all the Sciences' *Don Quixote*, part 1, cap 21).

Foresight, caution, thrift, prudence

1. **An tè cheanglas, 's è shiubhlas**.
   'He that binds travels (best)'.
   i.e. he who ties his burden properly will get along without stoppages.
   [*An té a cheanglaíos (= cheanglaíonn) is é a shiúlas (= shiúlann).*]

2. **An tè nach g-cuireann 'sa n-earrach, cha bhaineann se san fhoghmhar**.
   'He that does not sow in spring-time will not reap in the harvest-time'.
   [*An té nach gcuireann san earrach, cha bhaineann (= ní bhainfidh) sé san fhómhar.*]

3. **An tè chuireas, 's è bhaineas**.
   'He that sows will reap'.
   [*An té a chuireas (= chuireann) is é a bhaineas (= bhaineann).*]

4. **Amharc romhat sul a d-tabhraidh tu do leum**.
   'Look before you give a leap'.
   [*Amharc romhat sula dtabharfaidh★ tú do léim.*]

5. **Sèid sul a n-ndeòchaidh tu.**
   'Blow before you drink'.
   Alluding to hot broth, which may burn your mouth if you eat it incautiously; or to a drink, lest insects should be floating on the top; and applied as a warning against over-haste in anything.
   [*Séid sula ndeochfaidh★ tú .*]

6. **An tè nach g-caomhnaigh beagan, cha bhiann mòran aige**.
   'He that will not spare little, will not have much'.
   [*An té nach gcaomhnaíonn beagán, cha bhíonn (= ní bheidh) mórán aige.*]

7. **An tè nach g-cuiridh snaim caillidh se a cheud ghreim.**
   'He that does not tie a knot will lose his first stitch'.
   [*An té nach gcuirfidh* snaidhm caillfidh sé a chéad ghreim.*]

8. **Gearr an gead is foisge don scornach.**
   'Cut the gad nearest the throat'.
   This refers to a time when animals or prisoners in this country were hanged by a twisted *gad* (or withe) made of willow
   rods, before hemp ropes were used; and probably meant that
   if we wished to save the life of a culprit, we should cut the
   gad nearest his throat. Or, if there is a horse, fallen entangled
   in this primitive harness, and was in danger of being stran-
   gled, the same advice would suggest itself. It now signifies,
   'Do the thing first that is the most pressing need'.
   [*Gearr an gad is foisce don scornach.*]

9. **An tè nach g-cleachtann marcaigheacht, dear-
   madann na spuir.**
   'He that is not in the habit of riding, forgets the spurs'.
   This has many applications. Sometimes it means – A man
   not used to good company is at a loss how to behave.
   [*An té nach gcleachtann marcaíocht, dearmadann na spoir.*]

10. **Cuireann duine snaim le n-a theangaidh nach bh-
    fuasclochaidh 'fhiacla.**
    'A man ties a knot with his tongue that his teeth will not
    loosen'.
    That is when a man marries.
    [*Cuireann duine snaidhm lena theanga nach bhfuasclóidh a
    fhiacla.*]

11. **Fanann duine sona le sèun, agus bheir duine dona
    dubh-leum.**
    'The lucky man waits for prosperity, but the unlucky man
    gives a blind leap'.
    [*Fanann duine sona le séan, agus bheir (= tugann) duine dona dúléim.*]

12. **Cha n-diolaidh sì a cearc a rìamh 'sa lá fhliuch.**
    'She never sells her hen on a wet day'.
    A hen with wet feathers looks much smaller than when
    dry. The proverb recommends us to be cautious of having
    dealings with such people.
    [*Cha ndíolann (= Ní dhíolann) sí a cearc ariamh sa lá fhliuch.*]

13. **Is fearr pilleadh as làr an atha nà bathadh 'sa tuile.**
    'It is better to turn back from the middle of the ford than to be drowned in the flood'.
    Better stop than to lose it all. Said when any one repents a thing, and draws back at the last moment; as in the case of a marriage, when the couple are in the priest's house. Several Irish proverbs refer to fords in rivers, which were very important places before bridges were built.
    [*Is fearr filleadh as lár an átha ná bá sa tuile.*]

14. **Is searbh d'a ìoc an fìon ma's milis d'a òl.**
    'Wine is sweet in the drinking but bitter in the paying'.
    Spanish. *Al comer de los tocinos, cantan y hijos, al pagar sus a llorar.*
    'Whilst they eat the bacon, fathers and sons are merry, but when they pay for it they are sad'.
    [*Is searbh dá íoc an fíon más milis dá ól.*]

15. **Is còir nidh a thaisgidh le h-aghaidh na coise galair.**
    'It is right to keep something for the sore foot'.
    [*Is cóir ní a thaisceadh le haghaidh na coise galair.*]

16. **Is mairg a leigeas a rùn le cloidh.**
    'Wo to the man that entrusts his secret to a ditch'.
    English. *Walls have ears.*
    Spanish. *Tras pared ni tras (de) seto, no digas tu en secreto.*
    'Do not tell your secrets behind a wall or a hedge'.
    [*Is mairg a ligeas (= ligeann) a rún le claí.*]

17. **Ná cuir an t-uisge salach a mach go d-tiobhraidh tu an t-uisge glan a steach.**
    'Do not throw out the dirty water until you have brought in the clean'.
    [*Ná cuir an t-uisce salach amach go dtabharfaidh★ tú an t-uisce glan isteach.*]

18. **Is iomad tuisleadh o'n làimh go dti an bèul.**
    'There is many a slip from the hand to the mouth'.
    Spanish. *De la mano a la boca se pierde la sopa.*
    'From the hand to the mouth the soup is lost'.
    [*Is iomaí tuisle ón láimh go dtí an béal.*]

19. **Salachaidh aon chaora chlamhach sreud.**[d]
'A single scabby sheep will infect a flock'.
Latin. *Grex totus in agris unius scabie cadit.*
['In fields a whole herd falls dead through the infection of one (animal)'.]
[d]RMcA: The word usually given in Irish dictionaries for a 'flock' is *trèud;* but *srèud* is what I have always heard used in Ulster. O'Reilly gives *srèad.*★
[*Salóidh aon chaora chlamhach tréad.*]

20. **Is fearr aithreach agus fuireach nà aithreach agus imtheacht.**
'It is better to be sorry and stay than sorry and go away'.
Scotch. *Better rue sit nor rue flit;* also,
Fools are fain o' flittin' and wise men o' sittin'.
[*Is fearr aithreach agus fuireach ná aithreach agus imeacht.*]

21. **Rinne se an fèur, fad a's bhi an ghrìan suas.**
'He made hay while the sun was up'.
[*Rinne sé an féar fad agus a bhí an ghrian suas.*]

22. **An tè fhanas a bhfad a muigh, fuarann a chuid air.**
'The man that stays out long, his dinner cools'.
Applied to any one who stays too long from home: for instance, to O'Rourke, who was on a pilgrimage when his wife ran away with Dermod McMurrough, and caused the English invasion of Ireland.
[*An té a fhanas (= fhanann) i bhfad amuigh fuaraíonn a chuid air.*]

23. **Cuid an taisgeàir aig an g-caithteàir.**[e]
'The spender gets the property of the hoarder'.
English. *Fools build houses and wise men live in them.*
Latin. *Sic vos non vobis mellificatis apes.*
['In this way, bees, you make honey but not for yourselves'.]
[e]RMcA: 'All the masculine nouns which end in *òir* in other parts of Ireland are here pronounced *àir*'.★
[*Cuid an taisceora ag an gcaiteoir.*]

24. **Chan fhuair an madadh ruadh teachdaire a rìamh a b'fhearr nà è fèin.**
'The fox never found a better messenger than himself'.
[*Chan fhuair (= Ní bhfuair) an madadh rua teachtaire ariamh ab fhearr ná é féin.*]

25. **Is maith dhà òrus a bheith air do chuigeal**.
'It is good to have two stricks* of flax on your distaff'.
[*Is maith dhá abhras a bheith ar do choigeal.*]

26. **As a cionn a bhlichtear an bhò.**
'Out of her head the cow is milked'.
Signifying that, according to the manner a cow is fed, she
gives better or worse milk. You may expect to be served by
a man according as you treat him.
[*As a ceann a bhlitear an bhó.*]

27. **'Nuair a chrìonas slat, is deacair a sniomhadh.**
'When a rod withers, it is hard to twist'.
[*Nuair a chríonas (= chríonann) slat is deacair a sníomh.*]

28. **Is breàllan an tè nach nglacfadh airgead a d'fhu-
ralochadh air.**
'He is a fool that will not take money that is offered to
him'.
[*Is breallán an té nach nglacfadh airgead a d'fhorálódh air.*]

29. **Is maith an sèideadh sròine do dhuine, smug
fhaiceal air dhuine eile.**
'It is a good nose-blowing to a man to see snot on the nose
of another'.
A very homely way of recommending people to take
example by the faults or misfortunes of others.
Latin. *Felix quem faciunt aliena pericula cautum.*
['Happy is the one whom the dangers of another cause to
be cautious'.]
[*Is maith an séideadh sróine do dhuine smuga a fheiceáil ar
dhuine eile.*]

30. **Ni'l brigh 'san luibh nach bh'faghthar a n-àm.**
'There is no virtue in the herb that is not got in time'.
[*Níl brí sa luibh nach bhfaightear in am.*]

31. **Nà caill caora le luach pighine de tharra.**
'Do not lose a sheep for the sake of a pennyworth of tar'.
[*Ná caill caora le luach pingine de tharra.*]

32. **Is fusa sgapadh nà cruinniughadh.**
'It is easier to scatter than to gather'.
[*Is fusa scaipeadh ná cruinniú.*]

33. **Cha n-è là na gaoithe là na sgolba.**
'The windy day is not the day for fastening the thatch'.
The thatch on an Irish cottage is fastened down by a number of wattles or pointed rods of willow, called *sgolb*. The proverb signifies that a windy day is not the proper time for such work. It is applied in all cases where foresight is necessary.
[*Chan é (= Ní hé) lá na gaoithe lá na scolb.*]

34. **Nà dean crò a roimhe na h-arcaibh.**
'Do not build the sty before the litter comes'.
[*Ná deán cró roimh na harcaibh (= hairc).*]

35. **Nà beannuigh an t-ìasg go d-tiocaidh se a d'tìr.**
'Do not bless the fish till it gets to the land'.
[*Ná beannaigh an t-iasc go dtiocfaidh sé i dtír.*]

36. **Mur rinne tu do leabaidh, luidh uirrthi.**
'As you have made your bed, lie on it'.
Applied, for instance, to a bad marriage.
[*Mar a rinne tú do leaba(idh) luigh uirthi.*]

37. **Sin ag cur muinìghne a g-claidheamh briste.**
'That is putting trust in a broken sword'.
[*Sin ag cur muiníne i gclaíomh briste.*]

38. **Is beag a t-èibheall a lasas teine mhòr.**
'It is a small lighted coal that will kindle a great fire'.
Spanish. *De pequeña centella, gran hoguera.*
'A small spark makes a great fire'.
Scotch. *A sma' spark breeds meikle wark.*
[*Is beag an aibhleog a lasas (= lasann) tine mhór.*]

39. **Ma cheannaigheann tu droch-nidh, ceannochaidh tu a rìst go h-aithghearr.**
'If you buy a bad thing, you will soon buy again'.
Spanish. *Comprar lo que no has menester, y venderás lo que (no) podrás excusar.*
'Buy what you do not want, and you will sell what you cannot spare'.
Latin. *Si inutilia emas, necessaria vendes.*
['If you buy useless things you will sell things that are necessary'.]
[*Má cheannaíonn tú drochní, ceannóidh tú arís go hathghearr.*]

40. **Ni'l ò mheud**^f **an phràinn nach lughaide na gnothuidhe.**
    'The greater the hurry the less the work'.
    ^fRMcA: 'In other parts of Ireland *da mheud*; and so in similar phrases, as *da laighiod*'.
    [*Níl dá mhéad an phráinn nach lúide na gnóthaí.*]

41. **Ma shìneann tu le do làimh, cuairteochaidh tu le do chois.**
    'If you stretch out with your hand, you will seek out with your foot'.
    If you are too lavish with your hand, you may be driven to walk the road as a beggar.
    [*Má shíneann tú le do láimh, cuartóidh tú le do chois.*]

42. **Ma's milis a mhil, nà ligh-sa de'n drèasoig ì.**
    'Though honey is sweet, do not lick it off a briar'.
    [*Más milis an mhil ná lighse den dreasóig í.*]

43. **Nà cuntais na sicìnidh no go m-beidh siad leigthe.**
    'Do not count your chickens until they are hatched'.
    Latin. *Ante victoriam ne canas triumphum.*
    ['Do not sing of triumph before a victory'.]
    [*Ná cuntais na sicíní go mbeidh siad ligthe.*]

44. **Nì sgèul rùin è, ò chluinneas triùir è.**
    'It is no secret when three persons have heard it'.
    [*Ní scéal rúin é ó chluineas (= chluineann) triúr é.*]

45. **Thainig a tòn chun talamh eadar a dhà sdòl.**
    'The backside came to the ground between two stools'.
    [*Tháinig an tóin chun talaimh idir★ dhá stól.*]

46. **Faghann na h-eich bàs, fhad a's bhios a fèur a' fàs;**
    or,
    Gheibh na h'eich bàs, &c.
    'The horses die while the grass is growing'.
    English. *Live, horse, and you'll get grass*
    [*Faigheann na heich bás a fhad agus a bhíonn an féar ag fás.*
    Gheibh na heich bás a fhad agus a bhíos an féar ag fás.]

47. **Tarruing do lamh comh reidh a's thig leat as bèul a mhadaidh.**
    'Draw your hand out of the dog's mouth as easily as you can'.
    [*Tarraing do lámh comh réidh agus a thig leat as béal an mhadaidh.*]

48. **Sgèul a chuala mi-se,**
    a's chuir me a m-briotal faoi dhò,
    Go n-dean a beach dò fèin teach
    anns a g-ciùin ghrian-lò.
    'A story that I heard,
    and I committed it to memory twice,
    That the bee makes a house for itself
    on the sunshiny day'.
    [*Scéal a chuala mise*
    agus a chuir mé i bhfriotal faoi dhó
    Go ndéanann an beach dó féin teach
    sa gciúinghrianló. ★]

49. **Ni gheabhar an cù go n'imthigh an fiadh.**
    'The hound is not found until the deer is gone'.
    i.e. when one thing is found another is not forthcoming.
    [*Ní ghabhtar/fhaightear★ an cú go n-imí an fia.*]

50. **Sabhàlann greim a n-àm dhà ghreim.**
    'A stitch in time saves two stitches'.
    [*Sabhálann greim in am dhá ghreim.*]

51. **Is sleamhuin leac dorus tigh mòir.**
    'The door-step of a great house is slippery'.
    Alluding to the uncertainty of great men's favour.
    [*Is sleamhain leac dorais tí m(h)óir.* ★]

52. **Is farsuing bèul a bhothain.**
    'Wide is the door of the little cottage'.
    i.e. no house can be kept without expense. Said sometimes
    to deter from an imprudent marriage.
    [*Is fairsing béal an bhotháin.*]

Industry, perseverance, activity, energy, patience, and their opposites

53. **Cuidigheann Dia leis a tè a chuidigheas leis fèin.**
    'God helps him who helps himself'.
    French. *Aide-toi et Dieu t'aidera.*
    ['Help yourself and God will help you'.]
    [*Cuidíonn Dia leis an té a chuidíos (= chuidíonn) leis féin.*]

54. **Is fearr lùbadh nà briseadh.**
    'It is better to bend than break'.
    [*Is fearr lúbadh ná briseadh.*]

55. **Ma's fada an là, thig an oidche fa dheireadh.**
'Long as the day may be, the night comes at last'.
Italian. *Non vien dì, che non venga sera.*
['There is no day without an evening'.]
English. *The longest day will have an end.*
[*Más fada an lá t(h)ig (= tagann) an oíche faoi dheireadh.*]

56. **Buail an t-iarann fad a's ta se teith.**
'Strike the iron while it is hot'.
[*Buail an t-iarann fad agus atá sé te.*]

57. **Is fearr mall nà go brath.**
'Better late than never'.
[*Is fearr (go) mall ná go brách.*]

58. **Cha ghabhann dorn druidte seabhac.**
'A shut fist will not catch a hawk'.
[*Cha ghabhann (= Ní ghabhfaidh) dorn druidte seabhac.*]

59. **Chan fhaghthar saill gan saothar.**
'Fat is not to be had without labour'.
French. *Nul pain sans peine.*
['No bread without pain'.]
[*Chan (= Ní) fhaightear saill gan saothar.*]

60. **'Sè an t-èun maidne a gheabhas a phèisdeog.**
'It is the morning bird that catches the worm'.
[*Is é an t-éan maidine a gheobhas (= gheobhaidh)* an phéisteog.*]

61. **Is trìan de'n obair, tùs a chur.**
'Making a beginning is the one-third of the work'.
English. *What is well begun is half ended.*
French. *Ce n'est que le premier pas qui coute.*
['It is only the first step which costs'.]
Spanish. *Barba bien remojada, medio rapada.*
'A beard well lathered is half shaved'.
[*Is trian den obair tús a chur.*]

62. **Luidh le h-uan, a's èirigh le h-èun,**
O fhaiceas tu cleath agus fear 'n a dèigh,
Go bh-feicidh tu cruacha mònadh a's cocaidh fèir.
'Lie down with the lamb, and rise with the bird,
From the time you see a harrow and a man behind it,
Until you see stacks of turf and cocks of hay'.
i.e. from harrowing-time to hay-harvest.
[*Luigh le huan agus éirigh le héan
Ó fheiceas (= fheiceann) tú cliath agus fear ina diaidh
Go bhfeice tú cruacha móna(dh) agus cocaí féir.*]

63. **Dean sin mur a bheidheadh teine air do chraicionn.**
'Do it as if there were fire on your skin'.
[*Déan sin mar a bheadh tine ar do chraiceann.*]

64. **An tè is luaithe lamh, bìodh aige an gadhar bàn 's a fiadh.**
'He that has the quickest hand, let him have the white hound and the deer'.
English. *First come first served.*
The Irish proverb seems to refer to some incident in the old hunting expeditions of the Irish chiefs.
[*An té is luaithe lámh, bíodh aige an gadhar bán agus an fia.*]

65. **Is fearr èirigh moch nà suidhe mall.**
'Early rising is better than sitting up late'.
[*Is fearr éirí moch ná suí mall.*]

66. **Char fhag se cloch gan tionta.**
'He left no stone unturned'.
[*Char (= Níor) fhág sé cloch gan tiontú.*]

67. **Sgìste ghiolla an ghobha, ò na builg chun na h-inneora.**
'The leisure of the smith's helper, (that is) from the bellows to the anvil'.
[*Scíste ghiolla an ghabha, ó na boilg chun na hinneora.**]

68. **Ma's gasta an gearr-fhiadh, beirthear fa dheireadh air.**
'Though the hare is swift she is caught at last'.
[*Más gasta an giorria beirtear faoi dheireadh air.*]

69. **Is minic a bhi cù mall sona, a's cù dona'n a rith.**
'A slow hound has often luck when a swift hound has not'.
Alluding to dogs coursing a hare. Sometimes the hare, by a sudden turn, causes the foremost hound to run past her, when she is caught by a slower dog. It signifies that – 'Often he who plods steadily at home succeeds as well as one who roams about looking for business or profit.'
Italian. *Chi va piano va sano, chi va forte va alla morte.*
['Those who go slowly go safely, those who go quickly go towards death'.]
English. *The more haste the worse speed.*
[*Is minic a bhí cú mall sona agus cú dona ina rith.*]

70. **Is minic a rug fear a deich air a dà fhichid.**
'Many a time the man with the ten has overtaken the man with the forty'.
This proverb refers to card-playing. One of the usual Irish games is won by marking forty-five. A player, who at the commencement of a deal has only marked ten, while his opponent has marked forty, may still overtake him and win the game. The proverb is intended as an encouragement to persons engaged in any business.
[*Is minic a rug fear an deich ar an daichead.*]

71. **A n–dèigh a chèile tògthar na caisleàin.**
'By degrees the castles are built'.
A proverb which, no doubt, took its rise when the Irish, to their cost, saw the Anglo-Norman castles rising one after another round the English Pale.
[*I ndéidh (=ndiaidh) a chéile tógtar na caisleáin.*]

72. **Is èigin do leanabh lamhachan sul ma siubhalaidh se.**
'A child must creep before he walks'.
[*Is éigean don leanbh lámhac(h)án sula siúla sé.*★]

73. **Cha chruinnigheann cloch chasaidh caonach.**
'A rolling stone gathers no moss'.
Spanish. *Piedra movediza nunca moho la cobija.*
['A rolling stone gathers no moss'.]
This is a proverb found in almost all languages.
[*Cha (= Ní) chruinníonn cloch chasaidh caonach.*]

74. **Gheibh bèathach cheithre g–cos tuisleadh.**
'A four-footed beast will stumble'.
[*Gheibh (= Faigheann) beathach cheithre gcos★ tuisle.*]

75. **Faghann ìarraidh ìarraidh eile.**
'The seeking for one thing will find another'.
[*Faigheann iarraidh iarraidh eile.*]

76. **Mu'r**[†] **robh gnothuighe a mach acu, beidh a sàith gnothuighe a bhaile acu.**
'If they had no business abroad they have plenty of business at home'.
Said of persons idling their time, or going where they have no errand.
[†]RMcA: 'The common abbreviation of *muna*'.
[*Mura raibh gnóthaí amach acu beidh a sáith gnóthaí abhaile acu.*]

77. **Da m-beidheadh aon ribe air do chuigeal, cha deantà sin.**
'You would not do that if you had any flax on your distaff'.
Said of a woman spending her time foolishly.
[*Dá mbeadh aon ribe ar do choigeal cha (n)déanfá (= ní dhéanfá) sin.*]

78. **Is ionmhuin leis a chat ìasg, acht ni h-àill leis a chrùba fhliuchadh.**
'The cat likes fish, but does not like to wet her paws'.
[*Is ionúin leis an chat iasc, ach ní háil leis a chrúba a fhliuchadh.*]

79. **Is maith a saoghal è ma mhaireann se a bh-fad.**
'It is a very good time if it lasts'.
Addressed to a giddy thoughtless person.
[*Is maith an saol é má mhaireann sé i bhfad.*]

80. **Sè cuid an t-searraigh de 'n chliath a ta agad-sa.**
'You have the foal's share of the harrow'.
i.e. 'you are an idle spectator'; because, while the mare is drawing the harrow, the foal walks beside her doing nothing.
[*Is é cuid an tsearraigh den chliath atá agatsa.*]

81. **Ta uallach mhic lèisge ort.**
'You have the burden of the son of laziness on you'.
[*Tá ualach mhic leisce ort.*]

82. **Lèisge luidhe agus lèisge ag èirigh, sin mallachd Choluim-chille.**
'Laziness in lying, and laziness when risen, this is the curse of Columb-kille'.
[*Leisce ag luí agus leisce ag éirí sin, mallacht Cholm Cille.*]

83. **Is trom an t-uallach an fhallsachd.**
'Laziness is a heavy burden'.
[*Is trom an t-ualach an fhalsacht.*]

84. **Ghnidh codladh fada tòn lom.**
'Long sleep makes a bare back'.
[*Ghní (= Déanann) codladh fada tóin lom.*]

85. **Budh mhaith an teachdaire le cur a g-coinne an bhàis thu.**
'You would be a good messenger to send for Death'.
Because you would delay so long on the road.
[*Ba mhaith an teachtaire le cur i gcoinne an bháis thú.*]

86. **Eisd le tuile na h-amhna, a's gabhaidh tu breac.**
'Listen for the flood of the river, and you'll catch a trout'.
Wait patiently, and you will see the result.
[*Éist le tuile na habhann(a)⋆ agus gabhfaidh tú breac.*]

87. **Eisd le gaoith na m-beann go d-traoghthaidh na h-uisgidh.**
'Listen to the wind of the mountains until the waters ebb'.
Let the storm blow by.
[*Éist le gao(i)th na mbeann go dtraoithe na huiscí.*]

88. **Ni fiù an sògh an tè nach bh-fulaingidh an-ndòigh tamull.**
'He that will not bear adversity for a while does not deserve prosperity'.
Latin. *Dulcia non meruit qui non gustabit amara.*
['The one who will not taste what is bitter does not deserve things that are sweet'.]
[*Ní fiú an só an té nach bhfulaingíonn andóigh tamall.*]

89. **Is fada an ròd nach m-biann casadh ann: –** and,
Is direach an bothar nach m-biann càsadh ann.
'It is a long road (or a straight road) that has no turn in it'.
[*Is fada an ród nach mbíonn casadh ann.*
Is díreach an bóthar nach mbíonn casadh ann.]

90. **Is faide go bràth nà go bealtuinn.**
'It is longer to the day of judgment than to May-day'.
i.e. there is time enough yet.
[*Is faide go bráth ná go Bealtaine.*]

91. **Is subhailce an fhoighid nach d-tugann nàire.**
'Patience is a virtue that causes no shame'.
[*Is suáilce an fhoighid (= fhoighne) nach dtugann náire.*]

92. **An nidh nach fèadar a lèigheas, is èigin 'fhulaing.**
'What cannot be cured must be borne'.
[*An ní nach féidir a leigheas is éigean a fhulaingt.*]

93. **Is olc an ghaoith nach sèididh go maith do dhuine èigin.**
'It is a bad wind that does not blow well for somebody'.
[*Is olc an ghaoth nach séidfidh⋆ go maith do dhuine éigin.*]

94. **Chan 'uil† tuile ò mheud nach d-traoghann.**
'However great the flood, it will ebb'.
[*Chan fhuil (= Níl) tuile dá mhéad nach dtraoitheann (= dtránn).*]
†RMcA: 'Universally employed instead of *Ni'l* of the other provinces'.★
Or, more poetically expressed:
Ni'l tuile da mhèud nach d-tèid seall tamuill a d-tràigh.
[*Níl tuile dá mhéad nach dtéann seal tamaill i dtrá.*]

95. **Nachar leòr do dhuine dhona a dhichioll a dheanamh.**
'Is it not enough for a poor man to do his best?'
[*Nachar/Nár leor do dhuine d(h)ona a dhícheall a dhéanamh?*★]

96. **Cha bhiann imirce gan chaill.**
'There is no removal without loss'.
English. *Three removes are as bad as a fire:* and,
I never saw an oft-removed tree,
Nor yet an oft-removed family,
That throve so well as those that settled be.
[*Cha (= Ní) bhíonn imirce gan chaill.*]

97. **Foghnaidh go leòr comh maith le fèusda.**
'Enough serves as well as a feast'.
[*Fónaidh (= Fónann) go leor comh maith le féasta.*]

98. **Is fearr teine bheag a ghoras nà teine mhòr a losgas.**
'A little fire that warms is better that a large fire that burns'.
[*Is fearr tine bheag a ghoras (= ghorann) ná tine mhór a loscas (= loisceann).*]

99. **Is fearr leith-bhuilìn nà a bheith falamh gan aran.**
'Half a loaf is better than being entirely without bread'.
[*Is fearr leathbhuilín ná bheith folamh gan arán.*]

100. **Is fearr pèire maith bonn nà dhà phèire uachdar.**
'One good pair of soles is better than two pair of upper leathers'.
[*Is fearr péire maith bonn ná dhá phéire uachtar.*]

101. **Is beag a rud nach fearr nà diùltadh.**
'It is a small thing that is not better than refusal'.
[*Is beag an rud nach fearr ná diúltú.*]

102. **An ùair is gainne an meas 's è is fearr a bhlas.**
'When the fruit is scarcest, its taste is sweetest'.
Italian. *In tempo di carestìa è buono íl pan vecciato.*
['In time of famine bread of vetch is good'.]
[*Nuair is gainne an meas is é is fearr a bhlas.*]

103. **Is maith an t-annlann an t-ocras.**
'Hunger is a good condiment'.
Latin. *Optimum condimentum fames*
['Hunger is the best condiment'.] –and,
Jejunus rarò stomachus vulgaria temnit.
['A hungry stomach rarely despises common fare'.]
Italian. *Appetito non vuol salsa.*
['Hunger needs no sauce'.]
Spanish. *A la hambre no hay pan malo.*
['For hunger there is no (such thing as) dirty bread'.]
English. *Hungry dogs will eat dirty puddings.*
[*Is maith an t-anlann an t-ocras.*]

104. **Is fearr marcaigheachd air ghabhar nà coisigheacht ò fheabhas.**
'Riding on a goat is better than the best walking'.
[*Is fearr marcaíocht ar ghabhar ná coisíocht dá fheabhas.*]

105. **Is fearr dìomhaineach nà ag obair a n-asgaidh.**
'Better be idle than working for nothing'.
[*Is fearr díomhaoineach ná ag obair in aisce.*]

106. **Is fearr fuigheall nà bheith air easbhuidh.**
'Better have the leavings than nothing at all'.
[*Is fearr fuíoll ná bheith ar easpa.*]

107. **Is fearr 'na aonar nà bheith a n-droch-chuideachd.**
'It is better to be alone than in bad company'.
[*Is fearr ina aonar ná bheith i ndroch-chuideachta.*]

108. **Nà dean beagan de do mhèis.**
Gan fios nach pèisd a bheidheadh d'a meas;
Ni fearr an mhìas mhèith
Nà 'n mhìas rèidh a d-tiocar leis.
'Do not make little of your dish,
For it may be an ignorant person who judges it;
The richest food is no better
Than the ready dish which suits one's purpose'.
[*Ná déan beagán de do mhéis★*
Gan fios nach péist a bheadh dá meas;
Ní fearr an mhias mhéith
Ná an mhias réidh a dtiocfar leis.]

109. **Cha n-è gach aon n-duine d'ar òrduigh Dia sponòg airgid ann a bhèul.**
'It is not every one that God ordained should have a silver spoon in his mouth'.
[*Chan é (= Ní hé) gach aon duine dár ordaigh Dia spúnóg airgid ina bhéal.*]

110. **Cha lugha do mhaoin nà do mhuirighin.**
'Your means are not less than your family'.
i.e. though you are poor, your family is small.
[*Cha (= Ní) lú do mhaoin ná do mhuirín.*]

111. **Is fearr an t-slàinte bhocht nà na tàinte air chnoc.**
'Better is health with poverty, than whole herds of cattle on the hills'.
English. *Health is better than wealth*
[*Is fearr an tsláinte bhocht ná na táinte ar chnoc.*]

112. **Is fearr paiste nà poll,**
Is fearr lom nà lèun,
Is fearr maol nà bheith gan cheann,
A's diabhal ann acht sin fèin.
'Better a patch than a hole;
Better be bare than utterly destitute
Better be bald than without a head,
But the devil a much more than that!'.
Scotch. *Better a clout nor a hole out.*
[*Is fearr paiste ná poll,*
Is fearr lom ná léan,
Is fearr maol ná bheith gan cheann,
Agus diabhal ann ach sin féin.]

113. **Ma's dona maol, is mìle measa mallog.**
'If baldness is bad, a scald head is a thousand times worse'.
[*Más dona maol is míle measa mullóg.* *]

114. **Is fearr suidhe gearr nà seasamh fada.**
'A short sitting is better than a long standing'.
[*Is fearr suí gearr ná seasamh fada.*]

115. **Iomarcaidh d'aon nidh, 's ionann sin 's gan aon nidh.**
'Too much of one thing is the same as nothing'.
Latin. *Ne quid nimis:* and, *Est modus in rebus.*
['No excess in anything' and 'There is moderation in things'.]
Scotch. *Ower meikle water droon'd the miller.*
[*(An) iomarca d'aon ní, is ionann sin agus gan aon ní.*]

116. **Is fearr teacht a n-deireadh cuirme nà a d-toiseach troda.**
'Better to come at the end of a feast than the beginning of a fight'.
[*Is fearr teacht i ndeireadh coirme ná i dtosach troda.*]

117. **Is maith an gearran nach m-baineann tuisle ùair èigin dò.**
'It is a good horse that does not stumble sometimes'.
English. *'Tis a good horse that never stumbles.*
And a good wife that never grumbles.
[*Is maith an gearrán nach mbaineann tuisle uair éigin dó.*]

118. **Sùil le cùitiughadh a mhilleas a cearbhach.**
'It is the hope of recompense that ruins the card-player'.
[*Súil le cúiteamh a mhilleas (= mhilleann) an cearrbhach.*]

119. **Is fearr fuighleach madaidh nà fuighleach mogaidhe.**
'Better the leavings of a dog than the leavings of a mocker'.
[*Is fearr fuílleach madaidh ná fuílleach magaí.* *]

120. **Cha d-tuigear feum an tobair no go d-tèid se a d-tràigh.**
'The value of the well is not known till it dries up'.
                    'For it so falls out,
That what we have we prize not to the worth
Whilst we enjoy it: but, being lack'd and lost,
Why then we rate the value'. Shakespeare.
[*Cha dtuigtear (= Ní thuigtear) feidhm an tobair nó go dtéid (= dtéann) sé i dtrá.*]

121. **Beagan sìl de'n athruigh chòir**
A's beagan bò a bh-fèur maith
Beagan càirde a d-tigh an òil
Sin na trì bheagain is fearr air bith.
'A little seed of the right sort,
A few cows on good pasture,
And a few friends in the tavern;
These are three best little things in the world'.
[*Beagán síl den athraigh (= earra) chóir*
Agus beagán bó i bhféar maith
Beagán cairde i dtigh (= i dteach) an óil
Sin na trí bheagán is fearr ar bith.]

122. **Cùradh mo chroidhe ort, a bhothain,**
     'S tù nach m-biann a choidch' acht a g-cothan;
     Acht càil bheag bhuideach de do shochar
     Moch no mall a thigim
     Gur b'ionnad is fusa damh mo chosa 'shìneadh.
     'The plague of my heart on you, little cottage
     It is you that are constantly in disorder;
     But one little advantage you have, –
     No matter how late or how early I come,
     It is in you I can easiest stretch my legs'.
     English. *There's no place like home.*
     Italian. *Ad ogni uccello il suo nido è bello.*
     ['To every bird his nest is beautiful'.]
     [*Cúradh mo chroí ort, a bhotháin,*
     Is tú nach mbíonn choíche ach i gcothán*
     Ach cáil bheag bhídeach de do shochar
     Moch nó mall a thigim (= thagaim)
     Gurb ionat is fusa dom mo chosa a shíneadh.]

123. **Is fearr falamh nà droch-sgeul.**
     'Better (come) empty than with bad news'.
     [*Is fearr folamh ná drochscéal.*]

Discretion, prudence, self-restraint

124. **An tè nach ngabhaidh comhairle, glacaidh se comhrac.**
     'He who will not take advice will take a quarrel'.
     [*An té nach ngabhfaidh comhairle glacfaidh sé comhrac.*]

125. **Lèig dò fuaradh 'sa g-craiceann a'r theith se ann.**
     'Let him cool in the skin that he warmed in'.
     i.e. let an angry man cool before you reply.
     [*Lig dó fuarú sa gcraiceann ar théigh sé ann.*]

126. **Nà taisbean do fhiacal 's an àit nach d-tig leat greim a bhaint a mach.**
     'Do not show your teeth where you cannot give a bite'.
     [*Ná taispeáin d'fhiacail san áit nach dtig leat greim a bhaint amach.*]

127. **Ma's maith leat sìochaint, cairdeas, a's moladh,
Eisd, faic, is fan balbh.**
'If you wish for peace, friendship, and praise,
Listen, look, and be dumb'.
Latin. *Audi, vide, tace; si vis vivere in pace.*
['Listen, see, be silent; if you wish to live in peace'.]
French. *Oye, vois, et te taise, Si tu veux vivre en paix.*
['Listen, look, and keep quite, if you wish to live in peace'.]
Spanish. *Ver, Oir, y callar.*
['Look, listen, and keep quiet'].
[*Más maith leat síocháin, cairdeas agus moladh
Éist, feic is fan balbh.*]

128. **Nà labhair gach nidh do b'àill leat, le h-eagal go g-
cluinfeà nidh nar bh'àill leat.**
'Do not say everything you like, lest you hear a thing you
would not like'.
[*Ná labhair gach ní ab áil leat le heagla go gcluinfeá ní nárbh áil leat.*]

129. **Da fhaide a's bheidheas tu a muigh, nà beir droch-
sgèul a bhaile ort fèin.**
'As long as you are from home, never bring back a bad
story about yourself'.
[*Dá fhaide agus a bheas (= bheidh) tú amuigh ná beir drochscéal
abhaile ort féin.*]

130. **Thèid focal le gaoith, a's thèid buille le cnàimh.**
'A word goes to the winds, but a blow goes to the bones'.
English. *Soft words break no bones.*
[*Théid (= Téann) focal le gao(i)th agus théid buille le cná(i)mh.*]

131. **Chan sgèul rùin a chluinneas triùir.**
'A story that three people hear is no secret'.
Spanish. *Puridad de dos, puridad de Dios: Puridad de tres, de todos es.*
'A secret between two is God's secret; a secret between
three is everybody's'.
[*Chan (=Ní) scéal rúin ó chluineas (= chluineann) triúr.*]

132. **Cha deanann balbhan brèug.**
'A dumb man tells no lies'.
Spanish. *En boca cerrada no entran moscas.*
'Into a shut mouth flies do not enter', and
Oveja que bala bocado pierde.
'The sheep loses a mouthful when it bleats'.
[*Cha (n)déanann (= Ní dhéanann) balbhán bréag.*]

133. **Is olc nach ngabhaidh comhairle, acht is mìle measa a ghabhas gach uile chomhairle.**
'He is bad that will not take advice,
but he is a thousand times worse who takes every advice'.
[*Is olc nach ngabhfaidh comhairle ach is míle measa a ghabhfas (=
ghabhfaidh) gach uile chomhairle.*]

134. **Is furas beagan cainte a leasughadh.**
'It is easy to mend little talk'.
Latin. *Non unquam tacuisse nocet.*
['It never harms to have been silent'.]
[*Is furasta beagán cainte a leasú.*]

135. **Is binn beul 'n a thosd.**
'A silent mouth sounds sweetly'.
[*Is binn béal ina thost.*]

136. **Nà bi 'g 'ul eadar a craiceann 's a crann.**
'Do not go between the tree and its bark'.
i.e. do not intermeddle between near relations, such as man
and wife, &c.
[*Ná bí ag dul idir an craiceann agus an crann.*]

137. **Is fearrde do'n m-brò a bhreacadh gan a bhriseadh.**
'The mill-stone is the better of being picked, but not
broken'.
It is better to mend a thing than throw it away: or, you
ought not to go about a business too violently.
[*Is fearrde don mbró a breacadh gan a briseadh.*]

138. **Nà luadh gach nidh do chifear duit,
Is beag an dioghbháil a ghni an tochd;
Eisd le comhairle dhuine ghlic,
Tuig, a's lèig mòran tharad.**
'Do not talk of every thing you may see,
'Tis little harm that silence does;
Listen to the advice of a wise man –
Understand, but let much pass you, (without remark)'.
[*Ná luaigh gach ní a tchífear (= fheicfear) duit
Is beag an díobháil a ghní (= dhéanann) an tost,
Éist le comhairle dhuine ghlic
Tuig agus lig mórán tharat.*]

139. **Biann marbhadh duine eadar dhà fhocal.**
'The killing of a man may be between two words'.
The mistake of a single word may produce serious conse-
quences.
[*Bíonn marú duine idir dhá fhocal.*]

Procrastination

140. **Is èasgaidhe neòin nà maidin.**
'Evening is more active than morning'.
i.e. do the thing at once, for in the morning some obstacle
may arise.
Latin. *Carpe diem.*
['Pluck the day'.]
[*Is éasca nóin ná maidin.*]

141. **Is mithid a bheith bogadh na ngad.**
'It is time for you to be softening the *gads*'.
It is time to prepare for departure.
[*Is mithid bheith ag bogadh na ngad.*]

142. **Nà cuir do ghnothuighe ò 'n-diugh go d-ti a màireach.**
'Do not put off your business from to-day til
to-morrow'.
[*Ná cuir do ghnóthaí ó inniu go dtí amárach.*]

143. **Thainig tu an là a n-dèigh an aonaigh.**
'You have come the day after the fair'.
Latin. *Post festum venisti.*
['You have come after the festival'.]
[*Tháinig tú an lá i ndéidh (=ndiaidh) an aonaigh.*]

144. **'Sè trìall na g-cearc ag 'ul go h-Albainn.**
'That is (like) the intended journey of the hens to
Scotland'.
The children, when they hear the hens cackling at night,
say they are talking about going back to Scotland, where
they came from. There is an old Irish tune called '*Triall
na g-cearc go h-Albainn*' ['The journey of the hens to
Scotland']. This proverb is applied to persons who are
continually talking of doing a thing, but never do it.
[*Is é triall na gcearc ag dul go hAlbain.*]

145. **Fàl fa'n ngort a n-dèigh na fòghala.**
'Putting a fence round the field after the robbery'.
Italian. *Serrar la stalla quando s'han perduti i buovi.*
['To close the byre when the cattle are missing'.]
Spanish. *Después de vendimias cuévanos.*
'After the vintage, the baskets to gather the grapes'.
Para el mal que hoy acaba, no es remedio el de mañana.
'The remedy of to-morrow will not serve for the evil of
to-day'.
La casa quemada, acudir con el agua.
'When the house is burnt, to have recourse to water'.
[*Fál fán ghort* (= *um an ngort*) *i ndéidh* (=*ndiaidh*) *na foghla.*]

146. **A n-dèigh 'aimhleis do chithear a leas do'n Eirionnach.**
'After misfortune the Irishman sees his profit'.
i.e. he sees what he ought to have done, when too late.
[*I ndéidh* (=*ndiaidh*) *a aimhlis*★ *a tchítear* (= *a fheictear*) *a leas
don Éireannach.*]

Experience, knowledge

147. **Is maith an t-eòlaidhe deireadh an lae.**
'The end of the day is a good director'.
[*Is maith an t-eolaí deireadh an lae.*]

148. **Fa choin–fheasgar aithnighear fear.**
'About evening a man is known'.
i.e. after he has done his day's work.
[*Fá choineascar a aithnítear fear.*]

149. **Is fearr an chiall cheannaighthe nà a faghail a n-asgaidh.**
'Sense that is bought is better than what is got for noth-
ing'; and:
[*Is fearr an chiall cheannaithe ná a fáil in aisce.*]

150. **'Sì an chìall cheannaighthe is fearr.**
'Bought sense is the best'.
[*Is í an chiall cheannaithe is fearr.*]

151. **Is a g-cionn na bliadhna innsidheas iasgaire a thàb-
hachd.**
'It is at the end of the year that the fisherman can tell his
profits'.
[*Is i gceann na bliana a insíos* (= *insíonn) iascaire a thábhacht.*]

152. **Biann eagla na teine air a leanabh dòithte.**
'A burnt child fears the fire'.
Spanish. *El gato escaldado del agua fria huye.*
'The scalded cat flies from cold water'.
[*Bíonn eagla na tine ar an leanbh dóite.*]

153. **Is mall gach cos air chasan gan eòlus.**
'On an unknown path every foot is slow'.
[*Is mall gach cos ar chasán gan eolas.*]

154. **Moladh gach duine an t-ath mur gheabhaidh se è.**
'Let every man praise the ford as he finds it'.
Spanish. *Cada uno cuenta de la feria, como le va en ella.*
'Everyone speaks of the fair as he finds it'.
[*Moladh gach duine an t-áth mar a gheobhaidh/ghabhfaidh sé é.*]

155. **Mol a dheireadh.**
'Praise the end of it'.
i.e. see how it ends before you say anything.
Latin. *Exitus acta probat.*
['The result is proof of one's action'.]
Spanish. *Nadie se alabe, hasta que acabe.*
'Let no one boast until he has finished'.
English. *Don't halloo til you are out of the wood.*
[*Mol a dheireadh.*]

156. **Is maith a sgèulaidhe an aimsir.**
'Time is a good historian'.
English. *Time will tell.*
Latin. *Tempus omnia revelat.*
['Time reveals all things'.]
[*Is maith an scéalaí an aimsir.*]

157. **Is fearr eòlus an uilc nà an t-olc gan eòlus.**
'Better is knowledge of evil than evil without knowledge'.
He who knows what is wrong is more likely to avoid doing it.
[*Is fearr eolas an oilc ná an t-olc gan eolas.*]

158. **Cha ghabhar sean-èun le càbh.**
'An old bird is not to be caught with chaff'.
Latin. *Annosa vulpes haud capitur laqueo.*
['An aged fox is not captured by a snare'.]
[*Cha (= Ní) ghabhtar seanéan le cabha.*]

159. **Mol do ghad, 's na mol do shlat;**
    oir is iomadh slat àluinn nach snìomhann.
    'Praise your *gad* and not your rod;
    for many a beautiful rod will not twist'.
    Another allusion to the general use of willow rods for a
    variety of purposes.
    [*Mol do ghad agus ná mol do shlat, óir is iomaí slat álainn nach
    sníomhann.*]

160. **Is trom an t-uallach aineòlas.**
    'Ignorance is a heavy burden'.
    [*Is trom an t-ualach aineolas.*]

161. **Cruthughadh na putòige a h-ithe.**
    'The proof of a pudding is the eating of it'.
    [*Cruthú na putóige a hithe.*]

162. **Is àrd gèim bò air a h-aineòlas.**
    'The lowing of a cow is loud in a strange place'.
    Latin. *Bos alienus subinde prospectat foras.*
    'The strange ox looks frequently to the door'.
    Spanish. *El buey bravo, en tierra agena, se hace manso.*
    'The fierce ox becomes tame on strange land'.
    [*Is ard géim bó ar a haineolas.*]

Hope, reliance on providence

163. **Char òrduigh Dia bèul gan biadh.**
    'God never ordained a mouth to be without food'.
    Said sometimes to persons who complain of having too
    many children.
    [*Char (= Níor) ordaigh Dia béal gan b(h)ia.*]

164. **Char dùnadh dorus a rìamh nar fosgladh dorus eile.**
    'There was never a door shut but there was another opened'.
    Spanish. *Cuando una puerta se cierra, ciento se abren.*
    'When one door shuts, a hundred open'.
    [*Char (= Níor) dúnadh doras ariamh nár (f)osclaíodh doras eile.*]

165. **Char dhruid Dia bearn a rìamh nach bh-fosgoladh**
    se bearn eile.
    'God never closed one gap, that he did not open another one'.
    Spanish. *Dios que da la llaga, da la medicina.*
    'God who gives the wound, gives the cure'.
    [*Char (= Níor) dhruid Dia bearna riamh nach n-(bhf)osclódh sé
    bearna eile.*]

166. **Char uaith na madaidh deireadh na bliadhna go fòill.**
'The dogs have not eaten up the end of the year yet'.
i.e. have patience, you have still time enough.
[*Char uaigh (= Níor ith)*★ *na madaí deireadh na bliana go fóill.*]

167. **Is fearr muinighin mhaith nà droch-aigneadh.**
'Good hope is better than bad intention'.
[*Is fearr muinín mhaith ná drochaigne.*]

168. **Ta ìasg 's a bh-fairge ni's fearr nà gabhadh a rìamh**
'There is a fish in the sea better than ever was caught yet'.
[*Tá iasc sa bhfarraige níos fearr ná a gabhadh riamh.*]

169. **An ùair a thig cabhair, thig dhà chabhair.**
'When help comes, two helps come'.
English. *It never rains but it pours.*
[*Nuair a thig (= thagann) cabhair, thig dhá chabhair.*]

170. **Is breitheamh mall Dia,**
Nach dearna 'rìamh acht an chòir;
Chuir se Cormac a mach 's a t-sliabh,
A's lèig se an diabhal le n-a thòin.
'God is a slow judge,
Who never did anything but justice;
He put Cormac out on the mountain,
And let the devil at his back'.
Said on the downfall of a bad man; or when any one who
has long practised villainy with impunity, at last meets his
deserts. Who the Cormac was, that is named in the proverb,
is not known.
[*Is breitheamh mall Dia*
Nach ndearna riamh ach an chóir;
Chuir sé Cormac amach sa tsliabh,
Agus lig sé an diabhal lena thóin.]

171. **Cha bhiann Dia le mi-rùn daoine.**
'God takes no part in the bad designs of men'.
[*Cha (= Ní) bhíonn Dia le mírún daoine.*]

172. **Is maith Dia go là, a's nì fearr nà go brath.**
'God is good until day, and yet no better than he is until
the day of judgment'.
i.e. God's providence watches over us at all times.
'*Trust in God, and keep your powder dry*' – Oliver Cromwell.

The Spaniards have a proverb something like this last:
A Dios rezando, y con el mazo dando.
'Praying to God, and working with the hammer'.
[*Is maith Dia go lá, agus ní fearr ná go bráth.*]

173. **An nidh nach n-ithtear a's nach ngoidtear, gheabhar è.**
'The thing that is not eaten, and not stolen, will be found'.
[*An ní nach n-itear agus nach ngoidtear, gheofar é.*]

174. **Is farsuing Dia 's a g-cumhanglach.**
'In the narrow strait God's providence is wide'.
[*Is fairsing Dia sa gcúnglach.*]

175. **Is minic a bhi dubhach mòr air bheagan fearthana.**
'Tis often there has been great darkness with little rain'.
[*Is minic a bhí dubhach mór ar bheagán fearthainne.*]

Honour, disgrace, shame

176. **Is beò duine a n-dèigh a dhaoine,**
acht ni bèo è a n-dèigh an náire.
'A man may live after his kindred, but not after his shame'.
[*Is beo duine i ndéidh (=ndiaidh) a dhaoine,*
ach ní beo é i ndéidh (=ndiaidh) a náire.]

177. **Is ùaisle onoir nà òr.**
'Honour is more noble than gold'.
[*Is uaisle onóir ná ór.*]

178. **Is fearr paiste nà poll, acht is onoraigh poll nà paiste.**
'A patch is better than a hole, but a hole is more honourable than a patch'.
[*Is fearr paiste ná poll, ach is onóraí poll ná paiste.*]

179. **Is beag a rud a shalaigheas brighiste,**
agus ni lugha a thuilleas dìomadh.
'It is a little thing that dirties a pair of breeches,
but not less than what deserves reproach'.
[*Is beag an rud a shalaíos (= shalaíonn) bríste*
agus ní lú a thuilleas (= thuilleann) díomua.]

180. **Glacaidh gach dath dubh, acht ni ghlacaidh an dubh dath.**
'Every colour will take black, but black will take no colour'.
[*Glacfaidh gach dath dubh ach ní ghlacfaidh an dubh dath.*]

181. **Làn duirn de shògh, agus làn baile de nàire.**
'The full of a fist of gain, and the full of a village of shame'.
For example, when a single egg is stolen.
[*Lán doirn de shó agus lán baile de náire.*]

182. **Ma's mòr do chliù, cha mhaith.**⋆
'Though your fame is great, it is not good'.
[*Más mór do chlú cha m(h)aith (= ní maith).*]

183. **Is bùaine cliù nà saoghal.**
'Reputation is more lasting than life'.
[*Is buaine clú ná saol.*]

184. **Is fearr diol tnu nà diol truaighe.**
'It is better (to be) an object of envy than an object of pity'.
[*Is fearr díol tnútha ná díol trua.*]

Humility

185. **Is fàlta duine a g-clùid dhuine eile.**
'A man is shy in another man's corner'.
[*Is fálta duine i gclúid duine eile.*]

186. **Ghnidh suidhe ìsioll goradh àrd.**
'A low seat makes a high warming'.
[*Ghní (= Déanann) suí íseal goradh ard.*]

187. **Is minic a fagadh an tè bu mhò mheisneach, a's thainig a deireòil saor.**
'Many a time the most confident person has been left in the lurch, when the humble one has got off safe'.
As in battle, where the strong man may be slain, and the weak escape.
'The race is not to the swift, nor the battle to the strong' .– Bible.
[*Is minic a fágadh an té ba mhó misneach agus a tháinig an dearóil saor.*]

188. **'Sì an dìas is truime is ìsle chromas a cionn.**
'The heaviest ear of corn is the one that lowliest bends its head'.
A beautiful metaphor, implying that the man who has most knowledge is always the most modest.
[*Is í an dias is troime is ísle a chromas (= chromann) a ceann.*]

189. **Fear falamh a bheidheas gan nidh,**
     Suidheadh sìos a bh-fad o chàch;
     O mheud a maise bhios 'n a chorp,
     Is iomadh lochd a chithear 'n a làr.
     'He that has nothing,
     Let him sit far below the rest (of the company);
     Be he ever so handsome in his person,
     many a fault will be seen in him'.
     [*Fear folamh a bheas (= bheidh) gan ní*
     Suíodh síos i bhfad ó chách;
     Dá mhéad an mhaise a bhíos (= bhíonn) ina chorp
     Is iomaí locht a tchítear (= fheictear) ina lár.]

Courage, confidence, self-reliance

190. **Nà biodh do theangaidh fa do chrios.**
     'Do not keep you tongue under your belt'.
     i.e. speak out boldly
     [*Ná bíodh do theanga faoi do chrios.*]

191. **Nà seachain a's nà h-agair an cath.**
     'Do not either shun or provoke a fight'.
                                        'Beware
     Of entrance to a quarrel, but being in
     Bear it, that th' opposer may beware of thee' – Shakespeare.
     [*Ná seachain agus ná hagair an cath.*]

192. **Beidh nidh ag an sàrachan, 'n ùair a bhios an**
     nàireachan falamh.
     'The pertinacious man will get something when the
     shame-faced will go empty'.
     Latin. *Audaces fortuna juvat timidosque repellat.*
     ['Fortune favours the daring and repels the timid'.]
     Spanish *Al hombre osado la fortuna (le) da la mano.*
     'To the bold man fortune gives her hand'.
     English. *Faint heart never won fair lady.*
     [*Beidh ní ag an (t)sárachán nuair a bhíos (= bhíonn) an*
     náireachán folamh.]

Truth, sincerity, and the reverse

193. **Is fearrde a dhearcas brèug fiadhnuise.**
     'A lie looks the better of having a witness'.
     [*Is fearrde a dhearcas (= dhearcann) bréag fianaise.*]

194. **Bìann an fhirìnne searbh go minic.**
'Truth is often bitter'.
[*Bíonn an fhírinne searbh go minic.*]

195. **An lus nach bh-fuighthear, 'sè 'fhòireas.**
'The herb that cannot be got is the one that suits'.
Applied to persons who offer to give or lend a thing, but
unluckily it cannot be found.
[*An lus nach bhfaightear is é a fhóireas (= fhóireann).*★]

196. **Cha deanann bodach brèug 's a chlann a lathair.**
'A clown does not tell lies when his children are present'.
Because they might contradict him.
[*Cha (n)déanann (= Ní dhéanann) bodach bréag agus a chlann
i láthair.*]

197. **Cha deachaidh se air sgath an tuir leis.**
'He did not go behind the bush with him'.
i.e. he spoke out bluntly.
[*Cha dteachaidh (= Ní dheachaigh) sé ar scáth an toir leis.*]

198. **Meallann a fear brèugach a fear sanntach.**
'The liar deceives the greedy man'.
[*Meallann an fear bréagach an fear santach.*]★

199. **Ni fiù sgèul gan ughdar èisdeachd.**
'A story without an author is not worth listening to'.
[*Ní fiú scéal gan údar a éisteacht.*]

200. **Mhionnochadh se poll thrìd chlàr.**
'He would swear a hole through a plank'.
[*Mhionnódh sé poll t(h)rí(d) chlár.*]

Honesty, justice

201. **Nà bain leis an nidh nach m-baineann duit** (or, **leat**).
'Do not meddle with what does not concern you'.
[*Ná bain leis an rud nach mbaineann duit (or leat).*]

202. **Ghoideadh se an ubh o'n chorr, a's a chorr fèin fa
dheireadh.**
'He would steal the egg from the crane, and the crane her-
self at last'.
The crane is said to be remarkable for her vigilance.
[*Ghoidfeadh sé an ubh ón chorr agus an chorr féin faoi dheireadh.*]

203. **Saoileann gaduidhe na g-cruach gur sladaidibh an sluagh.**
'The man that steals stacks thinks all the world thieves'.
A thorough thief believes no one to be honest.
[*Síleann gadaí na gcruach gur sladaithe an slua.*]

204. **Eugcòir os cionn gach eugcòir,**
eugcòir a dheanamh air dhuine mhaith.
'Injustice beyond all injustice,
wronging the good man'.
[*Éagóir os cionn gach éagóra,*
éagóir a dhéanamh ar dhuine mhaith.]

205. **An uair a thuiteas rògairidh a mach, tiocaidh duine macanta air a chuid féin.**
'When rogues fall out, an honest man will get his own'.
[*Nuair a thitfeas (= thitfidh) rógairí amach tiocfaidh duine macánta ar a chuid féin.*]

206. **Is beag a ta eadar an chòir a's an eugcòir.**
'There is but little between justice and injustice'.
i.e. it is as easy to do a just as an unjust action.
[*Is beag atá idir an chóir agus an éagóir.*]

207. **Cuir an ceart 'roimh an bh-fèile.**
'Put justice before generosity'.
[*Cuir an ceart roimh an bhféile.*]

208. **Cuntas glan fhagas càirde buidheach**
A charas Criosd,* cuir a nall an fheòirlìn.
'Clear accounts leave friends thankful;
So, gossip, hand me over the farthing'.
Italian. *Conti chiari, amici cari.*
'Clear accounts make dear friends'.
Scotch. *Aft countin' keeps frien's lang thegither.*
English. *Short accounts make long friends.*
French. *A vieux comptes, nouvelles disputes.*
['Old (unpaid) accounts lead to new disputes'.]
[*Cuntas glan a fhágas (= fhágann) cairde buíoch;*
A chara as Críost, cuir anall an fheoirling.]

Pride, self-sufficiency, boastfulness, selfishness, wilfulness

209. **Saoileann gach èun gur b'è a chlann fèin is deise air a g-coill.**
'Every bird thinks her own young ones the handsomest in the wood'.
Latin. *Suum cuique pulchrum*
['One's own is beautiful to oneself'.] and,
Sua quisque laudat.
['Each one praises what is his'.]
Spanish. *Cada buhonero alaba sus agujas.*
'Every pedlar praises his needles'.
[*Síleann gach éan gurb é a chlann féin is deise ar an gcoill.*]

210. **Is teann gach madadh air a charnan féin.**
'The dog is bold on his own little heap'.
French. *Chien sur son fumier est hardi.*
['A dog is hardy on its own dunghill'.]
Scotch. *A cook is crouse on his ain midden.*
Spanish. *Cada gallo canta en su muladar.*
['Every cock crows on its own dunghill'.]
[*Is teann gach madadh ar a charnán féin.*]

211. **Is teann an madadh gearr a n-àit a m-biann a thathaigh.**
'The cur is bold in the place where he is well known'.
[*Is teann an madadh gearr in áit a mbíonn a thaithí.*]

212. **Ni aithnigheann a mhuc a bhios 'sa chrò a mhuc a bhios dul a ròd.**
'The pig in the sty does not recognize the pig going along the road'.
[*Ní aithníonn an mhuc a bhíos (= bhíonn) sa chró an mhuc a bhíos ag dul an ród.*]

213. **Sin ag deanamh sglèipe os cionn sglàmhaireachd.**★
'Putting on show over meanness'.
Said when a poor farmer puts on fine clothes.
[*Sin ag déanamh scléipe os cionn sclamhaireachta.*]

214. **Ni thuigeann an sàthach an seang.**
'The satiated man does not understand (the feelings of) the hungry man'.
[*Ní thuigeann an sá(tha)ch an seang.*]

215. **Biann duilleabhar àluinn a's toradh searbh air chrann na sgèimhe.**
'The tree of beauty has handsome foliage and bitter fruit'.
[*Bíonn duilliúr álainn agus toradh searbh ar chrann na scéimhe.*]

216. **'N uair a bhios bolg a chait làn, ghnidh se crònan.**
'When the cat's belly is full, she purrs';
[*Nuair a bhíos (= bhíonn) bolg an chait lán, ghní (= déanann) sé crónán.*] and

217. **Is mur gheall air fèin a ghnidheas a cat crònan.**
'It is on her own account the cat purrs'.
Spanish. *Halaga la cola el can, no por ti, sino por el pan.*
'The dog wags his tail, not for you but for the bread'.
[*Is mar gheall air féin a ghníos (= dhéanann) an cat cnónán.*]

218. **Cha chuimhnigheann a fear cìocrach a chù go m-beidh a bhrù fèin làn.**
'The hungry man does not remember his hound till his own belly is full'.
[*Cha (= Ní) chuimhníonn an fear cíocrach a chú go mbeidh a bhroinn féin lán.*]

219. **Seòl do shean–mhathair lachanaidh a bhleaghan.**
'Teach your grandmother to milk ducks'.
Latin. *Delphinum natare doces, vel aquilam volare.*
['You teach a dolphin to swim or an eagle to fly'.]
[*Seol do sheanmháthair lachain a bhleán.*]

220. **Gach duine a' tarruing uisge air a mhuileann fèin.**
'Every man drawing the water to his own mill'.
[*Gach duine ag tarraingt uisce ar a mhuileann féin.*]

221. **Is mian leis a chlèireach mìas mhèith comh maith leis an t-sagart.**
'The clerk likes a fat dish as well as the priest'.
Spanish. *Cuando el abad lame el cuchillo, mal para el monacillo.*
'When the curate licks the knife, it is bad for the clerk'.
[*Is mian leis an chléireach mias mhéith comh maith leis an tsagart.*]

222. **Is maith fa sheòladh an bhothair an tè a bhios olc fa aoidheachda.**
'He who is bad at giving lodging is good at showing the road'.
[*Is maith fá sheoladh an bhóthair an té a bhíos (= bhíonn) olc fá aíocht.*]

223. **Is maighistreas a luchog air a thigh fèin.**
'The mouse is mistress in her* own house'.
[*Is máistreas an luchóg ar a tigh (= teach) féin.*]

224. **'Sì a chneadh fèin is luaithe mhothuigheas gach duine.**
'It is his own wound that every man feels the soonest'.
[*Is é a chneá féin is luaithe a mhothaíos (= mhothaíonn) gach duine.*]

225. **Is mòr an caolach a bhi air do bheagan arbha.**
'There is a great deal of rubbish in your small quantity of corn'.
[*Is mór an caolach a bhí ar do bheagán arbha.**]

226. **Molaidh an gnìomh è fèin.**
'The deed will praise itself'.
Italian. *Dal detto al fatto, v' è un gran tratto.*
['From the word to the deed there is a great distance'.]
[*Molfaidh an gníomh é féin.*]

227. **Torann mòr air bheagan ola.**
'Much noise for little wool'.
English. *Much cry and little wool, as the devil said when shearing the pig.*
Scotch. *Mair whustle nor woo', as the souter said when shearin' the soo.*
Spanish. *Cacarear y no poner huevo.*
'To cackle and lay no egg'.
[*Torann mór ar bheagán olla.*]

228. **Leig fad an aghastair leis.**
'Let him have the length of the halter'.
[*Lig fad an adhastair leis.*]
or **Teilg an t–aghastar fa n–a chionn.**
'Throw the halter over his head'.
i.e. let him take his full swing.
English. *Give him rope enough, and he will hang himself.*
[*Teilg an t-adhastar fána cheann.*]

229. **Saoileann se gur b'è fèin an chloch a caitheadh leis a g–caislean.**
'He thinks that he himself is the very stone that was hurled at the castle'.
i.e. he was the one who bore the brunt. This proverb seems to allude to the stone cannon-balls used for artillery in the 15th and 16th centuries.
[*Síleann sé gurb é féin an chloch a caitheadh leis an gcaisleán.*]

230. **Is binn gach èun ann a dhoire fèin.**
'Every bird is melodious in his own grove'.
[*Is binn gach éan ina dhoire féin.*]

231. **Chan ùaisle mac righ nà a chuid.**
'The son of a king is not nobler than his food'.
Often said by a person who happens to come in unexpectedly on another who is in the act of cooking his own food; as much as to say, 'You need not be ashamed'. The saying took its origin in an anecdote which is told of one of the O'Neills, the Ulster chieftains. A bard on one occasion having entered a room without ceremony, discovered the chief toasting a cake for himself. O'Neill looked ashamed of his occupation; but the bard instantly addressed him in these impromptu lines:
Is tu-sa an tighearna O'Nèill,
A's mi-se mac t-sèin mhic Cuirc;
Tiontamaois a t-sudog air aon,
Chan uaisle mac righ nà a chuid.
['You are the Lord O'Neill
and I the son of Seán Mac Cuirc
Let us both turn the bannock
A king's son is no more noble than his food'.
Is tusa an Tiarna Ó Néill
Agus mise mac Sheáin mhic Cuirc★
Tiontaimis an tsudóg ar aon
Chan uaisle mac rí ná a chuid.]
Italian. *A tavola non bisogna aver vergogna.*
'At table one need not be ashamed'.
[*Chan uaisle (= Ní huaisle) mac rí ná a chuid.*]

Against trusting to appearances

232. **Bìann adharca mòra air bhà a bh-fad ò bhaile.**
'Cows far from home have long horns'.
We value things at a distance, or out of our reach, more than they deserve.
English. *Far away birds have fine feathers.*
Latin. *Omne ignotum pro magnifico est.*
['Everything unknown is taken as magnificent'.
Bíonn adharca móra ar bha i bhfad ó bhaile.]

233. **Is glas na cnuic a bh–fad uainn.**
'Distant hills appear green'.
[*Is glas na cnoic i bhfad uainn.*]

234. **Cha dheanann aon àilleog samhradh.**
'One swallow does not make a summer'.
[*Cha ndéanann (= Ní dhéanann) aon fháinleog amháin
samhradh.*]

235. **Suairc an taobh a muigh agus duairc an taobh a
stigh.**
'Civil outside and churlish inside'.
[*Suairc an taobh amuigh agus duairc an taobh istigh.*]

236. **Is minic gràna greannmhar, a's èadan deas air
mhìsteàir.**
'Often an ugly person is agreeable, and a mischievous one
has a handsome face'.
[*Is minic gránna greannmhar agus éadan deas ar mhisteoir.* ★]

237. **Troid chaoracha maola.**
'A fight between hornless sheep'.
i.e. a mock-fight; said of persons appearing to be very
angry with each other, but not so in reality.
[*Troid chaorach* ★ *maol.*]

238. **Ma's olc a dath, is maith a dreach.**
'Though the complexion is bad, the countenance is good'.
[*Más olc an dath is maith an dreach.*]

239. **Taisbean an laogh biadhta, acht nà taisbean an nidh
a bhiadhtaigh è.**
'Show the fatted calf, and not the thing that fattened him'.
[*Taispeáin an lao biata ach ná taispeáin an ní a bhiataigh é.*]

240. **Ghnidh aran cam bolg direach.**
'Crooked bread makes a straight belly'.
Alluding to oaten cakes, which become crooked when
toasted at the fire on the *'maide aràin'*. Many a person or
thing, though rough and unsightly, is good notwithstanding.
[*Ghní (= Déanann) arán cam bolg díreach.*]

241. **Cha chluinnean se an nidh nach binn leis.**
'He does not hear what is not pleasing to him'.
[*Cha (= Ní) chluineann sé an ní nach binn leis.*]

242. **Is anamh bhios teangaidh mhilis gan gath ann a bun.**
'A sweet tongue is seldom without a sting at its root'.
[*Is annamh a bhíos (= bhíonn) teanga mhilis gan ga ina bun.*]

243. **Blichtear na bà buidhe, a's òltar a g-cuid boinne,
Agus thèid na bà bàna gan sàl chun a bhaile.**
'The yellow cows are milked, and their milk is drunk;
While the white cows come back from the fair, and no bid
for them'.
Yellow cows are said to give better milk than white cows,
and therefore sell better in the fair. The proverb is applied
to women, and hints that a girl with an uninviting exterior
may make a better wife than a handsome one.
[*Blitear na ba buí agus óltar a gcuid bainne,
Agus théid (= téann) na ba bána gan sál★ chun an bhaile.*]

244. **Biann borb faoi sgèimh.**
'A violent disposition may be under a beautiful form'.
[*Bíonn borb faoi scéimh.*]

245. **Biann cluanaidhe a n-deagh-chulaidh.**
'A deceiver may be dressed in fine clothes'.
[*Bíonn cluanaí i ndea-chulaith.*]

246. **Cionn èireòige air shean-cheirc.**
'A pullet's head on an old hen'.
A hen's age can never be told by her head. The proverb is
applied to an elderly woman dressing herself with a showy
cap, more suitable for a young one.
[*Ceann eireoige ar sheanchirc (= sheanchearc).*]

247. **Ainm gan tàbhacht.**
'The name without the substance'.
[*Ainm gan tábhacht.*]

248. **Is maith an sgeul (*or,* an greann) a lìonas bolg.**
'It is a good story (or, jest) that fills the belly'.
[*Is maith an scéal (or an greann) a líonas (= líonann) bolg.*]

249. **Cha lìontar an bolg le caint.**
'The belly is not filled by talking'.
English. *Fair words butter no parsnips*; and,
Many words will not fill a bushel.
Latin. *Fabulis venter non expletur.*
['The belly is not filled by stories'.]
[*Cha (= Ní) líontar an bolg le caint.*]

250. **Beiridh cearc dhubh ubh bhàn.**
'A black hen lays a white egg'.
Spanish. *Tierra negra buen pan lleva.*
'Black land produces good bread'.
[*Beiridh (= Beireann) cearc dhubh ubh bhán.*]

Sobriety

251. **An ùair a bhios an deòch a stigh, biann a chiall a muigh.**
'When drink is in, sense is out'.
Italian. *Vino dentro, senno fuori.*
['Wine within, sense without'.]
Spanish. *Do entra (el) beber, sale saber.*
'When drink enters wisdom departs.'
[*Nuair a bhíos (= bhíonn) an deoch istigh, bíonn an chiall amuigh.*]

252. **Is cuma liom cumann bean leanna.**
'I do not care for the friendship of an ale-wife'.
[*Is cuma liom cumann bean leanna.*]

253. **Is giorra deòch na sgeul.**
'A drink is shorter than a story'.
[*Is giorra deoch ná scéal.*]

Poverty

254. **Is iomad gron a chithear air a duine bhocht.**
'Many a defect is seen in the poor man'.
[*Is iomaí cron a tchítear (= fheictear) ar an duine bhocht.*]

255. **Milleann a bhoichtineacht a choingeall.**
'Poverty destroys punctuality'.
[*Milleann an bhochtaineacht an c(h)oinníoll.*]

256. **Ta gob a phòcain air a chapàn aige.**
'He has the mouth of his poke on the baking dish'.
Equivalent to the next proverb, 'He is from hand to mouth'.
The *capan* is the wooden dish or bowl in which poor people knead their bread. The proverb says that the mouth of the beggar's 'poke' (*i.e.* the last of the meal) is always in the dish.
[*Tá gob a phocáin ar an chapán aige.*]

257. **Chan'uil aige acht o'n làimh go d-ti an beul.**
'He has nothing but from hand to mouth'.
[*Chan fhuil (= Níl) aige ach ón láimh go dtí an béal.*]

258. **Is ball buan do'n donas an nàire.**
'Shame is a constant accompaniment of poverty'.
[*Is ball buan don donas an náire.*]

259. **Brosnuigheann aire intleacht.**
'Necessity urges invention'.
[*Brostaíonn aire intleacht.*]

260. **Is iomad sift a dheanas duine bocht sul a sgabadh se tigh.**
'Many a shift the poor man makes before he will give up his house'.
[*Is iomaí seift a ghéanfas (= dhéanfaidh) duine bocht sula scaipe sé teach.*]

261. **Is buidh le bocht a bh-faghann.**
'The poor are thankful for what they get'.
[*Is buí le bocht a bhfaigheann.*]

262. **Is baile bocht, baile gan toit gan teine.**
'It is a poor village that has neither smoke nor fire'.
Spanish. *Casa sin chimenea, de muger pobre o yerma.*
'A house without a chimney is either inhabited by a poor woman, or empty'.
[*Is baile bocht baile gan toit gan tine.*]

263. **Is ionmhuin le Dia duine bocht sùgach,**
acht ni lugha air an diabhal nà duine bocht lùbach.
'God loves a cheerful poor man,
but he hates like the devil a dishonest poor man'.
Spanish. *Pobrete pero alegrete.*
'Poor but merry.'
[*Is ionúin le Dia duine bocht súgach,
ach ní lú air an diabhal ná duine bocht lúbach.*]

264. **Millidh an ainnis an t-iasacht.**
'Poverty spoils borrowing'.
English. *Poverty parts good company*
[*Millidh (= Milleann) an ainnise an t-iasacht.*]

265. **An tè bhios sìos buailtear clòch air,
a's an tè a bhios sùas òltar deòch air.**
'The man that is down has a stone thrown at him,
and the man that is up has his health drunk'.
[*An té a bhíos (= bhíonn) síos buailtear cloch air
agus an té a bhíos suas óltar deoch air.*]

266. **Cha seasann sac falamh.**
'An empty sack does not stand upright'.
[*Cha seasann (= Ní sheasaíonn) sac folamh.*]

267. **Ni baoghal do'n m-bacach an gaduidhe.**
'The beggar is in no danger from the robber'.
Latin. *Cantabit vacuus coram latrone viator.*
['The empty traveller will sing in the presence of a robber'.]
[*Ní baol don mbacach an gadaí.*]

268. **Cha robh se air faghail, 'n ùair a bhi an chìall da roinn.**
'He was not forthcoming when sense was distributed'.
Spanish. *Salamon pasó por su puerta cuando nació, mas no entró dentro.*
'When he was born, Solomon passed by his door and
would not go in'.
[*Cha (= Ní) raibh sé ar fáil nuair a bhí an chiall á roinnt.*]

269. **Cha robh se go maith, o rinne slat còta dò.**
'He was never good since the time that a yard (of cloth)
made a coat for him'.
i.e. he never was good since he was a boy.
[*Cha (= Ní) raibh sé go maith ó rinne slat cóta dó.*]

270. **Falaigheann gradh gràin, agus chi fùath a làn.**
'Love conceals ugliness, and hate sees many faults'.
[*Folaíonn grá gráin agus tchí (= feiceann) fuath a lán.*]

271. **'Sè an t-uisge is èadomhuine is mo tormàn.**
'It is the shallowest water that makes the greatest noise'.
Spanish. *Do va mas hondo el rio, hace menos ruido.*
'Where the river runs deepest it makes least noise'.
[*Is é an t-uisce is éadoimhne is mó tormán.*]

272. **Is beag a ghaoith nach ngluaisidh guaigìn.**
'It is a little wind that will not move a giddy-headed per-
son'.
[*Is beag an ghaoth nach ngluaisfidh guaigín.*]

273. **Chaithfeadh an tè gheabhas sùas leis eirigh go mòch.**
'The man who will overtake him must rise early'.
[*Chaithfeadh an té a gheobhadh suas leis éirí go moch.*]

274. **Is trèise an dùchas nà an oileamhuin.**
'A hereditary disposition is stronger than education'.
[*Is treise an dúchas ná an oiliúint.*]

275. **Is bùaine an buinneàn maoith nà an crann bromanta.**
'The soft twig is more durable than the stubborn tree'.
[*Is buaine an buinneán maoth ná an crann brománta.*]

276. **Is iomadh taod a thig ann a là earraigh.**
'Many a sudden change takes place in a spring day'.
A pleasing metaphor, applied to the fickleness of youth.
[*Is iomaí taod a thig (= thagann) i lá earraigh.*]

277. **Is mian le h-amadan imirce.**
'A fool is fond of removing'.
[*Is mian le hamadán imirce.*]

278. **Is minic a fuaras comhairle ghlic ò amadan.**
'Tis often a good advice has been got from a fool'.
[*Is minic a fuarthas comhairle ghlic ó amadán.*]

279. **Gach cat a n-dèigh a chineàil.**
'Every cat after its kind'.
[*Gach cat i ndéidh (=ndiaidh) a chineáil.*]

280. **An ùair a ghlaodhas a sean choileach, foghlumaidh an t-òg.**
'When the old cock crows, the young one learns'.
[*Nuair a ghlaos (= ghlaonn) an seanchoileach, foghlaimídh (= foghlaimíonn) an t-óg.*]

281. **Ta gò a n-aghaidh gò, agus camadh a n-aghaidh caim, agus casadh a n-aghaidh na gangaide.**
'There is deceit against deceit, and crook against crook, and twist against the screw'.
Said of any person more than usually 'crooked' in his disposition.
[*Tá gó in aghaidh gó, agus camadh in aghaidh caim agus casadh in aghaidh na gangaide.*]

282. **Ta nios mò nà a phaidireacha aige.**
'He knows more than his Pater-noster.
[*Tá níos mó ná a phaidreacha aige.*] and

283. **Ta nios mò nà mìola ann a cheann.**
'He has more than lice in his head'.
[*Tá níos mó ná míol(t)a ina cheann.*]

284. **Ta fios aige ca mheùd gràinne pònair a ghnidh cùig.**
'He knows how many beans make five'.
Spanish. *Saber cuantas púas tiene un peine.*
'To know how many teeth there are in a comb'.
[*Tá a fhios aige cá mhéad gráinne pónaire a ghní (= dhéanann) cúig.*]

285. **Briseann an dùchas tre shùilibh a chait.**
'The natural disposition of a cat bursts out through her eyes'.
[*Briseann an dúchas trí shúilibh (=shúile) an chait.*]

286. **Thug se ò dhùchas è, mur thug a mhuc a rùtail.**
'He got it from nature, as the pig got the rooting in the ground'.
He inherits the quality, or vice, from his parents.
[*Thug sé ó dhúchas é mar a thug an mhuc an rútáil.*]

287. **Aithnigh cù gèur a lòcht.**
'A sharp hound knows his fault'.
Most people are aware of their own faults.
Spanish. *Cada uno sabe donde le aprieta el zapato.*
'Every one knows where the shoe pinches him'.
[*Aithnídh (= Aithníonn) cú géar a locht.*]

288. **Guid è dheanadh mac a chait acht luchòg a ghabhàil?**
'What would the son of a cat do but catch a mouse?'
Italian. *Chi da gatta nasce sorici piglia.*
['A cat's offspring catch mice'.]
[*Cad é a dhéanfadh mac an chait ach luchóg a ghabháil?*]

289. **Gach eùn mur óiltear è, ars' an chuach a' dul 's a neanntàig.**
'"Every bird as he has been reared" said the cuckoo, as she went into the nettle'.
[*'Gach eán mar a oiltear é', arsa an chuach ag dul sa neantóig.*]

290. **Gach eùn mur oiltear è, a's an uiseag chun na mòna.**
'Every bird as he has been reared, and the lark to the moor'.
Latin. *Quo semel est imbuta recens servabit odorem testa diu.*
['The shell-fish will preserve for a long time the smell with which it has been recently saturated'.]
[*Gach éan mar a oiltear é agus an (fh)uiseog chun na móna.*]

291. **Budh dual do laogh an fhiaidh, rith a bheith aige.**
'It is natural for the fawn of a deer to have fleetness'.
[*Ba d(h)ual do lao an fhia rith a bheith aige.*]

292. **An rud fhàsas 's a g-cnàimh, ni fèadar a dhìbirt as a bh-feòil.**
'The thing that grows in the bone is hard to drive out of the flesh'.
Latin. *Naturam expellas furca, tamen usque recurrat.* – Horace
['You may drive nature out with a fork, however it will constantly recur'.]
[*An rud a fhásas (= fhásann) sa gcnáimh ní féidir a dhíbirt as an bhfeoil.*]

293. **Chan 'uil amadan air bith is measa nà sean-amadan.**
'There is no fool worse than an old fool'.
[*Chan fhuil (= Níl) amadán ar bith is measa ná seanamadán.*]

294. **An tè is mò fhosglas a bhèul, 'sè is lugha fhosglas a sporàn.**
'The man that opens his mouth the most, opens his purse the least'.
[*An té is mó a (fh)osclaíos (= osclaíonn) a bhéal is é is lú a fhosclaíos a sparán.*]

295. **Da d-treabhadh se an tìr, chaithfeadh se an rìoghachda.**
'Though he would plough a whole country, he would spend a whole kingdom'.
i.e. a hard worker, but as great a spender.
[*Dá dtreabh(f)adh sé an tír, chaithfeadh sé an ríocht.*]

296. **'Sè an carr falamh is mò a ghnì toran.**
'It is the empty car that makes the most noise'.
[*Is é an carr folamh is mó a ghní (= dhéanann) torann.*]

297. **'Sè an t–uisge ciuin is doimhne a ritheas.**
'It is the smooth water that flows the deepest'.
Spanish. *Del agua mansa me libre Dios, que de la recia me guardaré yo.*
'From the smooth water, Lord deliver me; from the rough
I shall guard myself'.
[*Is é an t-uisce ciúin is doimhne a ritheas (= ritheann).*]

298. **Bèul eidhnàin, a's croidhe cuilinn.**
'A mouth of ivy, and a heart of holly'.
[*Béal eidhneáin agus croí cuilinn.*]

299. **Bìann a donas a m–bun na stiocaireacht.**
'Bad luck attends stinginess'.
[*Bíonn an donas i mbun na stiocaireachta.*]

300. **An Laighneach laoigheach,**
An Mumhaineach spleaghach,
An Conachtach bèul–bhinn
'S an t–Ultach beadaidh.
'The Leinster-man is sprightly,
The Munster-man boastful,
The Connaught-man sweet-tongued,
And the Ulster-man impudent'.
[*An Laighneach laoidheach*★
An Muimhneach spleách
An Connachtach béalbhinn
Agus an tUltach beadaí.]

301. **Tabhartus Ui–Nèill, 's a dhà shùil 'n a dhèigh.**
'O'Neill's gift, and his two eyes looking after it'.
Said when any one unhandsomely reminds another of an
obligation conferred by himself.
[*Tabhartas Uí Néill agus a dhá shúil ina dhiaidh.*]

302. **Roinn mur do dhaoine, a's nà fag thu fèin falamh.**
'Share as your family do, so as not to leave yourself empty'.
i.e. your people always took good care of themselves.
[*Roinn mar do dhaoine agus ná fág thú féin folamh.*]

303. **Da g–cuirinn gruaig mo chinn faoi n–a chosa, cha**
sàsochadh se è.
'If I were even to put the hair of my head under his feet, it
would not satisfy him'.
[*Dá gcuir(f)inn gruaig mo chinn faoina chosa, cha sásódh (= ní
shásódh) sé é.*]

304. **Is fiata feargach gach lag-neartmhar.**
'Every feeble man is irritable'.
[*Is fiata feargach gach lagneartmhar.*]

305. **An tè d'uaith an fheòil, òladh se an brot.**
'He that has eaten the flesh-meat may drink the broth too'.
Said when the leavings of anything are offered.
[*An té a d'uaigh* (= d'ith) an fheoil, óladh sé an brat.*]

306. **An tè a bhualadh mo mhadadh, bhualadh se mè fèin.**
'He that would beat my dog would beat myself'.
[*An té a bhuailfeadh mo mhadadh, bhuailfeadh* sé mé féin.*]

Manners, behaviour, civility

307. **Cha mhilleann deagh-ghlòr fiacal.**
'A sweet voice does not injure the teeth'.
French. *Douces paroles n'écorchent pas la langue.*
['Sweet words will not scrape the tongue'.]
[*Cha (= Ní) mhilleann dea-ghlór fiacail.*]

308. **Chan fhaghann fear mogaidh modh.**
'The mocker is never respected'.
[*Chan (= Ní) fhaigheann fear magaidh modh.*]

309. **Cùairt go h-anamh go tigh do charaid, a's fanach gearr goirid ann.**
'Pay visits to your friend's house seldom, and stay but a short time there'.
Spanish. *A casa de tu tía, mas no cada día.*
'Go to your aunt's house, but not every day'. and
El huésped y el pez a los tres días hiede.
'A guest and a fish stink on the third day'.
[*Cuairt go hannamh go tigh (= teach) do charad agus fanacht gearr gairid ann.*]

310. **Aidigheann a tosdach.**
'The silent man confesses'.
[*Admhaíonn an tostach.*]

311. **Cha n-è an tè 'chomhnuidheas a d-tigh gloine, is còir a cheud chloch a chaitheadh.**
'He that lives in a glass house is not the one who ought to throw the first stone'.
Spanish. *El que tiene tejado de vidrio, no tire piedras al de su vecino.*
'He whose house is tiled with glass must not throw stones at his neighbour's'.
[*Chan é an té a chónaíos i dtigh gloine is cóir an chéad chloch a chaitheamh; or*
Ní hé an té a chónaíonn i dteach gloine is cóir an chéad chloch a chaitheamh.]

312. **Thig se gan ìarraidh mur thig a dò-aimsir.**
'He comes like the bad weather, uninvited'.
[*Thig (= thagann) sé gan iarraidh mar a thig an do-aimsir.*]

313. **Nà cuir do chorran a ngort gan ìarraidh.**
'Do not bring your reaping-hook to a field without being asked'.
[*Ná cuir do chorrán i ngort gan iarraidh.*]

314. **Ta sneag an cheapaire nar uaith tu ort.**★
'You have got the hiccup from bread and butter that you never ate'.
i.e. you are meddling with what does not concern you – or, you are taking offence at a thing not intended for you.
[*Tá snag an cheapaire nár uaigh (= ith) tú ort.*]

315. **Cha robh tu a riamh gan Diarmaid agad.**
'You were never without Dermot along with you'.
There is always something going astray with you. Also said to a person who has a habit of doing or saying a particular thing on all occasions.
[*Cha raibh (= Ní raibh) tú ariamh gan Diarmaid agat.*]

316. **Nà cuir do ghob a g-cuideachta gan ìarraidh.**
'Never thrust your beak into company without invitation'.
Spanish. *A boda ni bautizado, no vayas sin ser llamado.*
'Do not go to a wedding nor a christening unless you are invited'.
[*Ná cuir do ghob i gcuideachta gan iarraidh.*]

317. **Cha d-tainig fear an eadarsgàin saor a rìamh.**
'The intermeddler never came off safe'.
[*Cha dtáinig (= Níor tháinig) fear an eadarscáin*★ *saor ariamh.*]

318. **An tè is measa beàirt a's bèusa**
     Is lìa bheir tò-bhèum do gach aon neach;
     Is lèur dò locht gach duine ann 'èudan
     'S nì lèur dò an làn-locht a n-damantar fèin thrid.
     'The man who himself is the worst in deeds and disposition,
     Is the very one who calumniates everbody;
     He sees each man's fault plainly in his countenance,
     But he cannot perceive the greater fault that condemns himself'.
     [*An té is measa birt (= bearta) agus béasa*
     Is lia a bheir (= thugann) toibhéim do gach aon neach;
     Is léir dó locht gach duine ina éadán
     Agus ní léir dó an locht a ndamnaítear é féin tríd.]

319. **A ghreideàl a' tabhairt tòn dubh air a b-pota.**
     'The griddle calling the pot "black bottom"'.
     [*An ghrideall ag tabhairt tóin dubh ar an bpota.*]

320. **Comhairle charaid gan a h-ìarraidh, chan fhuair si**
     a rìamh an meas budh chòir di.
     'A friend's advice not asked for, was never valued as it deserved'.
     Latin. *Ad consilium ne accesseris antequam voceris.*
     ['Do not approach for advice before you are summoned'.]
     Scotch. *Come na to the council unca'd.*
     [*Comhairle charad gan a hiarraidh chan fhuair (= ní bhfuair) sí*
     ariamh an meas ba chóir di.]

321. **An tè a bhios 'n a mhaighistear, aithneochar è.**
     'The man who is the master is (easily) known'.
     [*An té a bhíos (= bhíonn) ina mháistir aithneofar é.*]

Friendship, choice of companions

322. **An tè a luidheas leis na madraidh, èireochaidh se**
     leis na dearnadaidh.
     'He that lies down with the dogs will rise up with the fleas'.
     He that touches pitch shall be defiled therewith. – Ecclesiasticus.
     Evil communications corrupt good manners. – St. Paul.
     [*An té a luíos (= luíonn) leis na madraí, éireoidh sé leis na*
     deargnaídí (= dreancaídí).]

323. **Is maith an sgathan sùil charad.**
     'The eye of a friend is a good looking-glass'.
     [*Is maith an scáthán súil charad.*]

324. **A n-am na ciorra aithnighear an charaid.**
'In time of need the friend is known'.
English. *A friend in need is a friend indeed.*
Spanish. *Amigo del buen tiempo, múdase con el viento.*
'A friend in prosperity changes with the wind' – and
Ahora que tengo oveja y borrego, todos me dicen: ¡en hora buena estéis Pedro!.
'Now that I have got a ewe and a lamb, everbody wishes
me "good day, Peter"'.
Latin. *Amicus certus in re incerta cernitur.* – Cicero
['A steadfast friend reveals himself in time of uncertainty'.]
– and
Ubi opes, ibi amici.
['Where there is wealth, there are friends'.]
[*In am na cearra aithnítear an charaid (= an cara).*]

325. **Bain le ruincìn, a's bainidh an ruincìn leat.**
'Meddle with the peevish man, and he will meddle with you'.
[*Bain le ruincín agus bainfidh an ruincín leat.*]

326. **Thèid gach èun le n' alt fein.**
'Every bird goes along with its own flock'.
[*Théid (= Téann) gach éan lena ealta féin.*] and:

327. **Eunlaith an aon eite a n-èinfheacht ag eitiollaigh.**
'Birds of one feather flying together'.
Latin. *Similis similem delectat.*
['Like delights in like'.]
Spanish. *Cada oveja con su pareja.*
['Every bird with its kind'.]
[*Éanlaith an aon eite in éineacht ag eiteallaigh (= eitilt).*]

328. **Bog a bodach a's bain beum as;**
    òl a ghloine a's bi reidh leis.
'Humour the clown, and take your turn out of him;
drink his glass, and have done with him'.
[*Bog an bodach agus bain béim as;*
ól a ghloine agus bí réidh leis.]

329. **Cha robh caora chlamhach air a t-srèud a rìamh,**
    nar mhaith leithi comràda bheith aici.
'There never was a scabby sheep in a flock
that did not like to have a comrade'.
[*Cha (= Ní) raibh caora chlamhach ar an tréad ariamh*
nár mhaith léi comrádaí a bheith aici.]

330. **Ni h-eòlus gan iontuigheas.**

'There is no knowing a person without living in the same house with him'.

Latin. *Homini ne fidas, nisi cum quo modium salis absumpseris.*

['Do not trust a man unless it is one with whom you have consumed a measure of salt'.]

[*Ní heolas gan aontíos.*]

331. **Na trèig do charaid air do chuid.**

'Do not desert your friend for your meat'.

[*Ná tréig do chara ar do chuid.*]

332. **Bhearaidh aon mhadadh a mhàin air mhadaidh an bhaile tafann.**

'A single dog will set all the dogs in the village a-barking'.

[*Bhéarfaidh (= Tabharfaidh) aon mhadadh amháin ar mhadaí an bhaile tafann.*]

Women, love, courtship, marriage

333. **An àit a m-biann mna biann caint,
a's an àit a m-biann gèidh biann callàn.**

'Wherever there are women there is talking;
and wherever there are geese there is cackling'.

Italian. *Dove sono donne ed ocche, non vi sono parole poche.*

['Where there are women and geese, the words are not few'.]

English. *Many women, many words.*

[*An áit a mbíonn mná bíonn caint agus an áit a mbíonn géanna bíonn callán.*]

334. **Is foisge do bhean leithsgeal nà bràiscin.**

'A woman has an excuse readier than an apron'.

[*Is foisce do bhean leithscéal ná práiscín.*]

335. **Triùir nach bh-fulaingeann altrum, sean-bhean, cearc, agus caora.**

'There are three things that do not bear nursing, an old woman, a hen, and a sheep'.

i.e. who are not thankful for being nursed.

[*Triúr nach bhfulaingíonn altram, seanbhean, cearc agus caora.*]

336. **Rùn caillighe a' sgollaireacht.**
'The secret of an old woman scolding'.
i.e. no secret at all, for a scolding woman will let it out in her rage.
[*Rún caillí ag scallaireacht.* *]

337. **Is bean gan leithsgeal gan sgìste, bean gan phìopa gan phàisde.**
'The woman has neither excuse nor rest who has not a pipe nor a child'.
[*Is bean gan leithscéal gan scíste, bean gan phíopa gan pháiste.*]

338. **Is maith a bhean ì, acht char bhain si a bròga di go foìll.**
'She is a good wife, but she has not taken off her shoes yet'.
i.e. she has not been proved yet: - speaking of a new wife.
[*Is maith an bhean í ach char (= níor) bhain sí a bróga di go fóill.*]

339. **Biann na mna falta, char lèig an nàire dòibh na fir a dhiùltadh.**
'Women are shy, and shame prevents them from refusing the men'.
Scotch. *Do as the lasses do: say 'Na,' and tak' it.*
[*Bíonn na mná fálta, char (= níor) lig an náire dóibh na fir a dhiúltú.*]

340. **Chan 'uil ach pleiseàm dram a thabhairt do chailligh.**
'It is nothing but folly to treat an old woman to a dram'.
[*Chan fhuil (= Níl) ach pléiseam dram a thabhairt do chailligh*]

341. **Praiseach bhuidhe na ngort chuireas mna na Midhe le h-olc.**
'It is the yellow *preshagh* that brings the Meath women to harm'.
In former times, when cabbages were not generally culti-vated in Ireland, the wild kail (called in Irish *Praiseach*), was often made use of as a kitchen vegetable. The proverb alludes to the practice of the women who, in going out in the evening to gather it in the fields, made this an excuse for meeting their lovers.
[*Praiseach bhuí na ngort a chuireas (= chuireann) mná na Mí le holc.*]

342. **An rud reamhar do'n mhnaoi bhreòite.**
'Give the dainty bit to the sickly woman'.
[*An rud ramhar don mhnaoi (= bhean) bhreoite.*]

343. **Glacann droch-bhean comhairle gach fir acht a fir fèin.**
'A bad wife takes advice from every man but her own husband'.
[*Glacann drochbhean comhairle gach fir ach a fir féin.*]

344*. **Cha n-è cossa a mathar a nigh si.**
'It was not her mother's feet that she washed'.
Said when a daughter turns out badly, *i.e.* 'she was not a good daughter, and will have no luck'.
[*Chan é (= Ní hé) cosa a máthar a nigh sí.*]

345. **Fuarann gradh go grod.**
'Love cools quickly'.
[*Fuaraíonn grá go grod.*]

346. **Is anamh earrach gan fuacht.**
'Spring is seldom without some cold'.
There is no youthful love without occasional coolness.
[*Is annamh earrach gan fuacht.*]

347. **Is olc a bhean tigh, inghean na caillighe èasgaidh.**
'The daughter of an active old woman makes a bad house-keeper'.
Spanish. *Madre piadosa cría hija merdosa.*
'An indulgent mother makes a sluttish daughter'.
Scotch. *A busy mither maks a dawly dochter.*
[*Is olc an bhean tí iníon na caillí éasca.*]

348. **Losg si a gual a's cha dearna si a goradh.**
'She burnt her coal and did not warm herself'.
Said when a woman makes a bad marriage.
[*Loisc sí a gual agus cha dtearna (= ní dhearna) sí a goradh.*]

349. **Nà gabh bean gan locht.**
'Never take a wife who has no fault'.
Because there is no such thing to be found.
[*Ná gabh bean gan locht.*]

350. **Ceannsuigheann gach uile fhear droch-bhean acht a fear fèin.**
'Every man can control a bad wife but her own husband'.
Latin. *Facile omnes cum valemus aegrotis consilia damus.*
['When we are able to, all of us can easily give advice to those who are all sick'.]
[*Ceansaíonn gach uile fhear drochbhean ach a fear féin.*]

351. **Chan'uil de bheann aici air, acht urad a's bheidheadh ag madadh dhà bhliadhna air a mhathair.**
'She has only as much regard for him as a two-year-old dog has for his mother'.
[*Chan fhuil (= Níl) de bheann aici air ach oiread agus a bheadh ag madadh dhá bhliain ar a mháthair.*]

352. **Ma chuaidh si chun a t-srotha, ni leis a discleàd.**
'If she went to the stream, it was not with the dish-clout'.
Said of a girl seduced by a person of higher rank, or of one who marries unexpectedly, but improves her condition. An excuse for frailty.
[*Má chuaigh sí chun an tsrutha, ní leis an discleád★.*]

353. **Faisiùn mna na cille le mna na tuaithe, alpàn chuca a's millìn uatha.**
'The usual custom of the nuns with the country-women – they recieve a great lump, and they give a small one in return'.
Alluding to nuns (and ecclesiastics in general) who were in the habit of giving presents of small value, in the expectation of receiving greater.
English. *Throwing a sprat to catch a salmon.*
[*Faisean mhná na cille le mná na tuaithe,*
alpán chuca agus millín uathu.]

354. **Is teòide do'n m-brat a dhùbladh.**
'A blanket is the warmer of being doubled'.
Said when relations marry.
[*Is teoide don mbrat a dhúblú.*]

355. **Aithnighear fear na cuaròige air fàithche a measg chàich.**
'The husband of the sloven is known in the field amidst a crowd'.
[*Aithnítear fear na cuaróige★ ar faiche i measc cháich.*]

356. **Fàl fa'n meur 's gan ribe fa'n tòin.**
'A ring on the finger and not a stitch of clothes on the back'.
[*Fál fán m(h)éar agus gan ribe fán tóin.*]

Family ties

357. **Ma's fogus damh mo chòta, is foisge nà sin damh mo lèine.**
'Though my coat is near me, my shirt is still nearer'.
Spanish. *Más cerca está la camisa que el sayo.*
'The shirt is nearer than the coat'.
[*Más fogas dom(h) mo chóta is foisce ná sin dom(h) mo léine.*]

358. **An easgainn ag ithe a 'rubaill.**
'The eel eating her own tail'.
Speaking ill of our own relations.
[*An eascann ag ithe a rubaill (= heireabaill).*]

359. **Is olc seanadh an èin a thrèigeas a h-èunlaith fèin.**
'The bird has little affection that deserts its own brood'.
[*Is olc seanadh an éin a thréigeas (= thréigeann) a héanlaith féin.*]

360. **Is tibhe fuil nà uisge.**
'Blood is thicker than water'.
Spanish. *Más vale onza de sangre que libra de amistad.*
'An ounce of blood is worth more than a pound of friendship'.
[*Is tibhe fuil ná uisce.*]

361. **Ma's dubh, ma's odhar no donn,**
Is d'a meannan fèin bheir a gabhar a fonn.
'Whether it be black, dun, or brown,
it is its own kid that the goat loves'.
[*Más dubh, más odhar no donn,
Is dá meannán féin a bheir (= thugann) an gabhar a fonn★.*]

362. **Saoileann an prèachan gur b'è èin fèin is deise anns a choill.**
'The crow thinks his own young ones the most beautiful in the wood'.
English. *All her geese are swans.*
Latin. *Suum cuique pulchrum.*
['One's own is beautiful to oneself'.]
[*Síleann an préachán gurb é a éin féin is deise sa choill.*]

Children

363. **Suidhe mhic a d-tigh an athara, suidhe leathan socair;**
Acht suidhe an athar' a d-tigh a mhic, suidhe cruinn corrach.
'The son's seat in his father's house is wide and steady,
But the father's seat in his son's house is round and shaky'.
[*Suí an mhic i dtigh (= i dteach) an athar(a)★, suí leathan socair;*
Ach suí an athar i dtigh an mhic, suí cruinn corrach.]

364. **A dhaoine grinne, an d-tuigeann sibh cùrsa na cloinne,**
Dar linn-ne budh leòibh-san, a's da m-ba leòibh-san ni h-ar linn-ne.
'Ye wise men, are you aware of the nature of children?
Anything we have is theirs, but what they get is not ours'.
[*A dhaoine grinne, an dtuigeann sibh cúrsa na clainne?*
Dar linne ba leo(fa)san agus dá mba leofasan níor linne.]

365. **An tè chaomhnas a t-slat, milleann se a mac.**
'He who spares the rod spoils the boy'.
[*An té a chaomhnaíos (= chaomhnaíonn) an tslat milleann sé an mac.*]

366. **Clann na n-daoine sona, adhbhar na n-daoine dona.**
'The children of lucky men are the materials of future unlucky men'.
Latin. *Heroum filii noxii.*
['The sons of heroes are harmful'.]
[*Clann na ndaoine sona ábhar na ndaoine dona.*]

367. **An nidh a chi an leanabh, 'sè a ghnidh an leanabh.**
'The thing the child sees is what the child does'.
Spanish. *Lo que se aprende en la cuna, siempre dura.*
'What is learned in the cradle always lasts'.
[*An ní a tchí an leanbh is é a ghní an leanbh.★*]

368. **Char bhris cearc na n-èun a sprogaille a rìamh.**
'A hen with chickens never yet burst her craw'.
Because she starves herself to give all to her chickens – said of a mother.
Scotch. *Bairn's mither burst never.*
[*Char (= Níor) bhris cearc na n-éan a sprochaille ariamh.*]

369. **Is beag a bhuailtear an leanabh nach dean gearan.**
'It requires little beating to make a child cry'.
[*Is beag a bhuailtear an leanbh nach ndéanann gearán.*]

370. **Is fearr mathair phòcàin nà athair seistrigh.**
'A begging mother is better than a ploughing father'.
The beggar-woman is fonder of her children than the father.
[*Is fearr máthair phocáin ná athair seisrí.*]

371. **Is minic a thig saoi ò dhaoi.**
'Often a clown's son is a gentleman'.
[*Is minic a thig (= thagann) saoi ó dhaoi.*]

372. **'Sè a leanabh fèin a bhaisteas a sagart air tùs.**
'The priest christens his own child first'.
Often said as a kind of excuse for serving one's self first. I
do not know the origin of the proverb.
[*Is é a leanbh féin a bhaisteas (= bhaisteann) an sagart ar (d)tús.*]

Personal appearance

373. **Cha robh bolg mòr fial a rìamh.**
'A big belly was never generous'.
Latin. *Venter obesus non gignit mentem subtilem.*
['An obese belly does not produce a subtle mind'.]
[*Cha (= Ní) raibh bolg mór fial ariamh.*]

374. **Chan 'uil si beag deas no mòr gràna.**
'She is neither small and pretty, nor big and ugly'.
i.e. she is worse than either.
[*Chan fhuil (= Níl) sí beag deas ná mór gránna.*]

375. **Fear dubh, dana; fear fionn, glìdeamhuil;**
Fear donn, dùalach; fear ruadh, sgigeamhuil.
'A dark-haired man is bold, a light-haired one timid;
A brown-haired man has luxuriant hair, and a red-haired is
a scoffer'.
English. *Fair and foolish, black and proud,*
Long and lazy, little and loud.
Scotch. *Grey-eyed greedy, brown-eyed needy.*
Black-eyed never blin', til it shame a' its kin; and
Fair folk are aye fuzzionless.
Spanish. *Asno cojo, y hombre rojo, y el demonio, todo es uno.*
'A lame ass, a red-haired man and the devil are all one'.
[*Fear dubh dána; fear fionn glídiúil;*
Fear donn dualach; fear rua scigiúil.]

376. **'Sè an t-èadach a ghni an duine.**
'The clothes make the man'.
English. *The tailor makes the man;* and
Fine feathers make fine birds.
But on the contrary,
Italian. *L'abito non fa il monaco.*
['The garb does not make the monk'.]
[*Is é an t-éadach a ghní (= dhéanann) an duine.*]

377. **Fòiridh fear odhar do bhean rìabhach.**
'A sallow man suits a swarthy woman'.
[*Fóiridh (= Fóireann) fear odhar do bhean riabhach.*]

378. **Is fearr greim de choinin nà dhà ghreim de chat.**
'One bit of a rabbit is worth two bits of a cat'.
Applied in various ways: as for instance, to a little man who
is abler at anything than a big fellow; or to one who prefers
a small drop of whiskey to a glass of beer.
[*Is fearr greim de choinín ná dhá ghreim de chat.*]

379. **Is maith a comhartha Criosdaidhe, brighiste bàna.**
'White breeches are a good indication of a Christian'.
This must allude to some local story.
[*Is maith an comhartha Críostaí bríste bána.*]

380. **Cionn mòr air bheagan cèille.**
'Big head and little sense'.
But the Scotch Highlanders have a proverb more in accor-
dance with phrenology –
Ceann mòr air dhuine glic, a's ceann ceirce air amadan.
'A big head on a wise man, and a hen's head on a fool'.
[*Ceann mór ar bheagán céille.*]

381. **Biann dùil le bèul fairge, acht cha bhiann le bèul
uaighe.**
'There is hope from the mouth of the sea, but not from the
mouth of the grave'.
Spanish. *A la muerte no hay cosa fuerte.*
'Nothing is strong against death'.
Italian. *A ogni cosa c'é rimedio fuorché alla morte.*
['There is a remedy for everything except death'.]
[*Bíonn dúil le béal farraige ach cha (= ní) bhíonn le béal
uaighe.*]

382. **Cha d-tig an bàs gan adhbhar.**
'Death does not come without a reason'.
[*Cha dtig (= Ní thagann) an bás gan ábhar.*]

383. **Ta se a nois a staid na firinne, agus sinn-ne air staid na brèige.**
'He is now in the state of truth, and we are in the state of untruth'.
[*Tá sé anois i staid na fírinne agus sinne i staid na bréige.*]

384. **Cabhair an bhochtàin, bèul na h-uaighe.**
'The poor man's relief is the mouth of the grave'.
[*Cabhair an bhochtáin béal na huaighe.*]

385. **Biann sùil le muir, acht cha bhiann sùil le cill.**
'There is hope from the sea, but no hope from the cemetery'.
[*Bíonn súil le muir ach cha (= ní) bhíonn súil le cill.*]

386. **Tinneas fàda a's èug ann a bhun.**
'A long illness, and death at its close'.
i.e. Death will end the longest illness.
[*Tinneas fada agus éag ina bhun.*]

387. **Eug a's imirce a chlaoidheas tigheabhas.**
'Death and removals upset housekeeping'.
[*Éag agus imirce a chloíos (= chloíonn) tíos.*]

Fate, predestination, things to be expected

388. **An tè a m-beidh se 'n a chineamhuin a chrochadh, ni bhàithtear go bràth è.**
'He whose fate it is to be hanged will never be drowned'.
[*An té a mbeidh sé ina chinniúint a chrochadh, ní bháitear go bráth é.*]*

389. **An tè a'r 'n-dàn dò an donas, is dò fèin a bhaineas.**
'If a man be doomed to have bad luck, it is on himself (only) it falls'.
[*An té ar i ndán dó an donas is dó féin a bhaineas (= bhaineann).*]

390. **Deireadh gach luinge, bathadh,**
     A's deireadh gach àiche, losgadh;
     Deireadh gach cuirme, caitheamh,
     A's deireadh gach gàire, osna.
     'The end of every ship is drowning,
     And the end of every kiln is burning;
     The end of every feast is wasting,
     And the end of every laugh is sighing'.
     Shakespeare applies the word '*drown*' to inanimate objects,
     thus –
     'deeper than ever did plummet sound
     I'll *drown* my book' – *The Tempest*.
     –'to drown my clothes, and say I was stripped
     – *All's Well that Ends Well*.
     Spanish. *Cantarillo que muchas veces va a la fuente o dexa el*
     asa o la frente.
     'The pitcher that goes often to the well leaves either its
     handle or its mouth'.
     [*Deireadh gach loinge bá(thadh),*
     Agus deireadh gach áithe loscadh;
     Deireadh gach cuirme caitheamh,
     Agus deireadh gach gáire osna.]

391. **Fa bhun a chrainn a thuiteas a duilleabhar.**
     'It is at the foot of the tree the leaves fall'.
     Curses are apt to fall on the very person who has uttered
     them.
     [*Fá bhun an chrainn a thiteas (= thiteann) an duilliúr.*]

392. **Tar èis stoirme thig sith.**
     'After a storm comes a calm'.
     [*Tar éis stoirme thig (= tagann) síth.*]

393. **Cha dùal sagart gan chleìreach, a's cha dùal**
     Domhnach gan aifrionn.
     'It is not usual for a priest to be without a clerk, nor a
     Sunday without Mass'.
     Used when a person says 'Amen' on hearing another utter
     a self-curse.
     [*Cha (= Ní) dual sagart gan chléireach agus cha dual Domhnach*
     gan aifreann.]

394. **Chan 'uil coill air bith gan a losgadh fèin de chrìon-lach innti.**
'There is no forest without as much brushwood as will burn it'.
i.e. (as explained to me once by a man who had used the proverb) *'There is enough of sin in every man to burn him in hell'. The axe is the destroyer of the forest, but the forest itself furnishes the handle.* Ruckert *Widsom of the Bramins.*
Spanish. *Del monte sale quien el monte quema.*
'From the mountain issues what burns it'.
[*Chan fhuil* (= *Níl*) *coill ar bith gan a loscadh féin de chríonlach inti.*]

395. **Guid è bheitheà brath air chat acht pisìn?**
'What would you expect from a cat but a kitten?'.
[*Cad é a bheifeá ag brath ar chat ach pisín?*]

396. **'N uair fhagas na cait a baile, biann na luchògaidh a' rince.**
'When the cat leaves the village, the mice dance'.
Latin. *Absente fele saliunt mures.*
['When the cat is absent the mice dance'.]
Italian. *Quando la gatta non è in paese i topi ballano.*
['When the cat is not in town the mice dance'.]
[*Nuair a fhágas* (= *fhágann*) *na cait an baile, bíonn na luchóga ag rince.*]

397. **Cha duàl Sathairn gan griàn, 's cha dual Domhnach gan aifrionn.**
'It is not usual for Saturday to be without sunshine, nor Sunday without Mass'.
Meaning no day at all.
[*Cha* (= *Ní*) *dual Satharn gan grian agus cha dual Domhnach gan aifreann.*]

398. **Trath sguireas an lamh de shileadh, stadaidh an beal de mholadh.**
'When the hand ceases to scatter, the mouth ceases to praise'.
Scotch. *A fu' purse never lacks friends.*
[*An tráth a scoireas an lámh de shileadh, stadaidh an béal de mholadh.*
= *An tráth a scoireann an lámh de shileadh, stadann an béal de mholadh.*]

399. **An uair a bhios a cupàn làn, cuiridh se thairis.**
'When the cup is full, it will run over'.
A person full of evil thoughts is sure to let them out.
[*Nuair a bhíos (= bhíonn) an cupán lán, cuiridh (= cuireann) sé thairis.*]

400. **An tè fhalaigheas, 'sè a gheabhas.**
'He that hides will find'.
Spanish. *Donde perdiste la capa, ahí la cata.*
'Search for your cloak where you lost it'.
[*An té a fholaíos (= fholaíonn) is é a gheobhas (= gheobhaidh).*]

401. **Char fhadaigh dìs teine gan troid.**
'Two persons never fixed a fire without disagreeing'.
French. *Le potier au potier porte envie.*
['One potter makes another potter jealous'.]
English. *Two of a trade can never agree.*
[*Char (= Níor) fhadaigh dís tine gan troid.*]

402. **Dean maith air dheagh-dhuine a's gheabhaidh tu d'a reìr**
Acht ma ghnidhir maith air dhròch-dhuine, beidh an dròch-dhuine dò feìn.
'Do good to a good man, and you will receive a proper return;
But if you do good to a bad man, he will look to himself'.
[*Déan maith ar dhea-dhuine agus gheobhaidh tú dá réir.*
Ach má ghnít(h)ear (= dhéantar) maith ar dhrochdhuine, beidh an drochdhuine dó féin.]

403. **A bh-fad as amharc, a g-cìan as intinn.**
'Far out of sight, far out of mind'.
[*I bhfad as amharc, i gcian as intinn.*]

404. **Is furas fuineadh a n-aice mine (*or* a chois mine).**
'It is easy to make dough beside meal'.
[*Is furasta fuineadh in aice mine (or de chois mine).*]

405. **Is furas teine a lasadh a chois connaidh.**
'It is easy to light a fire beside faggots'.
[*Is furasta tine a lasadh de chois connaidh.*]

406. **Is furas fuileadh air chionn charrach.**
'It is easy to draw blood from a scald-head'.
It is easy to wound a tender spot. Applied in many ways.
[*Is furasta fuiliú ar cheann charrach.*]

407. **Ni luaithe craicionn na sean-chaoracha air an aonach nà craicionn na caoracha òige.**
'The skin of the old sheep does not go sooner to the fair than the skin of the young one'.
A young person is not more certain of life than an old one. 'Be not too confident in your youth and strength'. *The race is not to the swift, nor the battle to the strong.* – Bible.
French. *Aussitôt meurt veau comme vache.*
['A calf may die every bit as soon as a cow'.]
[*Ní luaithe craiceann na seanchaorach★ ar an aonach ná craiceann na caorach óige.*]

408. **An nidh nach bh-faicear no nach g-cluinthear, cha bhiann tracht air.**
'When a thing is neither seen nor heard of, there is no talk about it'.
[*An ní nach bhfeictear nó nach gcluintear, cha (= ní) bhíonn trácht air.*]

409. **Is socair a chodlas duine air chneadh dhuine eile.**
'A man sleeps very soundly on another man's wound'.
[*Is socair a chodlaíos (= chodlaíonn) duine ar chneá dhuine eile.*]

410. **Ceathrar sagart gan a bheith sanntach,**
    Ceathrar Francach gan a bheith buidhe,
    Ceathrar grèusaidhe gan a bheith brèugach,
    Sin dà fhear dhèug nach b-fhuil 's a tìr
                            (*or* **s'a grìch**).
'Four priests that are not greedy,
Four Frenchmen that are not yellow,
Four shoemakers that are not liars,
These are twelve men not in the country'.
Spanish. *Cien sastres, y cien molineros, y cien tejedores, son tres cientos ladrones.*
'A hundred tailors, a hundred millers, and a hundred weavers, are three hundred thieves'.
[*Ceathrar sagart gan a bheith santach,*
Ceathrar Francach gan a bheith buí
Ceathrar gréasaí gan a bheith bréagach
Sin dáreag nach bhfuil sa tír (or *sa gcrích*).]

411. **Ma thuiteann cloch le fànaidh, is annsa g-carnàn a stadaidh si.**
'If a stone rolls down the slope it is on the heap below it will fall'.

If a man falls from a position for which he is not fitted, he finds his level. Applied also to persons who are so habitually unlucky that if anything unfortunate happens they are sure to have a share.

[*Má thiteann cloch le fána(idh) is sa gcarnán a stadfaidh sí.*]

412. **Cha dual toit gan teine, 's cha dual teine gan daoine.**
'There is not usually smoke without fire, nor fire without people'.

French. *Nul feu sans fumée.*
['No smoke without fire'.]
Spanish. *Donde fuego se hace, humo sale.*
'Where the fire is made, smoke arises'.
Latin. *Flamma fumo est proxima.*
['A flame is very close to smoke'.]

[*Cha (= Ní) dual toit gan teine agus cha dual tine gan daoine.*]

413. **Cha dual grìan gan sgàile.**
'There is not usually sunshine without shadow'.

[*Cha (= Ní) dual grian gan scáil(e).*]

414. **Is de'n g-cat a t-earbull.**
'The tail is (part) of the cat'.

A man may be expected to resemble the family he comes from.

[*Is den gcat an t-eireaball.*]

Impossible, unlikely, or absurd things

415. **Cleath fhada (***or***, claidheamh fada) a làimh claodhaire.**
'A long pole (*or* a long sword) in the hand of a coward'.

Good tools are lost on a person who cannot use them properly.

[*Cleath fhada (or claíomh fada) i láimh cladhaire.* *]

416. **Mur madadh a' tafan a n–aghaidh na gealaighe.**
'Like a dog barking at the moon'.
Applied to useless talking.
Italian. *I ragli dell'asino non entrano in cielo.*
['A donkey's bray is not heard in heaven'.]
English. *Every ass likes to hear himself bray.*
Latin. *Vox et præterea nihil.*
['A voice and nothing besides'.]
[*Mar mhadadh ag tafann in aghaidh na gealaí.*]

417. **Dhà nidh a theid a mògha, mòin air shlìabh, agus cìall ag duine bocht.**
'There are two things that go to loss, turf on a mountain, and intelligence in a poor man'.
Spanish. *Al desdichado, poco vale ser esforzado.*
'It avails little for the unfortunate man to be brave'.
[*Dhá ní a théid (= théann) amú, móin ar shliabh agus ciall ag duine bocht.*]

418. **Iomartas le chèile, luach chùig phonta chlaidheamh a's maide an doruis!**
'Such a comparison! a sword worth five pounds with a door–stick'.
Latin. *Fluvius cum mari certast*
['A river contends with the sea'.]
[*Iomartas le chéile, luach chúig phunt de chlaíomh agus maide an dorais.*]

419. **Sin a bheith baint na tùaighe as làimh an t–saoir.**
'That is like taking the axe out of the carpenter's hands'.
Said when an incompetent person takes any business out of the hands of one more fit.
[*Sin a bheith ag baint na tua as lá(i)mh an tsaoir.*]

420. **Nà bris do loirgìn air sdòl nach bh–fuil ann do shlighe.**
'Do not be breaking your shin on a stool that is not in your way'.
[*Ná bris do loirgín ar stól nach bhfuil i do shlí.*]

421. **Chan' uil annsin acht 'seachain an cionn is buain a muineal'.**
'That is merely avoiding the head and striking the neck'.
i.e. avoiding one bad thing, but doing one quite as bad.
Latin. *Incidis in Scyllam cupiens vitare Charybdim.*
['Wishing to avoid Charybdis, you fall into Scylla'.]
English. *To fall out of the frying-pan into the fire.*
Spanish. *Huyendo del toro cayó en el arroyó.*
'Flying from the bull he fell into the river'.
[*Chan fhuil* (= *Níl*) *ansin ach 'Seachain an ceann agus buain* (= *bain*) *an muineál'.*]

422. **Cha lìonann beannacht bolg.**
'A blessing does not fill a belly'.
Latin *Fabulis venter non expletur*
['A belly is not filled with fables'.] and
Ne verba pro farina.
['Words should not take the place of a meal'.]
English. *Many words will not fill a bushel.*
[*Cha* (= *Ní*) *líonann beannacht bolg.*]

423. **Nà tòg me go d-tuitidh me.**
'Don't lift me till I fall'.
English. *Don't take physic till you're sick.*
Latin. *Ne priùs antidotum quam venenum.*
['Do not take an antidote before poison'.]
[*Ná tóg mé go dtite mé.*]

424. **Sin tòn na muice meithe do ghrèisiughadh.**
'That is like greasing the rump of the fat hog'.
Spanish. *Al puerco gordo untarle el rabo.*
'To grease the fat hog on the breech'.
English. *To take coals to Newcastle.*
Latin. *In sylvam ligna referre*; and *Juxta fluvium puteum fodit.*
['To bring wood back into the forest' and 'One digs a well beside a river'.]
French. *Porter de l'eau à la mer.*
['To carry water to the sea'.]
Italian. *Veder lucciole per lanterne.*
['To mistake glow-worms for lanterns'.]
Spanish. *Llevar hierro a Viscaya.*
'To bring iron to Biscay'.
[*Sin tóin na muice méithe a ghréisiú* (= *ghréisceadh*).]

425. **Is feàrrde de'n chailleach a goradh, acht is misde di a losgadh.**
'The old hag is the better of being warmed, but the worse of being burned'.
We ought to be kind, but not over kind. Some say that this proverb refers to the burning of witches.
[*Is fearrde don chailleach a goradh ach is miste di a loscadh.*]

426. **Ni còir gearran èasgaidh a ghrèasughadh.**
'It is not right to urge an active horse'.
[*Ní cóir gearrán éasca a dhreasú.*]

427. **Cuartughadh an bhodaigh air an làir, agus è air a barr 'n a shuidhe.**
'The clown's search for the mare, and he sitting on her'.
[*Cuartú an bhodaigh ar an láir agus é ar a barr ina shuí.*]

428. **Cuartughadh gabhair gan fios a dhath.**
'Seeking for a goat without knowing its colour'.
Asking for what one knows nothing about.
[*Cuartú gabhair gan fios a dhatha.*]

429. **Cha d-tig uachtar air bhoinne an chait.**
'A cat's milk gives no cream'.
Addressed to a stingy person. There is no animal so fond of cream as a cat, and her own milk yields no cream.
[*Cha dtig (= Ní thagann) uachtar ar bhainne an chait.*]

430. **Cha d-tig le duine a bheith ag ithe mine a's a' feadalaigh air a bhall.**
'A man cannot whistle and eat meal at the one time'.
Latin. *Simul sorbere et flare difficile est.*
['It is difficult to drink and breathe at the same time'.]
Spanish. *Sorber y soplar, no se puede hacer a la par.*
'To sip and blow cannot be done at the same time'.
[*Cha dtig (= Ní thig) le duine a bheith ag ithe mine agus ag feadalaigh ar an bhall.*]

431. **Char chaill duine dona a chuid a rìamh.**
'An unlucky man never yet lost his property'.
Because he had none to lose.
[*Char (= Níor) chaill duine dona a chuid ariamh.*]

432. **Fear clumhaigh gan mhàla, agus bacach gan bhàta.**
'A feather-man without a bag, and a lame (beggar) without a stick'.
[*Fear clúmhaigh gan mhála agus bacach gan bhata.*]

433. **Ma fhaiceann tu cionn na muice air a mairt, nà h-aithris è.**
'If you see a pig's head on the cow, do not tell [it]'.
A wise man is cautious of mentioning strange things that he may see.
[*Má fheiceann tú ceann na muice ar an mart, ná haithris é.*]

434. **Budh dìomhain ìarraidh mèitheas air chait earraigh.**
'It is useless to look for fatness on a spring cat'.
[*Ba d(h)íomhaoin iarraidh méithis ar chat earraigh.*]

435. **Is maith a t-each a shàsuigheas gach marcach.**
'It is a good horse that pleases every rider'.
[*Is maith an t-each a shásaíos (= shásaíonn) gach marcach.*]

436. **Ag ìarraidh loirg air uisge, a's a' cuartughadh snathaide a measg cothain.**
'Looking for a track on the water, and seeking for a needle among litter'. ·
Latin. *In aere piscari, in mare venari.*
['To fish in the air, to hunt in the sea'.]
[*Ag iarraidh loirg ar uisce agus ag cuartú snáthaide i measc cocháin.*]

437. **Guid è a dubhairt Goll, acht gur deacair brighiste a bhaint de thòin lom.**
'What did Goll say? that it is hard to take breeches off bare hips'.
[*Cad é a dúirt Goll ach gur deacair bríste a bhaint de thóin lom.*]

438. **Rith na con a n-dèigh dà fhiadh.**
'The running of a hound after two deer'.
Latin. *Duos insequens lepores neutrum capit.*
['Following two hares, he captures neither'.]
Spanish. *Galgo que muchas liebras levanta ninguna mata.*
'The grey-hound that starts many hares kills none'.
[*Rith na con i ndéidh (=ndiaidh) d(h)á fhia.*]

439. **Is deacair gearr-fhiadh a chur as tum nach m-bìann se ann.**
'It is hard to drive a hare out of a thicket where she is not'.
[*Is deacair giorria a chur as tom nach mbíonn sé ann.*]

440. **Is deacair dàmhsa a chur roimhe shean-mhadadh.**
'It is hard to teach an old dog to dance'.
[*Is deacair damhsa a chur roimh* sheanmhadadh.*]

441. **Chan 'uil ann acht ag ìarraidh ola air a ngabhar.**
'It is just like seeking for wool on a goat'.
Latin. *Mulgere hircum;* and *Calvum vellere.*
['To milk a goat'. and 'To pluck one who is bald'.]
Spanish. *Buscar cinco pies al gato.*
'To look for five feet on a cat'.
[*Chan fhuil (= Níl) ann ach ag iarraidh olla ar an ngabhar.*]

442. **Bhearadh aon fhear a mhàin each chun uisge, acht ni bhearadh deichneabhar air òl.**
'One man could bring a horse to the water, but ten men could not make him drink'.
French. *On a beau mener le bœuf à l'eau, s'il n' a pas soif.*
['It is futile to lead an ox to the water if it is not thirsty'.]
[*Bhéarfadh aon fhear amháin each chun uisce ach ní bhéarfadh* deichniúr air ól.*]

443. **Ni choinnigheann an soitheach acht a làn.**
'A vessel will only hold the full of it'.
[*Ní choinníonn an soitheach ach a lán.*]

444. **Cha d-tig a bhaint as a t-sac acht a làn a bhìos ann.**
'We can only take out of the sack as much as there is in it'.
[*Cha dtig (= Ní thig) a bhaint as an tsac ach an lán a bhíos (= bhíonn) ann.*]

445. **N'il acht tafan gadhair a ngleann glas, a bheith tagradh le cionn gan eòlus.**
'It is like a hound barking in a green valley, to be arguing with an ignorant person, (*literally,* "with a head without knowledge")'.
[*Níl ach tafann gadhair i ngleann glas a bheith ag tagra le ceann gan eolas.*]

446. **Is tu fead air fuar lorg.**
'You are whistling on a cold track'.
Coming a day too late, or going on a useless errand.
[*Is tú fead ar fuarlorg.*]

447. **Cuairt fa bhùalaidh fhalamh.**
'Visiting an empty paddock'.
Said of any one who is disappointed in finding what he expected.
[*Cuairt fá bhuaile fholamh.* ★]

448. **Boinne ceirce a n-adharc mhuice, agus cleite cait d'a shùathadh.**
'Beaten up eggs in a pig's horn, and a cat's feather for mixing them'.
That is, an impossibility.★
[*Bainne circe in adharc mhuice agus cleite cait á shuaitheadh.*]

449. **Fuair se nead gearrain.**
'He has found a horse's nest'.
[*Fuair sé nead gearráin.*]

Trade, workmanship

450. **Is namhuid an cheird gan a foghluim ì.**
'A trade not (properly) learned is an enemy'.
[*Is namhaid an cheird gan í a fhoghlaim.* ★]

451. **Snaithe fàda an tailleair fhallsa.**
'The long stitch of the lazy tailor'.
[*Snáithe fada an táilliúra fhalsa.*]

452. **Mas olc a saor is maith a sgealbog.**
'Though the carpenter is bad, the shaving is good'.
English. *A carpenter is known by his chips.*
[*Más olc an saor is maith an scealpóg.*]

453. **'Si leith na ceirde an ùirleais.**
'The tools are the half of the trade'.
[*Is í leath na ceirde an uirlis.*]

454. **Chan fhuair droch-bhuanaidhe a riamh corran maith.**
'A bad reaper never got a good reaping-hook'.
[*Chan fhuair (= Ní bhfuair) drochbhuanaí ariamh corrán maith.*]

455. **Is fearr làn duirn de cheird nà làn duirn a dh' òr.**
'A handful of a trade is better than a handful of gold'.
A handfu' o' trade is worth a gowpen o' gowd.
[*Is fearr lán doirn de cheird ná lán doirn d'ór.*]

456. **Is minic a bhios rath air rapladh.**
'There is often luck with slovenliness'.
An excuse for roughly done work.
[*Is minic a bhíos (= bhíonn) rath ar rapla.*]

457. **Ta an dà iarunn dèag 's a teallach aige.**
'He has twelve irons in the fire'.
Said of any one who undertakes too much business at once.
[*Tá an dá iarann déag sa teallach aige.*]★

Good and bad luck

458. **Is fearr an t-àgh maith nà èirigh go moch.**
'Good luck is better than early rising'.
Many people are seen to succeed in the world without much exertion, while others who toil early and late are unsuccessful. This is attributed to 'luck'.
Scotch. B*etter be sonsie as soon up.*
[*Is fearr an t-ádh maith ná éirí go moch.*]

459. **Is fearr a bheith sona nà crìonna.**
'It is better to be lucky than wise'.
Italian. *Val più un' oncia di fortuna che cento di sapere.*
['Better one ounce of luck than a hundred of wisdom'.]
French. *Mieux une once de fortune qu'une livre de sagesse.*
['Better an ounce of luck than a pound of wisdom'.]
Scotch. *Gie a man luck and fling him in the sea.*
[*Is fearr a bheith sona ná críonna.*]

460. **Guid è a bhain dò? – an rud a bhi a g-cos na ceirce, (sin a mi-àgh).**
'What happened to him? What was at the hen's foot (that is, bad luck)'.
[*Cad é a bhain dó? an rud a bhí i gcos na circe (sin mí-ádh).*]

461. **Ma's fada a bhios an t-àgh, thig se fa dheireadh.**
'Though luck may be long in coming, it comes at last'.
English. *When things are at the worst they'll mend.*
[*Más fada a bhíos (= bhíonn) an t-ádh, thig (= tagann) sé fá (= faoi) dheireadh.*]

462. **Anns' a deireadh thig a biseach.**
'The luck comes in the end'.
[*Sa deireadh thig (= tagann) an biseach.*]

463. **Lèig an donas chun deiridh, a n–dùil s' nach d–tio-caidh se choidhche.**
'Leave the bad luck to the last, in hopes that it may never come'.
A dangerous advice, too often followed in Ireland.
English (Ulster). *Let the want come at the web's end.*
[*Lig an donas chun deiridh i ndúil agus nach dtiocfaidh sé choíche.*]

464. **Biann a mhi–àgh fèin a' brath air gach duine.**
'Every man has his own little bad luck awaiting him'.
[*Bíonn a mhí-ádh féin ag brath ar gach duine.*]

465. **Biann àgh air amadan.**
'A fool has luck'.
[*Bíonn ádh ar amadán.*]

466. **Fuair se air siubhal eadar cliath a's ursainn.**
'He got off betwixt hurdle and door-post'.
In former times the doors of cottages in Ireland were made, not of wood, but of wattled hurdles. The proverb signifies 'he had a hair-breadth escape'; or else, 'he got away secretly', because the hurdle-door in shutting made no noise.
[*Fuair sé ar shiúl idir cleith agus ursain.*]

467. **Chan mur shaoiltear a chrìochn'ar.**
'Things do not end as we expect'.
[*Chan (= Ní) mar a shíltear a chríochnaítear.*]

468. **Là fheil' Pàdruig earraigh,**
biann nead air gach coill,
breac air gach linn,
agus laogh boinionn ann gach airidh–bhò a n–Eirinn.
'On Saint Patrick's day, in the Spring,
there is always a nest in every wood
a trout in every pool,
and a heifer-calf in every dairy-cow in Ireland'.
[*Lá Fhéile Pádraig earraigh,*
bíonn nead ar gach coill,
breac ar gach linn,
agus lao baineann i ngach áiríbhó in Éirinn.]

469. **Gaoth ò dheas, teas a's toradh;**
Gaoth ò n-iar, iasg a's boinne;
Gaoth ò thuaith, fuacht a's feannadh;
A's gaoth ò n-ear, meas air chrannaibh.
'A wind from the south brings heat and produce;
A wind from the west, fish and milk;
A wind from the north, cold and flaying;
And a wind from the east, fruit on trees'.
[*Gaoth aneas teas agus toradh;*
Gaoth aniar, iasc agus bainne;
Gaoth aduaidh, fuath agus feannadh;
Agus gaoth anoir, meas ar chrannaibh (= chrainn).]

470. **An lonn dubh a sheineas go binn 's na Faoilligh,**
gulaidh se go cruaidh 's a Mart.
'The black-bird that sings sweetly in February
will lament bitterly in March'.
[*An lon dubh a sheinnfeas (= sheinnfidh) sna Faoilligh*
goilfidh sé go crua sa M(h)árta.]

471. **'Sè an sioc soinionn an earraigh,**
'Sè 'lionas fearantaidh le stòr;
B' fhearr cith cloch-shneachta a d-tùs an Iobràin
Nà leathad an aigeàin de 'n òr.
'Frost is the fair weather of spring-time,
And fills the lands with abundance;
Better a shower of hail in April
Than the breadth of the ocean of gold'.
[*Is é an sioc soineann an Earraigh,*
Is é a líonas (= líonann) fearainn le stór;
B'fhearr cith clochshneachta i dtús an Aibreáin
Ná leithead an aigéin den ór.]

472. **Fiach dubh foghmhair, agus feannog earraigh.**
'A black raven in Autumn, and a scald-crow in Spring'.
These are signs of good weather.
[*Fiach dubh fómhair agus feannóg earraigh.*]

473. **Nodhlaig ghlas agus roilig mhèith.**
'A green Christmas and a fat church-yard'.
[*Nollaig ghlas agus reilig mhéith.*]

474. **Ceatha Iobràin a neartuigheas na saorclann.**
'April showers strengthen the butter-cups'.★
Latin. *Imbribus innumeris campos humectat Aprilis.*
['April waters the fields with countless showers'.]
Spanish. *Mas vale un agua entre Abril y Mayo que los bueyes
y el carro.*
'A rain between April and May is worth more than the
oxen and the cart.'
Marzo ventoso y Abril aguanoso sacan a Mayo hermoso.
'A windy March and a rainy April make a fine May'.
English. *April showers make May flowers.*
[*Ceathanna Aibreáin a neartaíos (= neartaíonn) na sabhair-
cíní.★*]

475. **Trath 'ghoireas a chuach air a sgeathach lom,
dìol do bhò a's ceannaigh arbhar.**
'When the cuckoo cries on the bare thorn bush,
sell your cow and buy corn'.
[*An tráth a ghaireas (= ghaireann) an chuach ar an sceach lom,
Díol do bhó agus ceannaigh arbhar.*]

476. **Is bliadhain shòghmhuil shocharaidh
Bliadhan ròghmhuil sgeachairidh.**
'An abundant year of haws
is a prosperous and profitable one'.
Scotch. *A haw year is a braw year.*
[*Is bliain shóúil shochraí
Bliain róúil sceachairí.*]

477. **Oidhch' fheil' Finnìn finn
'Sè a thig rinn air an uair;
Agus là Padruig na bh-feart
A bheir neart do'n chloch fhuar.**
'At the festival of St. Finnan the fair
An edge comes on the weather;
And the festival of St. Patrick of the miracles
Gives new strength to the cold stone'.
French. *A la féte Saint Thomas
Les jours s'agrandissent d'un pas.*
['At the feast of St Thomas
the days lengthen by a footstep'.]
Saint Thomas's day is the shortest day in the year, and three

days before Christmas, when it is said that the weather always changes to bad: it improves about the 17th March, St. Patrick's day. St. Finnin who gives the old name to the festival, preserved in the proverb, was not a saint of the Roman calendar:★ St. Thomas's day was named in honour of Thomas à Becket.

[*Oíche Fhéile Finnín fhinn*
Is é a thig rinn ar an uair
Agus Lá Pádraig na bhFeart
A bheir (= thugann) neart don chloch fhuar.]

478. **Trì là lomartha an loinn,**
Trì là sgiuthanta an chlaibhreàin,
Agus trì là na bò riabhaighe.
'Three days for fleecing the black-bird,
Three days of punishment for the stone-chatter,
And three days for the grey cow'.
The first nine days of April are called the 'borrowing days'. The old legend relates that the black-bird, the stone-chatter, and the grey cow bid defiance to March after his days were over; and that, to punish their insolence, he begged of April nine of his days, three for each of them, for which he repaid nine of his own. A writer in the London *Notes and Queries* (vol v. p. 342) gives a different version: 'I remember, when a child in the North of Ireland, to have heard a very poetical explanation of the *borrowing days* of March and April. "Give me", says March "three days of warmth and sunshine for my poor young lambs while they are yet too tender to bear the roughness of my wind and rain, and you shall have them repaid when the wool is grown" '. The Scotch have a proverb on the *three* borrowing days, which is still heard in Ulster:★

March borrowed from April
Three days, and they were ill;
The first day was wind and weet,
The second day was snow and sleet,
On the third day cam sic a freeze
That it friz the bird's nebs till the trees.

Of course it is to be understood that this proverb, like many others relating to the weather, is only applicable to the 'Old Style'– the French have a proverb which refers to

the interchange of weather between March and April:
Quand Mars fait Avril, Avril fait Mars.
['When March behaves like April, April behaves like March'.]
[*Trí lá lomartha an loin*
Trí lá sciuthanta an chlochráin, *
Agus trí lá na bó riabhaí.]

479. **Ma thig a Mharta a steach mur a leomhan,**
thèid si a mach mur an uan.
'Though March comes in like the lion,
it goes out like the lamb'.
[*Má thig (= thagann) an Mhárta isteach mar an leo(mha)n*
*théid (= téann) sí *amach mar an (t-)uan.*]

480. **Is tuar fearthana alt àilleog.**
'A flock of swallows is a sign of rain'.
[*Is tuar fearthainne ealta fáinleog.*]

481. **Geimhreadh ceòthach, earrach ròghach,**
Samhradh rìabhach, agus foghmhar grìanach.
Geimhreadh ròghach, earrach ceòthach,
Samhradh grianach, agus foghmhar riabhach.
'A misty winter, a pleasant spring;
A variable summer, and a sunny autumn.
A pleasant winter, a misty spring,
A sunny summer, and a variable autumn'.
[*Geimhreadh ceoch, earrach reoch,*
Samhradh riabhach agus fómhar grianach -
Geimhreadh reoch, earrach ceoch,
Samhradh grianach agus fómhar riabhach.]

482. **Dearg a n-iar, is ionann è a's grian,**
Dearg a n-oir, is ionann è a's sioc.
'Red in the west (*i.e.* after sun-set) is a sign of sun-shine,
Red in the east is a sign of frost'.
[*Dearg aniar, is ionann é agus grian;*
Dearg anoir is ionann é agus sioc.]

483. **Bogha fliuch na maidne, bogha tirm an trathnòna.**
'A wet morning rain-bow, a dry evening rain-bow'.
[*Bogha fliuch na ma(i)dine, bogha tirim an tráthnóna.*]

484. **Dearg a n'ùas, fearthain a's fuacht,**
Dearg a n-oir, fearthain a's sioc,
Dearg a n-ìos, fearthain a's gaoth
Dearg a n-ìar tuineadh a's grian.
'Red in the south means rain and cold,
Red in the east, rain and frost,
Red in the north, rain and wind,
Red in the west, thawing and sun'.
[*Dearg anuas fearthainn agus fuacht,*
Dearg anoir, fearthainn agus sioc,
Dearg aníos, fearthainn agus gaoth,
Dearg aniar, tuineadh agus grian.]

485. **Rith con air a mònaidh, oidhche fhoghmhair ag**
tuitim.
'The closing in of an autumn evening is (like) the running
of a hound on a moor'.
An autumn night comes on quickly.
[*Rith con ar an m(h)ónaidh (= mhóin), oíche fhómhair ag titim.*]

486. **Nà mol a's nà di-mol goirt**
No go d-ti go rachaidh an mhi mheodhan thart.
'Neither praise nor dispraise growing crops, till the month
of June is over'.
The end of June tells the fate of the crops.
[*Ná mol agus ná dím(h)ol goirt*
Nó go dtí go rachaidh an Mhí Mheáin thart.]*

487. **Iobràn bog braonach a bheir boinne aige bà a's ag**
caoraigh.
'A soft dropping April brings milk to cows and sheep'.
[*Aibreán bog braonach a bheir (= thugann) bainne chuig* ba agus
chuig caoirigh.]

Allusions to superstitions and customs

488. **Beidh tu beò an bhliadhain so, a nois a bhìmoid a'**
tracht ort.
'You will live during this year, for we were just speaking of
you'.
Said when a person arrives just when others are talking of him.
[*Beidh tú beo an bhliain seo anois ó bhí muid ag trácht ort.*]

489. **A n–diùgh an Aoine a's (go soirbhidh Dìa dhòibh) cha chluin siad sinn.**
'This is Friday and (God prosper them!) they don't hear us'.
Alluding to the fairies. The Irish are averse to naming them directly.★
[*Inniu an Aoine agus (go soirbhí Dia dóibh) cha chluin (= ní chluineann) siad sinn.*]

490. **Aghaidh gach nidh fa dheas.**
'The front of everything to the South'.
A ploughman in Ireland uniformly turns his horses' heads to the south when yoking or unyoking them. The glass is always sent round at table from left to right, or with the course of the sun. This is a custom derived from pagan times; and the people say that all ancient graves placed to the south are those of pagans.
[*Aghaidh gach ní ó dheas.*]

491. **Cuir an gloine thart fa dheas.**
'Send round the glass to the south; or, to the right hand'.
[*Cuir an gloine★ thart fá dheas.*]

492. **Fios cionn fiaigh**
'The knowledge of the raven's head'.
The raven is believed to forebode.
[*Fios cheann féich.*]

493. **Fèuch nach n–dean tu droch–amharc air.**
'Take care lest you cast the evil eye on him'.
Referring to the superstition of the *Evil Eye*, which is still prevalent throughout the East, as well as in many parts of Europe.★
[*Féach nach ndéan (= ndéanfaidh) tú drochamharc air.*]

494. **Chuala me an chuach 's gan biadh ann mo bhroinn,
An cheud selide a' siubhal air a leac lom,
                              Uan dubh 's a tòn liom,
'S nach b'fhuras damh aithint nach n'èireochadh
                              an bhliadhain sin liom.**
'I heard the cuckoo when I had no food in my belly;
the first snail (that I saw) was creeping on a bare stone;
and I saw a black lamb with its rump towards me;
so it was easy for me to know that I would not prosper that
                                                        year'.

All believed to be bad omens.
[*Chuala mé an chuach agus gan bia i mo bhroinn,*
An chéad seilide ag siúl ar an leac lom,
Uan dubh agus a thóin liom
Agus nárbh fhurasta dom(h) a aithint nach n-éireodh an bhliain
sin liom?]

495. **Ni fearr dhuit Aoine throsgadh**
Nà dar-daol a losgadh.
'A Friday's fast is not better for you
than to burn a *dar-daol*'.
The *dar daol* or 'black jet', a small species of beetle,* is
superstitiously feared as unlucky and poisonous, and is
always thrown into the fire whenever it appears in a house.
[*Ní fearr duit Aoine a throscadh*
Ná daradaol a loscadh.]

496. **Ta cam roilig ann a chois.**
'He has the church-yard crook in his foot'.
That is,'he is *reel-footed*'.The superstition is that if a woman
at a funeral rubs the earth of a grave-yard off her foot, her
next child will be deformed in this manner.
[*Tá cam reilige ina chois.*]

497. **An rud a sgrìobhas a Pùca, leigheadh se fèin è.**
'What the *Pooka* writes, let him read it himself'.
[*An rud a scríobhas (= scríobhann) an Púca, léadh sé féin é.*]

498. **Ta se comh fior 's go bh-fuil Pùca, a g-Ceanadas.**
'It is as true as that there is a *Pooka* in Kells'.
[*Tá sé comh fíor agus go bhfuil Púca i gCeanannas.*]

499. **Dìa, a's Muire, a's Eòin baiste linn.**
'God, and theVirgin Mary, and John the Baptist be with us!'.
A very usual exclamation when any person is heard to
sneeze; as evil spirits are supposed to have power over
human being whenever this happens.
[*Dia agus Muire agus Eoin Baiste linn.*]

500. **Nà crèid feannog no fiach**
No Dìa brèige mna;
Moch no mall mur èireochas a ghrìan,
'S mur is toil le Dìa a bhìos a là.
'Do not believe the scald-crow nor the raven,

Nor any false deity of the women;
Whether the sun rises early or late
It is according to God's will the day will be'.

Among the Romans not a bird
Without a prophecy was heard;
Fortunes of empires often hung
On the magician magpie's tongue;
And every crow was to the state
A sure interpreter of fate' – Churchill
'Old crows settled on the path;
Dames from milking trotting home
Said the sign foreboded wrath,
And shook their heads at ills to come' – Clarke
[*Ná creid feannóg ná fiach*
Ná Dia bréige mná;★
Moch nó mall mar a éireos (= éireoidh) an ghrian
Is mar is toil le Dia a bhíos (= bhíonn) an lá.]

501. **Chuir si bioran suain ann a chionn.**
'She has put a *bioran suain*★ in his head (his hair)'.
Said of a profound sleeper. The *bioran suain* was a magical
pin that had the power of throwing a person into a deep
sleep.
[*Chuir sí biorán suain ina cheann.*]

502. **Tracht air a diabhal, agus taisbeanaidh se è**
fèin.
'Talk about the devil, and he will shew himself'.
[*Trácht ar an diabhal agus taispeánfaidh sé é féin.*]

503. **Baitear a long ann a n-aon pheacaidhe.**
'A ship is sunk on account of one sinner'.
This seems to refer to the Bible history of Jonah, on whose
account a tempest arose and the ship was endangered. So
lately as the year 1861, I heard this proverb applied by a
Donegal man, when mentioning to me that the ship had
been lost in which Hunter was emigrating after having
sworn informations against the people of Gweedore, who
had destroyed a number of sheep in revenge for being
deprived of some land.
[*Báitear an long in aon pheacaí.*]

504. **Cha deachaidh aon fhear a rìamh go h-Ifrionn gan
sè phighinidh air faghail bhàis dò.**
'No man ever went to hell without sixpence at the time of
his death'.
A relic of pagan mythology. So among the Romans it was
customary to put a small coin in the mouth of the corpse,
to pay Charon for ferrying it over the river Styx.
[*Cha dteachaidh (= Ní dheachaigh) aon fhear ariamh go
hifreann gan sé pingine ar fáil bháis dó.*]

Allusions to ancient history and tradition

505. **Urchar an daill fa'n dabhach.**
'The blind man's shot at the tub'.
A reference to an Ossianic story. One tradition is that Oisín
(Ossian), who was blind, threw an apple at Saint Patrick's
house-keeper, because she only gave him an ordinary
man's allowance to eat, through he was a giant in size. The
expression signifies a random hit, a blind man's cast.
[*Urchar an daill fán dabhach.*]

506. **Ta se comh brèugach le h-Oram.**
'He is as great a liar as Oram'.
A common saying in Louth and Meath. Origin unknown.
[*Tá sé comh bréagach le hOram.*]

507. **Ceathrar d' a d-tug Fionn fuath,
Cù truagh, agus each mall,
Tighearna tire nach m-bèidheadh glic,
A's bean fir nach m-beireadh clann.**
'There were four things that Fionn (MacCumhal) hated,
A worthless hound, and a slow horse,
A chieftain without wisdom,
And a wife that does not bear children'.
[*Ceathrar dá dtug (= dár thug) Fionn fuath,
Cú trua, agus each mall,
Tiarna tíre nach mbeadh glic,
Agus bean fir nach mbéarfadh★ clann.*]

508. **Trì h-iongantuis Bhaile Fhòir;
muileann gan sruth,
angcoire g-cloich,**

agus mainistear air fhàsach.
'The three wonders of Bally-ore:
a mill without a stream,
a hermitage,
and a monastery in a wilderness'.
Ballyore is in the County Louth.* The mill is driven direct
from the lake without a mill-course. I do not know what
the other parts of the proverb allude to.*
[*Trí hiontais Bhaile Fhobhair:*
Muileann gan sruth
Ancaire i gcloich*
Agus mainistir ar fhásach.]

509. **Ta se comh crionna 's go d-tiobhradh se breith**
     eadar Conall a's Eòghan.
     'He is so wise that he would decide between Conall and
     Eòghan'.
     Referring to the well-known historic dispute which ended in
     the division of Ireland between those two sovereigns.*
     [*Tá sé comh críonna agus go dtabharfadh sé breith idir Conall*
     agus Eoghan.]

510. **Sin deireadh le h-obair a Dreagaigh.**
     'That is an end to Drake's work'.
     Took its origin in the time of Queen Elizabeth, when
     some noted personage named Drake flourished in Meath,
     who has given name to Drakestown and Drake's fort.* It
     means 'there's an end of the business'.
     [*Sin deireadh le hobair an Dreagaigh.*]

Miscellaneous

511. **Is leùr do'n dall a bhèul.**
     'A blind man can see his mouth'.
     [*Is léir don dall a bhéal.*]

512. **Budh chòir an dàn a dheanadh go maith air tùs,**
     mur is iomad fear millte a thig air.
     'A poem ought to be well made at first,
     for there is many a one to spoil it afterwards'.
     [*Ba chóir an dán a dhéanamh go maith ar (d)tús,*
     mar is iomaí fear millte a thig (= thagann) air.]

513. **Is iomadh sgèul a thig ann a m-bliadhain;**
    'S is iomadh slìabh air bheagan bò;
    Is iomadh fear nar chìor cionn lìath;
    'S is iomadh fial air bheagan stòir.
    'Many a piece of news comes in a year;
    There's many a mountain with few cattle;
    Many a man never combed a grey head;
    And many a liberal man has little means'.
    [*Is iomaí scéal a thig (= thagann) i mbliain;*
    Agus is iomaí sliabh ar bheagán bó;
    Is iomaí fear nár chíor ceann liath;
    Agus is iomaí fial ar bheagán stóir.]

514. **Is fearr rith maith nà seasamh fada.**
    'A good run is better than a long stand'.
    English. *He that fights and runs away may live to fight another*
    day – Hudibras.
    Greek. Ἀνηρ ο φενγων και παλιν μαχησεται.
    (Qui fugiebat rursùs proeliabitur).
    ['The one who ran away will fight again'.]
    An excuse said to have been given by Demosthenes for
    having run away from the battle of Cheronaea and left his
    shield behind him.
    Spanish. *Mas vale que digan aqui hyó, que aqui murio.*
    'Better they should say, here he ran away, than here he
    died'.
    [*Is fearr rith maith ná seasamh fada.*]

515. **Tabhair a rogh do'n m-bodach, agus 's è a dìogadh**
    a thoghfaidh se.
    'Give a clown his choice and he will choose the worst'.
    [*Tabhair a rogha don mbodach agus is é an díogha a thoghfaidh*
    sé.]

516. **Is doiligh roghain a bhaint as a dìogadh.**
    'It is hard to make a choice out of the refuse'.
    [*Is doiligh rogha a bhaint as an díogha.*]

517. **Iall fada de leathar chàich.**
    'A long strap of other people's leather'.
    [*Iall fhada de leathar cháich.*]

518. **Is bog reidh gach duine fa chraicion dhuine eile.**
'Every man is very obliging with other men's hides'.
Latin. *Ex alieno tergore lata secare lora.*
['To cut broad reins from the hide of another'.]
These proverbs seem to belong to times when the skins of
animals were much used for domestic purposes.
[*Is bog réidh gach duine fá chraiceann duine eile.*]

519. **Iomad na lamh a bhaineas a cath.**
'It is the multitude of hands that gain the battle'.
English. *Many hands make light work.*
Latin. *Multorum manibus grande levatur onus.*
['A great burden is lightened by the hands of many'.]
[*Iomad na lámh a bhaineas (= bhaineann) an cath.*]

520. **Ni'l ò mheud a teachdaire nach mòide na
gnothuighe.**
'The greater the messenger the more important the affair'.
[*Níl dá mhéad an teachtaire nach móide na gnóthaí.*]

521. **Mol a mhònaidh a's seachain ì,
Càin an choill a's tathuigh ì.**
'Praise the moor but avoid it:
revile the wood but frequent it'.
[*Mol an mhónaidh (= mhóin) agus seachain í,
Cáin an choill agus taithigh í.*]

522. **Maith air shean n-duine, maith air àn-nduine,
agus maith air leanabh, trì neithe a thèid a mògha.**
'A good thing done for an old man, for an ill-natured man,
or for a child, are three good things thrown away'.
Because the one soon dies, the other is no man's friend, and
the child forgets the obligation.
French. *Ce qu' on donne aux méchants toujours on le regrette.*
['One always lives to regret what one gives to evil-doers'.]
[*Maith ar sheanduine, maith ar anduine
agus maith ar leanbh, trí nithe a théid (= théann) amú.*]

523. **An ùair 'ìosas a mhuc a sàith, èirigheann a biadh
searbh.**
'When the pig has eaten her fill, her food grows bitter'.
[*Nuair a íosas (= itheann)* an mhuc a sáith, éiríonn an bia
searbh.*]

524. **O chaith tu an choinneal, caith an t-orlach.**
'Since you have used up the candle, you may use up the inch'.
[*Ó chaith tú an choinneal, caith an t-orlach.*]

525. **Creach Peadar a's dìol Pòl.**
'Plunder Peter and pay Paul'.
[*Creach Peadar agus díol Pól.*]

526. **Na bain tuibhe de do thigh fèin le sglàtaidh a chur air thigh fir eile.**
'Do not take the thatch of your own house to put slates on another man's house'.
[*Ná bain tuí de do thigh (= theach) féin le sclátaí a chur ar thigh an fhir eile.*]

527. **Ta fuasgladh gach ceisde innti fèin.**
"The explanation of every riddle is contained in itself'.
[*Tá fuascladh (= fuascailt) gach ceiste inti féin.*]

528. **Teilg ailp a m-bèul a mhadaidh.**
'Throw a lump into the dog's mouth'.
Applied to a person who talks too much.
[*Teilg ailp i mbéal an mhadaidh.*]

529. **An fad a bhìos naosg air mòin, no cleite air a tòin, no gob uirthi.**
'As long as there is a snipe on a bog, or a feather on her tail, or a beak upon her'.
[*An fad a bhíos (= bhíonn) naosc(ach) ar móin, nó cleite ar a tóin, nó gob uirthi.*]

530. **An t-olc gan mhaith a d-tòin a chòimhigh.**
'The bad and no good on the back of a stranger'.
i.e. lay all the blame on the stranger. Said sarcastically.
[*An t-olc gan mhaith i dtóin an choimhthígh.*]

531. **An nidh a deir gach uile dhuine, caithidh se bheith fior.**
'The thing that everybody says must be true'.
Latin. *Vox populi, vox Dei.*
['The voice of the people, the voice of God'.]
[*An ní a deir gach uile dhuine, caithfidh sé bheith fíor.*]

532. **Cha n-è gach aon là a mharbhas Muiris bulog.**
   'It is not every day that Maurice kills a bullock'.
   [*Chan é (= Ní hé) gach aon lá a mharbhas (= mharaíonn)*
   Muiris bológ.]

533. **Comh cleachdta air a's bheidheadh fear mire air**
   chaitheadh sean-hata.
   'As well used to it as a madman is to wearing an old hat'.
   It is often remarked that insane people have a dislike to
   wear any proper covering on the head.
   French. *Tel cerveau tel chapeau.*
   ['The hat matches the head'.]
   [*Comh cleachta air agus a bheadh fear mire ar chaitheamh sean-*
   hata.]

534. **Is ionann 's a càs, a t-èug 's a bàs.**
   'To die and to lose one's life are much the same'.
   i.e. a distinction without a difference.
   English. *Six of the one and half-a-dozen of the other.*
   [*Is ionann agus an cás, an t-éag agus an bás.*]

535. **Astar bò ion-laoigh.**
   'The period of cow with calf'.
   i.e. three quarters of a year. Said of any long-winded affair.
   [*Aistear bó ionlao.*]

536. **Cha dearna se poll nar chuir mi-se tàirne ann.**
   'He did not make a hole that I did not drive a nail into'.
   Said when one person is arguing with another.
   [*Cha dtearna (= Ní dhearna) sé poll nár chuir mise tairne ann.*]

537. **Sin a chloch a n-àit na h-uibhe.**
   'That is the stone in place of the egg'.
   [*Sin an chloch in áit na huibhe.*] and:

538. **Sin a sòp a n-àit na sguaibe.**
   'That is the wisp in place of the besom'.
   i.e. getting anything bad in return for good.
   [*Sin an sop in áit na scuaibe.*]

539. **Ta do chuid 's do bhuidheachas agad.**
   'You have both your property and your thanks'.
   Said when a person offers a thing to another which he
   does not need.
   [*Tá do chuid agus do bhuíochas agat.*]

540. **An uile nidh ag ìarraidh a chòir fèin, agus a gaduidhe ag ìarraidh a chrochadh.**
'Everything demanding its due, and the thief his hanging'.
[*An uile ní ag iarraidh a chóra féin, agus an gadaí ag iarraidh a chrochta.*]

541. **Ta se mur dearnad ann a stocaidh.**
'It is like a flea in his stocking'.
[*Tá sé mar dhreancaid ina stoca.*]

542. **Tarruing rib as 'fhèasòig, a's fèuch fein an rachaidh leat.**
'Pull a hair out of his beard and see yourself if he'll go with you'.★
i.e. do not trust a man altogether until you try him.
[*Tarraing ribe as a fhéasó(i)g agus féach féin an rachaidh leat.*]

543. **D'ìosadh na caoraigh an fèur thrìd.**
'The sheep would eat the grass through it'.
Said of anything of a very flimsy texture.
[*D'íosfadh na caoirigh an féar tríd.*]

544. **Fear na bò 's an 'ruball.**
'The owner of the cow at her tail'.
Meaning that the person most interested in an affair takes the most prominent place.
[*Fear na bó sa ruball (= eireaball).*]

545. **Nà fag fuighleach tàilleair do dhèigh.**
'Do not leave a tailor's remnant after you'.
That is, a small remnant indeed.
[*Ná fág fuílleach táilliúra i do dhiaidh.*]

546. **Geinn d' ì fèin a sgoilteas a darach.**
'It is a wedge made from itself that splits the oak-tree'.
Said of a man who has been the cause of his own ruin.
[*Ging (= ding) di féin a scoilteas (= scoilteann) an dair.*]

547. **Ma bhris tu an cnàmh, char dhiùghail tu an smior.**
'Though you have broken the bone, you have not sucked out the marrow'.
i.e. you have done the most difficult part of the work but not finished it.
[*Má bhris tú an chnámh char (= níor) dhiúl tú an smior.*]

548. **A' mu'r robh ann acht a sagart a's a brathair, chaill mi-se mo chuid.**
'Although there was nobody present but the priest and the friar, still I have lost my property'.
Somebody present must have taken it.
[*Á mura raibh ann ach an sagart agus an bráthair, chaill mise mo chuid.*]

549. **O thigh an diabhail go tigh an deamhain.**
'From the house of the devil to the house of the demon'.
[*Ó thigh (= theach) an diabhail go tigh an deamhain.*] and:

550. **As a choire anns a teinidh.**
'Out of the pot into the fire'.
Latin. *Incidit in Scyllam cupiens evitare Charybdim.*
['Wishing to avoid Charybdis, he falls into Scylla'.]
[*As an choire (isteach) sa tine.*]

551. **As na sìor-thathaigh thig na cathaighe.**
'From frequent opportunities come temptations'.
[*As na síorthaithithe (a) thig (= thagann) na cathuithe.*]

552. **Is fearr suidhe ann 'aice nà suidhe ann 'àit.**
'It is better to sit beside it than in its (empty) place'.
Better take care of one's property than spend it.
English. *Better spare than spend.*
[*Is fearr suí ina aice ná suí ina áit.*]

553. **Dean taise le truaighe, a's gruaim le namhuid.**
'Have a kind look for misery, but a frown for an enemy'.
[*Déan taise le trua agus gruaim le namhaid.*]

554. **Nach è so saoghal fa seach, 'sa t-each air mhuin a mharcaigh.**
'Is not this a world of vicissitudes! – the horse is on top of the rider'.
[*Nach é seo saol fá seach agus an t-each ar mhuin an mharcaigh.*]

555. **An nidh is anamh, is è is iongantaighe.**
'The thing that is scarce is the most wonderful'.
[*An ní is annamh is é is iontaí.*]

556. **Focal amlàin, agus dealg labàin,
agus snaithe bog ola a ghearras go cnàmh,
na trì neithe is gèire air bith.**

'The saying of a fool, a thorn in mud,
and a soft woollen thread that cuts to the bone,
are the three sharpest things in the world'.
[*Focal amhláin*★ *agus dealg lábáin*
agus snáithe bog olla a ghearras (= ghearrann) go cnámh
na trí nithe is géire ar bith.]

557. **An tè 'bhìos buaidheartha, bìann se bogadaigh,**
    'S an tè 'bhìos aedharach, bìann se 'mogadh air.
    'The man who is troubled sits rocking himself,
    While the man who is cheerful makes game of him'.
    [*An té a bhíos (= bhíonn) buartha bíonn sé ag bogadaigh,*
    Agus an té a bhíos aerach bíonn sé ag magadh air.]

558. **Biodh a sligean aig Pàdruig a's mo chràg agam fèin.**
    'Let Patrick have the shell and me my own paw'.
    [*Bíodh an sligeán ag Pádraig agus mo chrág agam féin.*]

559. **An uair is cruaidh do'n chailligh, caithidh si rith.**
    'When the old hag is hard pressed she must run'.
    Italian. *Il bisogno fa trottar la vecchia.*
    ['Necessity makes the old hag trot'.]
    [*Nuair is crua don chailligh (= chailleach), caithfidh sí rith.*]

560. **Ta dhà chionn a teud a's cead a tharruing aige.**
    'He has got the two ends of the rope, and leave to pull'.
    i.e. 'he has it all his own way'; or, as the French would say,
    'he is master of the position'.
    [*Tá dhá cheann na téide agus cead a tarraingthe aige.*]★

561. **Is mòr òrlach de shròin duine no de nidh comh**
    beag leith.
    'An inch of a man's nose, or of anything as small, is a good
    deal'.
    [*Is mór orlach de shró(i)n duine nó de ní comh beag léi.*]

562. **Is mairg a chaillfidh ann uair onfa.**
    'Wo to those who are lost in time of a storm'.
    [*Is mairg a chaillfí in uair anfa.*]

563. **Ma ghradhann tu an t-aoileach, ni fhaic tu dùragan**
    ann.
    'If you are fond of dung, you see no motes in it'.
    [*Má ghránn tú an t-aoileach ní fheiceann tú dúradán/dúlagán ann.*]

564. **Deireadh gach sean-mhallacht, sean-ghearran bàn.**
'The end of every old curse is an old white horse'.
Meaning that the finishing stroke of ill luck is being served
with a law 'process'.
[*Deireadh gach seanmhallachta seanghearrán bán.*]

565. **Briseadh gach uile dhuine fuinneog dò fèin, mur
dubhairt an t-amadan.**
'Let every man break a window for himself, as the fool
said'.
[*'Briseadh gach uile dhuine fuinneog dó féin', mar a dúirt an t-amadán.*]

566. **Is iomadh glèus ceòil a bhìos ann, ars' an fear a robh
a trumpa maide aige.**
'There's many a sort of musical instrument, said the man
who had the wooden trump'.
[*'Is iomaí gléas ceoil a bhíos (= bhíonn) ann' , arsa an fear a raibh
an trumpa maide aige.*]

567. **Ta se comh daor le h-im na Fraince.**
'It is as dear as French butter'.
[*Tá sé comh daor le him na Fraince.*]

568. **Ni lia tir nà gnathas.**
'There are not more countries than there are customs'.
[*Ní lia tír ná gnás.*]

569. **Ni faghthar saoi gan locht.**
'Not (even) a nobleman is to be found without a fault'.
Latin. *Sine vitiis nemo nescitur.*
'No-one is born without faults'.]
[*Ní fhaightear saoi gan locht.*]

570. **Mac baintreabhaighe aig a m-bidh crodh,
searrach sean-làrach air fèur,
agus madadh muilleora aig a m-bidh min,
triùir is meanmnaigh air bith.**
'The son of a widow who has cattle,
the foal of an old mare at grass,
and the dog of a miller who has meal,
are the three merriest creatures living'.
[*Mac baintrí ag a mbíonn crodh,
searrach seanlárach ar féar,
agus madadh muilleora ag a mbíonn min,
triúr is meanmnaí ar bith.*]

571. **Is cruaidh an cath ò nach d-tig fear innsidh an sgèil.**
'It is a hard fought battle from which no man returns to tell the tale'.
[*Is crua an cath ó nach dtig (dtagann) fear inste★ an scéil.*]

572. **Fèudaidh an cat amharc air an righ.**
'A cat may look at the king'.
[*Féadaidh (= Féadann) an cat amharc ar an rí.*]

573. **An chearc a' dul ag ìarraidh an ghèidh.**
'The hen going to seek for the goose'.
Said when people give small presents in expectation of receiving greater ones.
English. *Throw a sprat to catch a salmon.*
French. *Donner un oeuf pour avoir un boeuf.*
['Giving an egg to get an ox'.]
[*An chearc ag dul ag iarraidh an ghé.★*]

574. **Sin a ghrideal a' tabhairt tòn dubh air a b-pota.**
'That is like the griddle calling the pot "black rump"'.
Spanish. *Dixo la sarten à la caldera, tirte allá cul negra.*
'The fying-pan said to the kettle, stand off, black bottom'.
[*Sin an ghrideall ag tabhairt tóin dubh ar an bpota.*]

575. **An chapall a phreabas 's è èimheas.**
'The mare that kicks is the one that squeals'.
i.e. he who has done the mischief is the one who makes the most noise about it.
[*An capall★ a phreabas (= phreabann) is é a éimhíos (= éimhíonn).★*]

576. **An tè 'bhrathas 's è mharbhas.**
'He that spies is the one that kills'.
[*An té a bhraitheas (= bhraitheann) is é a mharbhas (= mharaíonn).*]

577. **Maireann an chraobh air a bh-fàl, a's cha mhaireann an lamh a chuir i.**
'The tree in the hedge remains, but not so the hand that planted it'.
[*Maireann an chraobh ar an bhfál ach cha (= ní) mhaireann an lámh a chuir í.*]

578. **Loisgeann se a choinneal 's a da chionn.**
'He burns his candle at both ends'.
[*Loisceann sé an choinneal sa dá cheann.*]

168   *Robert Shipboy MacAdam*

579. **Is de 'n imirt mhaith a choimhead.**
   'Watching is a part of good play'.
   [*Is den imirt mhaith an coimhéad.*]

580. **Caithtear cuinm a n-dèigh Càsg.**
   'After Easter come feasts'.
   English. *There's a good time coming.*
   [*Caitear coirm★ i ndéidh (=ndiaidh) Cásca.*]

581. **'S è an gaduidhe is mò is fearr a ghnidh crochadair.**
   'It is the greatest thief that makes the best hangman'.
   English. *Set a thief to catch a thief.*
   [*Is é an gadaí is mó is fearr a ghní (= dhéanann) crochadóir.*]

582. **Is olc a breitheamh air dhathaibh dall.**
   'A blind man is a bad judge of colours'.
   [*Is olc an breitheamh ar dhathaibh (= dhathanna) dall.*]

583. **An t-seòid is dò-fhaghala, 'sè is àille.**
   'The jewel that is hardest to be got is the most beautiful'.
   [*An tseoid is dofhála is í is áille.*]

584. **Ta cead cainnte aig fear caillte na h-imeartha.**
   'The one who loses the game has the liberty of talking'.
   The conqueror may allow the vanquished the satisfaction
   of grumbling.
   [*Tá cead cainte ag fear caillte na himeartha.*]

585. **Ciall, foighid, is fàrus, a's nà dean aimhleas.**
   'Have sense, patience, and self-restraint, and do no mis-
   chief'.
   [*Ciall, foighid (= foighne) agus foras agus ná déan aimhleas.*]

586. **Goid ò ghaduidhe, faghail a n-asgaidh.**
   'To steal from a thief is to get for nothing'.
   [*Goid ó ghadaí, fáil in aisce.*]

587. **Aois crann darach:**
   Mìle blìadhan a' fàs,
   Mìle blìadhan a stàt,
   Mìle blìadhan air làr,
   A's mile bliadhan de bhàrr,
   Bainfear clar donn daraigh as a làr.
   'The age of the oak-tree:
   after a thousand years growing; viz. a thousand years flour-
   ishing,

a thousand years prostrate,
and a thousand years besides,
and even then a brown oak plank may be taken out of its middle'.
The wonderful durability of oak timber is well known.
[*Aois crann darach:*
Míle bliain ag fás,
Míle bliain i stát(?),
Míle bliain ar lár,
Agus míle bliain de bharr,
Bainfear clár donn darach as a lár.]

588. **Suan-ghoil do chathbhruith, agus cead raflaigh do'n bhrochan.**
'Let broth boil slowly, but let porridge make a noise'.
A housewife's proverb.
[*Suanghail do cháfraith agus cead ráflaidh don bhrochán.*]

589. **Chighim comh fada 's a chloch mhuilin leis a bh- fear a bhreacas ì.**
'I see as far into the mill-stone as the man that picks it'.
[*Tchím (= Feicim) comh fada sa chlo(i)ch mhuilinn leis an bhfear a bhreacas (= bhreacann) í.*]

590. **Fuair si fad a bhròige.**
'She has got the length of his shoe'.
i.e. 'she knows how to manage him'.
[*Fuair sí fad a bhróige.*]

591. **Cha troimid' an loch an lach,**
Cha troimid' an t-each an srian;
Cha troimid' an chaora an olan,
Cha troimid' an cholann an chiall.
'The lake is nothing the heavier of the duck,
Nor is the horse the heavier of the bridle;
The sheep is not the heavier of the wool,
Nor is the body the heavier of the understanding'.
[*Cha (= Ní) troimide an loch an lacha,*
Cha troimide an t-each an srian;
Cha troimide an chaora an olann
Cha troimide an cholainn an chiall.]

592. **Gnidh sparan trom croidhe èadtrom.**
'A heavy purse makes a light heart'.
[*Ghní (= Déanann) sparán trom croí éadrom.*]

593. **'Sè fear na fiadhnuise is mò chidh an racan.**
'It is the stander-by who sees the most of the quarrel'.
Latin. *Plus in alieno quam in suo negotio vident homines.*
['Men see more in the business of another than in their own'.]
English. *Lookers-on see the most of the game.*
[*Is é fear na fianaise is mó a tchí (= fheiceann) an racán.*]

594. **Ta se amhuil a's mala pioba, cha seineann se go m-beidh a bholg làn.**
'He is like a bag-pipe, he never makes a noise till his belly's full'.
French. *Jamais la corne-muse ne dit mot si elle n-a pas le ventre plein.*
['The bag-pipe never says a word on an empty stomach'.]
[*Tá sé amhail agus mála píbe, cha seinneann (= ní sheinnfidh) sé go mbeidh a bholg lán.*]

595. **As a g-cisteanach 'thig an fonn.**
'Out of the kitchen comes the tune'.
Spanish. *Cuando la sartén chilla, algo hay en la villa.*
'When the frying-pan makes a noise, there is something going on in the town'.
[*As an gcisteanach a thig (= thagann) an fonn.*]

596. **Is maith sgèul go d-tig sgèul eile.**
'One story is good till another one comes'.
[*Is maith scéal go dtig (= dtaga(nn)) scéal eile.*]

597. **Is fusa tuitim nà èirigh.**
'Falling is easier than rising'.
[*Is fusa titim ná éirí.*]

598. **Leigeann gach duine uallach air a ngearran èasgaidh.**
'Every one lays a burden on the willing horse'.
[*Ligeann gach duine ualach ar an ngearrán éasca.*]

599. **Gearr mo chionn a's cuir ceirín air.**
'Cut my head, and then put a plaster on it'.
Spanish. *Quebrásteme la cabeza, y ahora me untas el casco.*
'You first break my head, and then anoint my skull'.
[*Gearr mo cheann agus cuir ceirín air.*]

600. **Ma thrèigear a sean-fhocal, nì bhrèugn'ar è.**
'Though the old proverb may be given up, it is not the less true'.
[*Má thréigtear an seanfhocal ní bhréagnaítear é.*]

Notes

The Life and Times of
Robert Shipboy MacAdam (pp 1–71)

1. On the encroachment of many areas of the modern city districts on former townlands, see Deirdre Flanagan, in Hughes (1992). For the industrial development of Belfast, see Bardon (1982: chapters 4–6), Maguire (1993), and Agnew (1996).

2. *Cen. Ire* 1659 p 8 lists 589 inhabitants in Belfast (366 English and 223 Irish) with a further 120 inhabitants in the 'towne lands' belonging to Belfast. Robinson (1986: 9 §8) puts the population of Carrickfergus at 596 for this year.

3. In the medieval period Belfast was only noted for its small castle at the ford, a crossing point between what is modern Counties Antrim and Down. Thus in a *Pipe Roll* of Henry III (1262 AD) Belfast is referred to as 'Castle of the Ford' while in 1533 the town is styled 'Bealefarst, an old castle standing on a ford'. See Hughes (1992: 81–2).

4. Benn (1877: 108–9).

5. Bardon (1982: 31).

6. MS p 160. For a discussion of MacAdam's English-Irish dictionary see pp 47, 49–50.

7. *Dublin Penny Journal* 23/3/1833 p 310, cited Ó Buachalla (1968: 46).

8. 'In Memoriam Robert S. MacAdam' *Ulster Journal of Archaeology* second series, volume 1 (1895) p 152.

9. According to Beckett (1995: 3), there were three other MacAdam siblings who died at an early age.

10. For a plan and sketch of High Street Belfast in the late eighteenth century see Elliot (1989: plates 19 and 20, p 180).

11. Ó Buachalla (1968: 101) refuted the 1838 date proposed in the *Centenary Volume* of *The Belfast Natural History and Philosophical Society* p 90, as there is a reference to the Soho Foundry in *Matier's Belfast Directory, 1835–6*. Brett (1985: 18) suggested that this business opened 'about 1834'.

12. Brett (1985: 18, who also further refers (n 36) to H-R Hitchcock *Early Victorian Archictecture* (London 1954 p 527). On the Egyptian Prince Ibrahim Pasha see p 32.

13. de Paor (1990: 24).

14. For a summary of his life cf Froggatt (1981 and 1984), Ó Buachalla (1968: 17–19, especially p 18 n 7), Benn (1877: ii, 157–161) and Anderson (1888: 32–4 for a summary and plate of a bust, plus a photograph of his grave in Layd Graveyard, Cushendall facing p 60). The house were he was brought up still stands on the coast road between Waterfoot and Cushendall where a commemorative plaque, in Irish, has recently been erected.

15. On the career of Mary Ann McCracken see McNeill (1960).

16. Cited Ó Buachalla (1968: 77).

17. MacDonnell to Bunting, Bunting MSS No 14, cited Ó Buachalla (1968: 15 n 1).

18. Introduction to Bunting's *A General Collection of the Ancient Irish Music*.

19. Young, R 1894–5: 'The Irish Harpers in Belfast in 1792' *Ulster Journal of Archaeology* series 2, vol 1, 120–7 See also Hayward (1952: 71–4).

20. Now St Anne's Cathedral in Donegal Street.

21. Elliot (1989).

22. Carroll (1995).

23. *Dublin University Magazine* 29 (1847) 67, cited Ó Buachalla (1968: 23).

24. *Bolg an tSolair* or *Gaelic Magazine* described by Ó Snodaigh (1995: 63–4) as 'an 120-page miscellany of dialogue, poetry, translations, prayers and vocabulary. Lynch and Russell seem to have been its main begetters'. Unfortunately this publication only survived through a single issue. A limited edition was reproduced by the Linen Hall Library in 1995.

25. Ó Casaide (1930: 15ff).

26. For details on this poet see Hughes (1987).

27. Chitham (1986).

28. Lynch to Mary Ann McCracken in Bunting MSS, Main Library Queen's University Belfast, cited Ó Buachalla (1968: 38–9).

29. Anderson (1888: 32). Cf also on 5 October 1793 'That the Revd. Jas Bryson and Doctor M'Donnell be requested to solicit Donations of Books from such persons as they think proper' ibid. 18.

30. On the links between freemasons and the United Irishmen see Smyth (1993).

31. Anderson (1888: 91).

32. Fortunately four of his sermons have survived, Ó Snodaigh (1995: 55).

33. Ó Buachalla (1968: 55).

34. For the English translation of Bryson's version of the Deirdre story see Hughes and McDaniel (1988–9).

35. Ó Buachalla (1968: 54). For details of the Irish manuscript collection in Belfast Public Library see the catalogue compiled by Ó Buachalla (1962) and Appendix A in Ó Buachalla (1968: 275).

36. Details in Ó Buachalla (1968: 56–7).

37. Ó Snodaigh (1995: 57, citing Magee 1988, 56).

38. Walsh (1844: 146). On Walsh's involvement in the controversy of the Home Mission schools in Co Antrim see pp 36–9.

39. Ó Buachalla (1968: 59–64).

40. Moses Neilson was a native of Castlederg in Co Tyrone, according to Ó Snodaigh (1995: 57).

41. Dr Ó Duibhín has since informed me that this was cited by Robb (1946).

42. Jamieson (1959: 40).

43. Brady and Cleeve (1985: 320).

44. Originally printed in Dublin (P Wogan) this work has been recently reprinted (with a bilingual foreword by R Ó Bléine/Blaney) by Iontabhas Ulatch/Ultach Trust (Belfast 1990).

45. Ó Snodaigh (1995: 56).

46. Neilson (1808: ix–x).

47. Campbell (1991: 125).

48. The Book of the Royal Belfast Academical Institution (eds Fisher and Robb) pp 203–5, cited Ó Buachalla (1968: 47).

49. For a history of this school see Jamieson (1959). The word 'Royal' was inserted into the title in 1830 apparently in recognition of the restoration of a government grant in 1827. The initial grant was removed in 1816 when a number of the teaching staff toasted the success of the French Revolution as part of their St Patrick's Day celebrations. When this was reported to the government authorities they offered an ultimatum that the Academical Institution would have to chose between its freedom of conscience or its financial aid – the Institution opted for the former. The Book of the RBAI p 63.

50. For a history of the Academy, see Shearman (1935).

51. Cited by Ó Buachalla (1968: 30) and Ó Snodaigh (1995: 63).

52. On the history of this illustrious institution see Anderson (1888) and Killen (1990).

53. Anderson (1888: 35).

54. Ibid 95 and 42.

55. RJ Tennent's copy of this book is preserved in the Library of The Royal Belfast Academical Institution.

56. 'He had a private museum of geological specimens which was regarded as the best in Ireland'. Newmann (1993: 143).

57. 'The first two librarians were . . . James MacAdam, who stayed only one year before deciding he could not afford the time the post demanded, and the Reverend George Hill, who was librarian for thirty years and in many ways the founder of the Library'. Walker and McCreary (1994: 87).

58. Young MS 9/3 Queen's University Belfast, cited Ó Buachalla (1968: 179).

59. Moody and Beckett (1959: 122).

60. Fisher and Robb (1913: 246).

61. 'Another founder with similar [ie liberal and tolerant] views was James MacAdam, a prosperous ironfounder in the city, and father of the

Gaelic scholar Robert MacAdam'.
Campbell (1991: 125).

62. Ó Buachalla (1962: 27).

63. Anderson (1888: 95).

64. Rathlin Gaelic was a variety of Scottish Gaelic apparently introduced post-1575: 'Rathlin was depopulated in 1575, when the inhabitants (Gaelic-speaking Scots) were massacred by English soldiers under John Norris, so that the present dialect was introduced since that date'. O'Rahilly (1932: 164 n 2).

65. Wagner (1958, esp. xx–xxi) and Wagner and Ó Baoill (1969) which covered Ulster, Scotland and the Isle of Man. See also map in Hughes (1994: 610).

66. Bibliographical details in Hughes (1994: 619–20).

67. GB Adams (1964).

68. For details of this large-scale nineteenth-century Ordnance Survey, see Andrews (1974) , Ó Maolfabhail (1989) and Hughes (1991: 121–2).

69. See Hughes (forthcoming) – although for the corruption of modern Killinchy (Co Down) from its original Irish *Cill Duinsighe* 'Church of St Duinseach' to local Irish *Cill Inse* 'Church of the Island', see Hughes ibid.

70. Nevertheless the Ordnance Survey memoirs for Ulster have been computerised at the Institute of Irish Studies, Queen's University Belfast where an extensive publication programme has just been completed, see Day (1986).

71. *OSM* vol 17, p 4.

72. *OSL Down* p 46. On the reasonable quality of this speaker's Irish cf Toner/Ó Mainnín (1992: 2–3).

73. Ó Mainnín (1992: 11).

74. Cited Ó Casaide (1930: 54ff.).

75. Ó Tuathail (1933: xi).

76. *Historical Sketches of the Native Irish* in 1830. It would be true to say that Irish-speaking continued more vibrantly in Tyrone than any other area of the six counties in the twentieth century, with the possible exception of the Glens of Antrim. For a detailed discussion of Irish in Co Tyrone in the current century see Ó Conluain (1989).

77. *Sgéul fa bheatha agus pháis ár dTighearna agus ár Slánuightheora, Íosa Críost. Le h-ághaidh úsáide na nUlltach a n-Doire agus a d-T'r Eoghain, an a dteangaidh cuigeadhaigh féinn* – cited Ó Tuathail (1933: xii).

78. Newmann (1993: 127).

79. Parish of Aghagallon, Co Antrim Fair Sheets 1838 *OSM* vol 21, p 22.

80. *OSM* vol 13, p 58.

81. Neilson (1808: ix–x).

82. On the work of societies such as the Hibernian Bible Society, The Irish Evangelical Society (1814), the Irish Society for Promoting Education of the Native Irish through the Medium of their own Language (1818), see Hempton and Hill (1992: 52ff), and p 000.

83. *OSM* vol 9, p 84.

84. Cited Ó Casaide (1930: 56f).

85. Smith (1902).

86. Madden (1843: vol 2 pp 230–31, cited Ó Buachalla 1968: 40).

87. Newmann (1993: 250).

88. 'John Templeton, one of Russell's sincerest friends, lived until 1825. He continued his scientific work and maintained his interest in Dublin's Botanic Gardens. Just before his death he was reconciled with Dr McDonnell through the intermediacy of Mary Ann McCracken'. Carroll (1995: 224).

89. Chart (1931: 333). On the career of William Drennan, son of Presbyterian minister Rev Thomas Drennan, see Hayward (1952: 45–8).

90. One is reminded here of the British Prime Minister Lloyd George who employed Welsh-speaking nannies in London for his children.

91. McCall (1881: 52, 90, 110, 117, cited Ó Buachalla 1968: 75–6). On Lord Downshire's extension of an invitation to Philip Barron of Waterford to visit his brother Lord George Hill at Dublin Castle to view Irish manuscripts, see p 30. For Lord Hill's manuscripts on display as part of the British Association Exhibition in Belfast 1852 see p 53.

92. Public Records Office Northern Ireland D671/Bundle C 235, cited by Ó Buachalla (1968: 73).

93. Dr MacDonnell praised Anderson for his scholarly objectivity and balanced approach: 'The Book which your Lordship sent me is written with great prudence and circumspection for altho' the author be a Scotch Presbyterian yet one can never discern from his work to what sect he belongs. There is none of those absurd reproaches cast upon Papists, no predictions of their conversion, nothing said about Antichrist, the Babylonesh Lady and the beast with the ten horns'.

94. Ibid 74.

95. Ó Buachalla (1968: 71–2) reproduces the text of a copy of a letter (written in English and dated Ballynascreen 21 July 1828) from Feenachty to MacAdam on a report of his progress on this project: 'Now unless this recommendation from the clergy ['Mr Murphy the Parish Priest'] induce the people to come forward and attend we can do nothing else to render our endeavours successful. The truth is the people in general are so poor and distressed that they have not time to attend. They tell me that Winter would be the only time here for such an undertaking …'

96. Campbell (1991: 230).

97. Cited Ó Buachalla (1968: 74).

98. Deane (1924:65). On Rev R J Bryce, see of Blaney (1996: 133–43).

99. Original Irish cited in Ó Buachalla (1968: 86), my translation.

100. Ó hAilín (1969: 94). He was a brother of Sir Henry Winston Barron, Member of Parliament for Waterford.

101. *Ancient Ireland* vol 1, no 1, pp 5–6 (cited Ó Buachalla 1968: 76).

102. *Ancient Ireland* vol 1, Prospectus (cited Ó Buachalla 1968: 87).

103. Although the work (which resembles Neilson's grammar of 1808) is anonymous Ó Buachalla points out that the Queen's University copy includes a dedication 'To Prof. Stevelly from Robt. MacAdam one of the compilers', and he adduces evidence for Feenachty's part in the work from other sources.

104. The text of this letter (National Library G702) has been reproduced in Ó Buachalla (1968: 88).

105. Deane (1924).

106. R MacAdam to John Windele MS 4B6 RIA, pp 181–2, cited Ó Buachalla (1968: 78).

107. *OSL Co. Down* 5. However, it will be seen (p 56) that Robert MacAdam published many of O'Donovan's lectures in the *Ulster Journal of Archaeology* in the 1850s.

108. Not forgetting his reference to the pronunciation of German in a note in his Introduction to his *Six Hundred Gaelic Proverbs Collected in Ulster (Ulster Journal of Archaeology* ser 1, vol 6 (1858) n b – see p 180, n 8).

109. This latter talk is preserved as Young MS 9/17 in the Library of Queen's University Belfast. The above lists of talks delivered by Robert MacAdam to *The Belfast Natural History and Philosophical Society* and *The Belfast Literary Society* are based on Ó Buachalla (1968: 261).

110. *Irish Sketch Book* (London 1843), cited Walker and McCreary (1994: 2).

111. Ie *Maith agus Dearmad*, the Irish translation of Maria Edgeworth's *Forgive and Forget*.

112. National Library G702, cited Ó Buachalla (1968: 96).

113. *OSM* vol 13, p 52.

114. For details see Newmann (1993: 60–1) and Whitaker (1982). A biography of Delargy is in preparation by Professor S Ó Catháin, Department of Irish Folklore, University College Dublin.

115. For an edition of this valuable material see Watson (1984 and 1987). According to Watson (1984:77) Barney Bhriain MacAulay, 75 years old in August 1925, was 'born in Baile Ímonn, reared in Clonriach'. For a recording of this speaker by the German scholar Dögen in the early part of this century, see Ó Duibhín (forthcoming).

116. University College Galway Irish MS 66 p 5, cited Ó Buachalla (1968: 97).

117. Cited Ó Buachalla (1968: 99).

118. On John Windele (1801–86), see *Journal of the Cork Historical and Archaeological Society* 4 (1900) 35–9.
119. Cited Ó Buachalla (1968: 240).
120. Hempton and Hill (1992: 56).
121. Seoirse Ó Mhachaire, literally 'George from (the) Plain/Field'.The Ó of surnames, which means 'descendant, or grandson', should not cause aspiration to the following word, Ó Machaire.
122. Ó Buachalla (1968: 100ff.). For further details on Field see R. Blaney (1996).
123. Ó Casaide (1930: 66).
124. Ó Buachalla (1968: 120–1).
125. In the remainder of this section on the 'Bible War' in Co Antrim, citations are taken from O'Laverty vol 5, 500 ff and Ó Buachalla (1968: 103–13).
126. 'I was obliged to make false reports of their schools to the Directors as it was altogether falsehood from beginning to end as I thought the more we could take off them the better as St. Paul said he robbed other sects to establish his own'.
127. According to the *Belfast Newsletter* 4 March 1852.In his work *The Home Mission Unmasked* Walsh (1844: 90) estimated that the total costs of the Home Mission's operation was somewhere in the region of £4,000 per annum.
128. On the Rev Allen,see Blaney (1996: 86–9).
129. Beckett (1967: 1). On the manuscript in question, see Ó Buachalla (1968: 114).
130. Beckett (1987: 10).
131. Ó Buachalla (1962: 29).
132. Beckett (1995: 4).
133. Cited Ó Buachalla (1968: 115, 117, 120–1).
134. On the career of this colorful character, prone to presenting his own compositions to earlier Gaelic poets, see Duffy (1989).
135. Ó Buachalla (1968: 120, 119).
136. Ó Buachalla (1968: 132).
137. Both survive in the Belfast Public Library as MSS XXIII and XXIV, Ó Buachalla (1962: 17–20).
138. Letter printed in Ó Buachalla (1968:

213–4). See also pp 276–81 for an impressive list of the total MSS transcribed by Peadar Ó Gealacáin, and for a recent account of Ó Gealacáin's career, see Dawson (1992).
139. The full text of this long piece, *Fáilte Pheadair Uí Ghealacáin lena Eachtra agus lena Ráflaigh* ('A welcome to Peter Gallegan and the accounts of his rambles'), has been edited by Beckett (1987: 84–115).
140. English translation by Morris (1921: 5).
141. Letter in Ó Buachalla (1968:242–3).
142. Ibid (1968: 163)
143. Ibid (1968: 171).
144. Ibid (1968: 138).
145. Ibid 140–1.
146. Hedge-school educated John O'Daly (1800–78) of Co Waterford became a teacher of Irish in the Wesleyan College, Kilkenny, before moving to Dublin to set up as a bookseller and publisher. In addition he also wrote many books of interest to the revival of the Irish language, including *Reliques of Irish Jacobite Poetry* (1844) and *The Poets and Poetry of Munster* (1849). See Brady and Cleeve (1985: 184) and Welch (1996: 420).
147. For this correspondance see Ó Buachalla (1968: 194).
148. Ibid 198.
149. For a detailed treatment of Art Bennett's life, literary work and patrons see Ó Muirí (1994: 3–114). For an edition of his Irish-language poems see Ó Fiaich and Ó Caithnia (1979).
150. This is a relatively rare mention of MacAdam to the famine, although there are a few mentions of it in sentences in the dictionary, eg *Is mór an dul chun deiridh ata a mbarr na prátuidh a mbliadhna* (D24); *Thug an ghorta so dha thoradh maith* (P81). On the other hand, Hugh McDonnell treats the famine in some detail as may be seen from his letter (reproduced by Beckett (1967: 291–3)) and in an Irish poem on the potato blight, Beckett (1987: 46 ff., poem 11). Beckett (1987: 19–20) discusses McDonnell and the Famine, as does Mac Lochlainn (1995).

151. Ó Buachalla (1968: 174–5 and 215–6), my translation.
152. Beckett (1995: 8–9).
153. The full text of the Introduction is given by Beckett (1995: 14–23).
154. From his Introduction (my translation): *nuar a dhearfam dobh gur le mead mo ghean air mo thier dhuchais ⁊ le tesghra don teanguidh,* cited Beckett (1995: 14).
155. Beckett (1995) lists the likely dictionaries which MacAdam had in mind: O'Reilly *Irish-English Dictionary* (Dublin 1817); McCurtin *An Foclóir Bearla Gaoidheilge* (Paris 1732); O'Brien *Irish-English Dictionary* (Paris 1768); Foley *English-Irish Dictionary* (Dublin 1855); Thaddeus Connellan *An English-Irish Dictionary intended for use of schools* (Dublin, 1814) and *Irish-English Guide* (London, 1824).
156. Cited Beckett (1995: 14–15).
157. My translation – original in Beckett (1995: 16): *mur deir an scripture nach ar choir do neach dol chun cogaidh nó a thogbhal taoidh gan a mhuintir do aireamh ⁊ a chuid argid a chontas mar sin damhsa nir thinnsgan me an obair so go bhfuair me damh fein mur fhear cuidigh Aodh mhac domhnaill noch a labhair an geilge ona óge ⁊ rinne stedair cinnte de na hudair mur aon le bheith na bhard ⁊ fa mheis aige uasal ⁊ iosal air feith na heirinne fa na eoluis a dteanguidh a mhathara.*
158. Ó Buachalla (1968:179). The 'Repeal' is a reference by MacAdam to 'The Repeal of the Union', the topical debate of the day. On Hugh McDonnell's Irish-language compositions in relation to the Repeal of the Union and Daniel O'Connell (including 'O'Connell's Welcome to Dundalk, in 1843 and a lament on his death) see Beckett (1987: 17–8).
159. Queen's University of Belfast McAdam MSS 1/1108–9, cited Ó Buachalla (1968: 102 n 4).
160. Young MS 9/4.
161. Cited in Ó Buachalla (1968: 222).
162. McManus (1991: 46, and 48).
163. Ó Buachalla (1968: 223–4).
164. Verse cited in Ó Buachalla (1968: 220), my translation.
165. Royal Irish Academy MS 4B12 p. 999, cited Ó Buachalla (1968: 226).
166. Robert MacAdam in his opening passage of volume 1 of the *Ulster Journal of Archaeology* in 1852.
167. Moody and Beckett (1959: 116).
168. 'The professorship of the Celtic languages was held by O'Donovan till the latter's death in 1861, at the age of fifty-two. Having no students to teach, he spent most of his time in Dublin, translating the ancient laws of Ireland. But each summer term he came to Belfast and delivered six evening lectures open without fee to the public, on the language, manners, laws, and customs of the ancient Irish. Though the College could ill afford the luxury of a professor without students, both the president and the vice-president expressed to the 1857 commission their appreciation of O'Donovan's eminence as a scholar'. Moody and Beckett (1959: 170).
169. The professor of Irish at Cork was Owen Connellan, a convert to Protestantism who was appointed ahead of the dithering O'Donovan – Boyne (1987: 92–3). Beckett (1995: 10) reveals that Sligo-born Owen Connellan (1800–69), worked 20 years in the Royal Irish Academy before becoming Professor in Cork. His publications included an English translation of the *Annals of the Four Masters* (1846), although this version is much inferior to the magnificent edition published by O'Donovan.
170. The society in question was doubtless the *Kilkenny Archaeological Society* which began publishing its own journal *Transactions of the Kilkenny Archaeological Society*, vols 1–2 (1849–53). The publication still continues as *Journal of the Royal Society of Antiquaries of Ireland*, see Hughes and Hannan (1992: 262–3) for details.
171. Irish letter cited Ó Buachalla (1968: 238–9), my translation.
172. Boyne (1987: 93). Boyne also informs us that O'Donovan was appointed as examiner in Celtic languages in 1855 'at an additional salary

of £20 a year'. For a text of the first examination set by O'Donovan see Boyne pp 133–5 (Appendix 1).

173. Young MS 9/4, Queen's University of Belfast, cited Ó Buachalla (1968: 232).

174. For the full text of this poem see Beckett (1987: 76–9).

175. His tombstone in Layd graveyard begins:'Erected in Memory of James M'Donnell of Belfast and of Murlough, in this county – a Physician whose abilities and greater benevolence made him venerated in the Glens of Antrim, where he was born; and in Belfast where he died 1845 in his eighty second year . . .'

176. Ó Buachalla (1968: 252) points out that, in 1855, Peter Gallegan gave Eugene Gilbert Finnerty 16 of his Irish manuscripts in return for kindness the latter had shown to Peter and his remaining family: 'He lived near Kells, in the Co. of Meath and was very thankful to me for some little kindness which I conferred on him and on his only relative a niece since dead . . . He was one of the most noble-minded men, and honourable men that I have ever met'.

177. He died in a poorhouse on 31 March 1867, and is buried in Moyra graveyard near Falcarragh. His son-in-law wrote to MacAdam, 14 July 1867, thanking him 'for contributing £1 to the obsequies of poor Hugh'. Ó Buachalla (1968: 258 n 37). For an account of his teaching career see de Brún (1987: 81–3).

178. MacAdam to Windele RIA MS 4B22, cited Ó Buachalla (1968: 255–6).

179. On the career of Clare-born Eugene O'Curry (1792–1862), author of lectures on the *Manuscript Materials of Ancient Irish History* (1861) and many other seminal works on early Irish literary history and manuscripts, see de hÓir (1961) and Welch (1996: 416–7).

180. Moody and Beckett (1959: 170) note that Edinburgh-born Charles MacDouall (1813–83), the first Professor of Latin at Queen's 1849–50, said of O'Donovan:'we are all proud of his connection with us [ie Queen's College Belfast]', and described his work on the Irish language and Irish archaeology as 'celebrated all over Europe'. One may note that this claim of an outsanding international profile is certainly borne out by the showering of the many accolades upon O'Donovan such as his call to the Bar in London (1847) and his being made a Member of the Royal Irish Academy in the same year (with the Cunningham Gold Medal from the RIA following a year later). There was also the award of the honorary degree of LLD, conferred by Trinity College Dublin in 1850, and the extremely prestigious membership of the Royal Prussian Academy in 1856 – see Boyne (1987: 106).

181. Gregory (1914: 41).

182. On Windele see Welch (1996: 604) and n 118.

183. See Sir William Wilde in his *Report of the Census of 1851*.

184. Cork-born scholar William Reeves (1815–92) would also secure the *Book of Armagh* for Trinity College Dublin.

185. For full details of MacAdam's collection see Appendix D in Ó Buachalla (1968: 284–7).

186. His tombstone inscription (cited by de Paor 1990: 20) reads:'In memoriam Robert Shipboy MacAdam, born 1808, died 3rd January 1895. Editor of the Ulster Journal of Archaeology, 1853–1862'.

187. Bardon (1982: 112) draws attention to the sectarian strife which erupted in August 1864 in Belfast which included the burning of an effigy of Daniel O'Connell by Orangemen and a rampage by several hundred 'Catholic navvies' through Belfast only to be confronted by 'Protestant workers from the neighbouring Soho Foundry' who as Bardon reports 'surged out to repel the invaders, as a verse from a satirical Orange ballad recalled: '...But Och! We were chased by the boys of Soho'.

188. Ó Casaide (1930: 49).

189. Many of Ferguson's sketches from this period are housed in the Linen Hall Library, Belfast.

190. On Sir Samuel Ferguson see Lady Ferguson (1896). For his brief flirtation with the Young Irelanders and his co-founding of the Protestant Repeal Association in 1848, before reverting to Unionism following the collapse of Young Ireland, see Campbell (1991: 226–8), and Welch (1996: 346).

191. *Colla Ciotach* was a figure in Gaelic genealology (one of the three *Collas*) from whom the MacDonnells claimed their ancestry.

192. Letter cited Ó Buachalla (1968: 241).

193. On Hyde, see Dunleavy and Dunleavy (1991).

194. Eoin Mac Néill, or John MacNeill (1867–1945) was born in Glenarm, Co Antrim, and educated at St Malachy's College, Belfast, before going on to Dublin where he co-founded the Gaelic League, edited its newspaper *The Gaelic Journal* and played a central role in Dublin life at the turn of the century. A future Professor of Early Irish History at University College Dublin, he was also involved with the Irish Volun-

teers in 1916 and went on to be Minister of Education 1922–5. See Martin and Byrne (1973).

195. On Patrick Pearse (1879–1916), author, educationalist and leader of the 1916 Rising, declared President of the Provisional Republican Government, see Edwards (1979).

196. One feels that Byrne's statement here has not perhaps taken full account of the efforts of earlier bodies such as the Ulster Gaelic Society.

197. O'Byrne (1946: 201).

198. Bardon (1982: 335).

199. McGimpsey (1994: 11).

200. 'Is é is túisce a chuimhnimh ar bhéaloideas na ndaoiní a bhailiú, bíodh nár bronnadh an onóir sin air; is é is túisce a chuimhnimh ar "aithbheodhadh na teanga" bíodh nach bhfuil an chreidiúint sin tabhartha dó − eisean dáiríribh, "the First Gaelic Leaguer". Laoch agus fathach fir ab ea an fear seo − laoch agus fathach a ligeadh i ndearmad is i ndíchuimhne ámh.' Ó Buachalla (1968: 267), my translation.

The Proverb Collection of Robert Shipboy MacAdam: Introduction, AJ Hughes (pp 65–72)

1. No attempt has been made to expand the European examples or to cite more apt examples for some of MacAdam's parallels. For those interested in this aspect see Strauss (1995). AJ Hughes and F Williams have cited some of the MacAdam collection as part of the Irish material in the examples they have selected for the Irish-language section of Paczolay (1997).

2. *UJA* ser 1, vol 2 (1854) 126–9.

3. *UJA* ser 1, vol 6, p 177, reproduced p 79.

4. MacAdam in his Introduction to *Six Hundred Gaelic Proverbs Collected in Ulster* shows that he was aware of early efforts at proverb collection: 'It will be seen, on comparison, that, with very few exceptions, the proverbs in the present list differ entirely from all those already

printed, and which may be found in Hardiman's *Irish Minstrelsy*, *The Dublin Penny Journal,* and Bourke's *Irish Grammar'*. *UJA* ser, 1, vol 6, p 173 (see p 75). Boyne (1987: 136) cites a reference to O'Donovan's article 'Irish Proverbs' in *Dublin Penny Journal* no. 20, 10 November 1832, pp 158–9.

5. Fionnuala Williams, currently a leading authority on Irish proverbs has published a short appraisal of the MacAdam collection, observes: 'Mac Adam's proverb collection was the largest printed one that had ever been undertaken in Ireland'. Williams (1995: 344).

6. Ie Samuel Bryson (pp 9–10).

7. As discussed, *Sean-Fhocla Uladh* ['the Proverbs of Ulster'] was Morris' own work.

8. Morris (1921: 4).

9. For thumb-nail sketches see New-mann (1993:188) and Welch (1996: 447). See also Énrí Ó Muirgheasa (1874–1945), four Irish-language memorial lectures, delivered 1973–4.(*Éigse Fhearnmhaí,*undated).
10. Ó Muirgheasa (1976: xi).
11. *Irisleabhar na Gaedhilge* uimh. 95, Márta 1898.
12. Ó Muirgheasa (1907).
13. See, however,Williams (1995:354 n. 15 and 17) for discrepancies.
14. This is more or less the orthography in Dinneen's dictionary, the main Irish-English dictionary from 1927 to the appearance of Ó Dónaill's *FGB* in 1977.
15. Ó Muirgheasa omitted all English-language translations for his entire corpus in the 1931 edition of his work, a policy followed by Ó hUr-moltaigh for the 1976 revised edition.
16. *Seanfhocail Uladh* (1976).
17. As regards the Spanish material some slight changes have been made from MacAdam's originals on the advice of Dr Isabel Torres, Department of Spanish, Queen's University Belfast. Hispanicists should, therefore, check the original Spanish spelling used by MacAdam in the *Ulster Journal of Archaeology.*
18. This is, broadly speaking, in keeping with the policy adopted by Ó hUr-moltaigh (Ó Muirgheasa 1976: xv).
19. For example, numbers 1, 3, 16, 22, 27, 60, 62, 118, 129, 131, 151, 179, 188, 193, 205, 208, 212, 216, 217, 222,224,242,248,260,265 and 280.
20. For example, numbers 97, 250, 264, 287, 377, 398 and 592. Notes also *d'uaigh* 'ate' numbers 155, 305 and 314.
21. Standard Irish *déanann, tagann, téann, tugann.*
22. *UJA* ser 1,vol 6,p 173.Ó Muirgheasa (1907: xiii), without giving any spe-cific reasons, said of MacAdam's examples: 'They were collected by him chiefly in the counties ofAntrim, Derry and Donegal, prior to 1858'.
23. Ó Muirgheasa (1976: number 42b).
24. Quiggin (1906: 195 number 23), Stockman 1974:100 §196), de Búrca (1970: 90 number 80), Holmer

(1965:165 number 2) and Ó Cróinín (1980: 354 number 146).
25. As part of the story *An rí agus a pheata cait* ('The king and his pet cat'),Wag-ner and MacCongáil (1983: 28–32).
26. *Uair is crua don chailleach, caithfidh sí rith* 'Need makes the old wife trot' Pedersen (1995: story 30 pp 257–9 and 402–3).
27. Cf, for example, Ó Murchú (1989: 146–7) for a version from East Perthshire:
    Chuala mi a' chuthag gan nì mo
    bhroinn,
    Chonnaic mi an searrach is a thón
    rom,
    Chonnaic mi an tseilcheag air an leac
    lom,
    Dh'fhaithnich mi nach dtéideadh a'
    bhliadhna seo lium.
28. On the dialect boundary of Ulster from the River Drowse in Donegal to the Boyne, in Drogheda, see my notes to MacAdam's Introduction p 180.
29. For example, number 286 and 587 can be found in McDonnell's tract §26 and §57 of Beckett (1967).
30. For example, number 498 is found in McDonnell's poem *An Dochtúr Ó Ceallachán agus a Bhás.* Beckett (1987).
31. Cited Ó Buachalla (1968: 199).
32. In this respect one may note, from Bennett's same letter,one line further on: *ach an t-arán itear théid sé ar dear-mad* (ie 'eaten bread is soon forgot-ten'); or from his finish to the same: *Ach coimhnigh an seanfhocal, gur chaill tú an chaora d'easbhaidh an t-earra, mur cailleadh an t-each d'easbhaidh an chrú.* (ie 'Remember the proverb, that you lost the sheep for want of goods as the horse was lost for want of a shoe').
33. Hamilton (1974: 95).
34. The first story in the second edition of *An Grá agus an Ghruaim.* On Mac Grianna (1900–90), see Newmann (1993: 160). An English-language biography is also in preparation by P. Ó Muirí (Lagan Press).
35. Ó Muirgheasa (1976: 28 n 250).
36. Ó Muirgheasa (1907, 1931 and 1976). Ó Muirgheasa (1907) had 1637 proverbs plus a corpus of other

material 'Proverbial Literature from the Ulster Manuscripts' (pp 257–319), making a total of 2,280. In 1931 Ó Muirgheasa (p vii) informs us of an additional 300 proverbs added since then.

37. Ó Siochfhradha (1926 and 1984). For an English-language summary of this source see Williams (1986).

38. Ó Muirgheasa (1907: vi) reminds us of the earlier work for Scottish Gaelic: 'Our friends the Gaels of Scotland are far ahead of us in this respect. Over one hundred and twenty years ago (in 1785) Donald Macintosh, a Scotch episcopal clergyman, published over 1,300 Gaelic proverbs. In 1819 a second edition of the work appeared containing over 1,500 proverbs. And in 1882 Dr Alexander Nicolson re-edited this work, and added to the number of its sayings till they now reach the grand total of 3,900.'

39. Williams (1995: 349).

Introduction, Robert MacAdam (pp 73–9)

1. With the three exceptions of original notes by Robert MacAdam a, b, c (= numbers 6, 8 and 10) all other explanatory notes in this section have been added by AJ Hughes.

2. For an account of the census for this period see Fitzgerald (1984), and for a more recent assessment see Hindley (1990).

3. Ie *Irish Minstrelsy, or, Bardic remains of Ireland* published in 1831 by James Hardiman (1790–1855), a native speaker of Irish from Co Mayo who was librarian at Queen's College Galway, see Welch (1996: 237).

4. A reference to John O'Donovan's collection of Irish proverbs in *The Dublin Penny Journal* no 20, 10 November 1832, pp 158–9. See p 66.

5. Presumably a reference to the 1856 *College Irish Grammar* which was written by Fr Ulick Bourke (1829–1887), a native of Co Galway who was educated and ordained a priest in Maynooth College. Described by Brady and Cleeve (1985: 16) as 'one of the most influential of the Irish revivalists, through his teachings and writings'. See also Welch (1996: 58).

6. In *UJA* ser 1, vol 6 (1858) p 174, R MacAdam adds the following as note a: 'Trench on *The Lessons in Proverbs* p 48'.

7. In addition to *seanrá* ('old saying') the most common Irish term currently employed for 'proverb' appears to be *seanfhocal* ('old word'). One may also note *nathán*, defined by *FGB* as 'pithy proverbial saying; adage, aphorism; tag'.

8. In *UJA* p 175 MacAdam adds the following as note[b]: '*Ch* pronounced guttural like German *ch* in *noch*, or like the *gh* in our *lough*'.

9. MacAdam's fieldwork is quite valuable in attesting the occurrence of the negative particle *cha* (as opposed to *ní*) in the spoken Irish of counties Louth and Meath. Although Louth and Meath are currently administratively part of the province of Leinster, the occurrence of *cha* beyond the south-west border of modern nine-county Ulster in these latter two counties would tend to date this dialect feature of spoken Ulster Irish (ie *cha* (= Old Irish *nícon*) alongside, or in place of, *ní* – as opposed to the exclusive employment of *ní* in the rest of Ireland south of Ulster) back to the period when the boundary of Ulster ran from the river Drowse, in Co Donegal to the Boyne in Co Meath (or *ó Drobais co Bóind* as laid out in the twelfth-century Irish MS the *Book of Leinster*). See Hughes (1997: 246–7).

10. In *UJA* p 175 MacAdam adds the following as note[c]: '*Ní* and *cha* are used indiscriminately in the south-west of Donegal'.

11. On the distinction in French dialectology between *Langue d'Oui* and the *Langue d'Oc*, see von Wartburg (1971: 60–5).

12. On the negative particle *ní* (from Old Irish *ní*) and *cha*, or *chan* before

vowels (Old Irish *nícon*) plus *char* (from Old Irish *nícon-ro*) see Hughes (1994: 614–8).

13. It may well be that MacAdam's work, which was read and quoted by Professor TF O'Rahilly may have prompted the latter's view on the alleged widespread Scottish Gaelic infleunce on spoken Ulster Irish.

This latter theory, formulated by O'Rahilly (1932), was generally accepted, almost unquestioningly, for over half a century, although it was challenged by Ó Dochartaigh and Ó Buachalla in the mid 1970s (see, for example, Ó Dochartaigh 1985: 205–236), and Hughes (1997).

Linguistic Notes to the Proverbs (pp 80–170)

The following are intended as (a) a brief comment on some of the lexical items and (b) a brief account of some of the dialect features appearing in the corpus of proverbs gathered by MacAdam.

4–5 Alternatively present subjunctive *sula tabhra, sula ndeocha.*

7 *nach g-cuiridh* This may possibly be for *nach gcuirfidh* as RMcA does not seem to always have included *-f-* [-h-] for the future and conditional. For similar examples, see *gabhaidh* (133), *Ghoideadh* (202), *molaidh* (if not a consuetudinal present 226), *gluaisidh* (272), *bhualadh* (306), *bhéara(i)dh* (332, 442), *stadaidh* (411), *sheineas* and *gulaidh* (470), *nach m-beireadh* 507, *go d-tiobhradh* (509), *caithidh* (531 and 559) and *d'íosadh* (543).

17 Possibly pres. subj *go dtabhra*, see 4, 5.

19 The form *sréad* 'herd, flock' instead of *tréad* is common in Ulster dialects.

23 The pronunciation [-ar´] for *-óir* is quite common in Ulster Irish, cf. also *-óg* pronounced as [ag] Ó Dochartaigh (1987: 89 maps 4.1 and 4.2).

25 *abhras* 'strick'. The English word 'strick' appears to be a Scots word in Ulster English, cf. *streek* 'strick, a bundle of broken flax for scutching 18–19th cent.'. Robinson (1985: 678).

45 *eadar* Ulster Irish preserves the old form *eadar* 'between' (Old Irish *eter*) as opposed to *idir* in most other Irish dialects, although in East Ulster one also hears *eadra* (eg, Tyrone, Armagh etc.) see Hughes (1994: §12.2).

48 *anns a g'ciùin ghrian-lò* = *ciúin* + *grian* + *ló* dat. of *lá* 'day'.

49 Alternative *ní ghabhfar* or even *ní ghe-*

ofar (Std. Ir. *ní bhfaighfear* 'will not be got').

51 *leac dorus tigh mòir.* The non-aspiration of *móir* may possibly be an archaism as aspiration after old s-stem nouns was not the norm in early Irish.

60 Alternative *a ghabhfas.*

67 For *inneora* as a gen. sg. of *inneoir*, a variant of *inneoin* (gen. *na hinneonach*) cf. *FGB*. For the nominative *inneoir* in East Ulster cf. Ó Tuathail (1933: xxvi).

72 Possibly future *sula siúlfaidh.*

74 Alternative *beithíoch cheithre chos.*

86 *abhanna* is found as a gen. sg. in Ulster, see 327 below.

93 Possibly future *nach séidfidh*, cf. no. 7.

94 *Chan fhuil* v *Ní fhuil* or Std. Ir. *Níl.* On *cha, chan* see my note to MacAdam's introduction p 180, n 12.

95 *Nachar leòr* or *Nár leor* 'Would it not be enough/was it not enough . . .' For the form *nachar*, alongside *nár*, in East Ulster and in some Connaught dialects, see Hughes (1994: 617 3b) and Hughes (1997).

108 *mhéis* = dat sg. of fem. *mias.*

113 *Ma's dona maol, is mìle measa mallog.* 'If baldness is bad, a scald head is a thousand times worse'. An alternative interpretation might be to take *mallag* as equal to *FGB mullóg leathaigh* 'a heaped load of seaweed' and read 'If baldness is bad a head of untidy unkempt hair is worse'.

119 A version of this proverb, which I collected in mid-Donegal in 1979, was: *Is fearr fuíoll an mhadaidh ná fuíoll an mhagaidh* 'Better the leavings of the dog, than to be the butt of humour'.

122 *i gcothán* (or *i gcochán*) 'in straw', lit.

'in a mess with straw strewn on the ground'?

146 *aimhlis* is given in *FGB* as a varaint gen. sg. of *aimhleas* (Std Ir. gen. *aimhleasa*).

166 On *char uaigh* 'did not eat' see 314 below.

182 Note aspiration after *cha* of the copula in some Ulster dialects.

195 Alternatively read as a fut. *An lus nach bhfaighfear is é a fhóirfeas* (= *fhóirfidh*).

198 C. Beckett informs me that this appears in the Introduction to MacAdam's *Dictionary: chiem gach lá an fear breagach aige mealladh na bhfear sanntach.*

208 *FGB* has *cara as Críost* 'godparent'.

213 *FGB* has *sclamhaireacht* as a variant of *sclamhairt* 'abuse, scolding'. In MacAdam's Dictionary (P92) *Ghnidh se sgléip os cionn sglamhaireacht* is translated 'He is poor and proud'.

223 Note the use of 3 sg. masc. possessive pronoun with *luchóg* a fem. word, and see *gabhar* (no. 361) and *capall* (no. 575).

225 On the survival of archaic gen. sg. *arbha* in Ulster , as opposed to modern gen. *arbhair*, cf. Dinneen (sv *arbhar*) and Hughes (1994: 631–2 §5.10).

231 *Mac Cuirc* Probably *Mag Oirc* officials to O'Neill cf.: '*Mac Guirk, -Gurk Mag Oirc* (not *Mag Cuirc*). A Tyrone sept from Niall Naoighiallach numerous in that county . . .' MacLysaght (1972: 140).

236 The word *misteoir* is not in *FGB*, although Dinneen cites *misteoir* as a variant of *mistire* 'a sly fellow'.

237 *caoracha* According to O'Rahilly (1932: 214): 'When a gen. sg. ends historically in a non-palatal consonant, the tendency in Ulster Irish is to add –*a* to it, eg *athara, mathara, Éireanna, gualanna . . . cathracha*' – see also Hughes (1994: 631 §5.9). Evidence for these gen. forms (which go back at least as early as seventeenth-century MSS) is peppered throughout the examples gathered by MacAdam such as: *abhanna* (86), or *athara* (363). The form *caoracha*, however, (normal gen. *caorach*) seems to be a further example of this feature. The frequency of the form *caoracha* is also confirmed by nos. 407 and 363.

243 Could *sál* represent *tál* 'milk yield'?

300 *An Laighneach laoidheach* 'The Leinster-man is sprightly'. This form may relate to 'calf' (*lao*) or even to 'lay' (*laoi*), however it has been the subject of debate, even in the early literature as Ó Cuív (1989–90: 96–5) points out.

305 *d'uaigh* 'ate' see 314.

306 This proverb is also commonly heard in Donegal Irish as: *An té a bhuailfeadh mo mhadadh, buaileadh sé mé féin.* 'He that would beat my dog let him beat myself'.

314 Although *d'ith* is more usual for 'ate' in modern Irish, the form *d' uaidh, d'uaigh* (originally an old perfect of the verb 'to eat', Old Irish *do-foid/-doid*) is still found in some modern dialects, esp. Co Clare – Ua Súilleabháin (1994: 531 §8.74). See also nos. 166 and 305.

It is also noteworthy that the same proverb as no. 314 turned up in a collection of material from Tyrone (c.1950): *Tá snoig an cheapaire nar uaidh tú ort!* 'You have hiccough from the buttercake you never ate!'. Hughes (1994b: 140 sv. *ceapaire*).

317 *fear an eadarscáin* does not occur in *FGB* and would be equivalent to *fear na headrána*.

336 *scallaireacht*. does not occur in *FGB* as a headword and is equivalent to *scalladóireacht* 'scolding'.

344 Misprinted as 444 in *UJA*.

352 *discleád* seems to be a borrowing from Eng. *dishcloth*.

355 *cuaróg* does not occur in *FGB* or Dinneen in this sense, although in MacAdam's Dictionary (S51 and 52) we find *cuarog* 'sloven woman' 'slut' *cuarog* also a brogue. In this last sense cf. Irish *cuarán* 'a sandal'.

361 *gabhar* Note the the use of a feminine possessive adjective with *gabhar* a masc. noun. For the converse see *luchóg* (no. 223) and *capall* (no. 575).

363 For *athara* as an alternative gen. sg. in Ulster, as opposed to Std. Ir. *athar*, see 237 above.

367 = Std Ir. *An rud a fheiceann an leanbh is é a dhéanann an leanbh*. One may

note here that the proverb would lose its rhyme in Standard Irish.

388 Cf. MacAdam's Dictionary (D61).

407 On the gen. form *caorach* > *caoracha* see no. 237.

415 *claodhaire* MacAdam's spelling of the word as *claodhaire*, as opposed to *cladhaire* 'coward', is an example of the development of *-adh-* to *ao-*, or [ö:] > [λ:], in East Ulster; see Hughes (1989–90 and 1994b: 129–39).

440 *roimhe* In Ulster Irish the 3 sg. masc. form of the preposition is often used instead of the simple form (*roimh*). Notes also *chuige* for *chuig* in no. 487, and see Hughes (1994: 657–8).

442 *Bhearadh* on the absence of *-f-* (*bhéarfadh*) see 7. No. 442 may contain an example of the verb *breith* for *tabhairt*.

447 *fá bhuaile fholamh* or alternatively dat. sing. *fá bhuailidh fholaimh*.

448 Micheál A. Ó Murchú suggests to me that this was in fact an old remedy to cure those who were love-sick, while F Williams points out that that it is also part of the concoction made to revive a dead combatant in rhymers' plays.

450 *gan a foghluim í* Note this construction as opposed to *gan í a fhoghlaim*, or *gan a foghlaim*.

457 Cf. MacAdam's Dictionary (I55).

474 *na saorclann* 'buttercups' is an unusual form. It would appear that the meaning is 'primroses'.

477 *St Finnin* While MacAdam notes this saint is not in the Roman calendar, Farmer (1987) gives details of 'Finan Lobur' a sixth-century Irish abbot. The notes to *Félire Óengusso Céli Dé* 'The Martyrology of Óengus the Culdee' record the following for the 16 March (this saint's feast-day): *Finan lobur o Shurd Colum chille, nó ó Cluain mor Moedoc il-Laigniph, nó o Inis Faithlinn for Loch Lein hi Mumain*. 'Finan the leper, from Colum-cille's Swords or from Clúain mór Maedóic in Leinster, or from Inisfallen on Loch Léin in Munster'. Stokes (1905: 98–9).

478 *An chlaibhreàn* does not occur in the dictionaries and may possibly be for *cloichreán*, a variant of *clochrán*

'stonechat'. On the 'borrowing days' see Dinneen (*riabhach*) and Hughes (1991b).

479 According to *FGB* the word *Márta* 'March' can be either masc. or fem.

486 Cf. MacAdam's Dictionary (J).

487 On 3 sg. masc. *chuige* for simple prepostion *chuig* see no. 440. On the confusion of *chuig* and *ag* see Hughes (1994: 658).

489 On reluctance to name fairies directly and for the use of terms such as 'gentry', 'wee folk' etc, see Ó hEochaidh, Ní Néill and Ó Catháin (1977: 26–7).

491 *FGB* gives *gloine* as both fem. and masc.

493 The 'evil eye' is a very prevalent feature of Irish folk belief, see MacGabhann (1993).

495 *dardeel* is common in Ulster Eng. cf. *Concise Ulster Dictionary* (1996).

500 Ó Tuathail (1933: 148 no. 58) has a version from Tyrone resembling the wording of MacAdam's form but I have recorded, in 1984, the following variant in the Bluestack Mountains, Co Donegal:
Ná creid feadóg a's ná creid fiach
Agus ná tug aird ar bhriathra mná
Ná cá bith mar a shoillsigh(th)eas an ghrian – mar is toil le Dia a bhéas an lá.
'Believe not plover nor raven
And heed not the words of a woman
Nor how the sun shines –
As God pleases, the day will be'.

501 *biorán suain* '(in folktales) sleep charm' *FGB*.

507 *nach m-beireadh* possibly *nach mbeirfeadh* (see no. 7). On the future / conditional stem *b(h)eirfidh / bheirfeadh*, as opposed to *b(h)éarfaidh / bhéarfadh* see O'Rahlilly (1932: 224) and Hughes (1994: 650).

508 MacAdam's statement that 'Ballyore is in the County Louth' may be in need of review as it would appear that *Baile Fhóir* (or *Baile Fhobhair*) refers to Fore Abbey, in the parish of St Feighin's, barony of Fore, Co Westmeath. For the life of St Féichín of Fore (*Vita Sancti Abbatis de Fauoria*), see Plummer (1910), Farmer (1987: 156–7) and Ó hÓgáin (1990: 197–8).

Fiachra Mac Gabhann has kindly drawn my attention to an article by Greville-Nugent (1979) concerning the seven wonders of Fore: 'The monastery in a bog, the mill without a race, the water that flows underground, the tree that has three branches, the water that never boils, the stone raised by Fechin's prayers, the anchorite in a stone'. *angcaire i gcloich* 'an anchor in a stone?'.

509   The reference here is to *Conall Gulban* and *Eoghan* (two of the many sons of fifth-century king Niall of the Nine Hostages) from whom Tyrconnell, and Tyrone and Inishowen are named: *Tír Chonaill* 'Conall's Land' (or Donegal), *Tír Eoghain* 'Eoghan's Land' and *Inis Eoghain* 'Eoghan's Island'.

510   According to MacLysaght (1978: 90): 'This name is derived from an Old-English word meaning dragon. The Drakes of Drakestown, Co Wexford, are Cromwellian, but those of Drakerath and Drakestown, Co Meath are there since the thirteenth century'.

523   *íosas* could represent a future stem *íosfas* (cf. condit. *d'íosfadh* written as *d'íosadh* no. 543), although for *íos-* in the present tense of this verb, see Hughes (1994: 654).

542   This may also be translated: 'Pull a hair out of his beard and see if you succeed'.

556   *amlán* This word does not occur in *FGB*, but it appears to be a by-form of *amhlán* 'boor'.

560   Cf. MacAdam's Dictionary (S78).

571   The variant verbal noun *inseadh* 'to tell' is heard in East Ulster (as opposed to *inse*, or Std. Ir. *insint*). The form *insidh* represents a variant genitive which developed for verbal nouns ending in -*adh*, see Hughes (1994:646 §7.16a), and note *cloch chasaidh* 'rolling stone' no. 73.

573   The word *gé* is both fem. and masc. according to *FGB*.

575   The word *capall* (masc.) means 'mare' in northern dialects of Irish, cf. Wagner (1959: map 52). On it being fem. here (*an chapall*) cf. *luchóg* (no. 223) and *gabhar* (no. 361).

      The form *éimhíonn* 'cries' is related *FGB* *éimheach* 'crying, screaming, clamorous . . .'

580   RMcA had *cuinm* a variant dialect form for *cuirm*: Cf. *Chríochnuigh siad an pósadh le cuinm mhór.* (C23); *cuirm* 'entertainment' (E25), *do thabhairt cuinm* 'regale' (R23) 'revel . . . orgie' (R48).

589   In MacAdam's Dictionary (L4) this is translated: 'I see how the land lies'.

Index of proverbs in languages other than Irish

English: MacAdam's Introduction, 16, 23, 46, 55, 61, 64, 69, 96, 103, 111, 117, 122, 130, 155, 156, 169, 192, 208, 264, 324, 333, 353, 372, 375, 376, 401, 416, 421, 422, 423, 424, 452, 455(?), 461, 463 ('Ulster'), 474, 514, 519, 552, 573, 580, 581, 593.

French: MacAdam's Introduction, 53, 59, 61, 127, 208, 210, 307, 401, 407, 412, 424, 442, 459, 477, 478, 522, 533, 560, 573, 594.

Greek: 514.

Italian: 55, 69, 102, 103, 122, 145, 208, 226, 231, 251, 288, 333, 376, 381, 396, 416, 424, 459, 559.

Latin: 19, 23, 29, 39, 43, 88, 103, 115, 127, 134, 140, 143, 155, 156, 158, 162, 192, 209, 219, 232, 249, 267, 290, 292 (Horace), 320, 324 (one example and Cicero), 327, 330, 350, 362, 366, 373, 396, 412, 416, 418, 421, 422, 423, 424 (two examples), 430, 436, 438, 441, 474, 504 (Charon), 514, 518, 519, 531, 550, 569, 593.

Scotch: 20, 38, 112, 115, 208, 210, 320, 339, 347, 368, 375, 398, 455(?), 458, 459, 476, 478.

Scottish Gaelic: 380

Spanish: MacAdam's Introduction, 14, 16, 18, 38, 39, 61, 73, 103, 127, 131, 132, 145, 154, 155, 162, 164, 165, 172, 192, 209, 210, 217, 221, 251, 262, 263, 268, 271, 284, 287, 297, 309, 311, 316, 324, 327, 347, 357, 360, 367, 375, 381, 390, 394, 400, 410, 412, 417, 421, 424 (two examples), 430, 438, 441, 474, 514, 595, 599.

Sources named by MacAdam

Bible 187, 322 (Ecclesisaticus and St Paul), 407, 503 (Jonah)
Churchill 500
Clarke 500
Cromwell 172
Don Quixote (MacAdam's Introduction)
Drake 510
Hudibras 514
Hunter 503.
Pope (MacAdam's Introduction)
Ruckert Wisdom of the Bramins 394
Russell (MacAdam's Introduction)
Shakespeare 191, 390
Young (MacAdam's Introduction)

Irish Word Index to Irish Proverbs

lán 181, 216, 218, 270, 399, 443, 444,
    445, 594
lao 'young deer' 291, 'calf' 239, 468, 535
laoidheach 300
lár 189, 587
lasadh 38, 405
láthair 196
le 364
leaba 36
leac 51, 494
léamh 487
léan 112
leanbh 72, 152, 367, 369, 372, 522
leann 252
leas 146
leasú 134
leath 99, 453
leathan 363
leathar 517
leigheas 92
léim 4, 11
léine 357
léir 318, 511
leisce 81, 82
leithead 471
leithscéal 334, 337
leomhan 479
leor 95, 97
lí 42
lia 318
liath 513
ligint 16, 43, 125, 138, 170, 228, 339,
    463, 598
linn 468
líonadh 248, 249, 422, 471
loch 591
locht 189, 287, 318, 349, 569
loirgín 420
loisceadh 98, 348, 390, 394, 425, 495,
    578
lom 84, 112, 437, 475, 494
lomartha 478
lon dubh 470, 478
long 390, 503
lorg 436, 446
lorga 420
lú 110, 179, 263, 294
lua 138

luach 31, 418
luath 224, 407
lúbach 263
lúbadh 54
luchóg 223, 288, 396
luí 36, 62, 82, 322
luibh 30
lúide 40
lus 195

má 55, 68, 182, 402, 452, 462
mac 81, 231, 288, 363, 365, 570
Mac Coirc (?) 231
macánta 205
madadh 47, 119, 166, 210, 211, 306, 322,
    332, 351, 416, 440, 528, 570; cf. cú
madadh rua 24
magadh 308, 557
magaí 119
maide 418, 566
maidin 60, 140, 483
mainistir 508
mairg 16, 562
mairstean 79, 577
maise 189
máistir 321
máistreás 223
maith 25, 28, 79, 85, 93, 97, 100, 103,
    117, 121, 127, 147, 156, 167, 172, 182,
    204, 221, 222, 238, 248, 269, 323, 329,
    338, 379, 402, 435, 452, 453, 458, 512,
    514, 522, 530, 579, 595; cf. *fearr*
mála 432, 494
mall 57, 65, 69, 122, 153, 170, 500, 507
mallacht 82, 564
maoin 110
maol 112, 113, 237
maoth 275
marbhadh 139, 532, 576
marcach 435, 554
marcaíocht 9, 104
mart 433
Márta 470, 479
máthair 344, 351, 370; sean-mh. 219
méad 94, 189, 520
mealladh 198
meán cf. *mí*
meanmach 570

tuath 353
tuí 526
tuigbheáil 120, 138, 214, 363
tuile 13, 18, 86, 94
tuilleadh 'to earn' 179
tuineadh 484
tuisleadh 74, 117
tús 61, 373, 512, 513

uachtar 100, 429
uaidh 'ate' 166, 305, 314
uaigh 381, 384
uair 'time' 117, 562

uair 'weather' 477
ualach 81, 83, 160, 598
uan 62, 479, 494
uasal 177, 231
údar 199
uibh 202, 250, 537
uile 133, 350, 531, 540, 565
uirlis 453
uisce 17, 87, 220, 271, 297, 360, 436, 442
Ultach 300
urchar 505
ursain 466

English Word Index to Irish Proverbs

frown 553
fruit 102, 215, 469
full 181, 217, 218, 399, 443, 594

gad 8, 141, 159
gain 181, 519,
game 584
gap 165
gather 32
generosity 207
generous 373
gentle 371
get 261, 590
giddy 272
gift 301
give 260, 353
give up 600
glass 311, 328, 491
go away 20
goat 104, 361, 428, 441
God 53, 109, 163, 165, 170, 171, 172,
    174, 263, 489, 499, 500
gold 177, 455, 471
Goll 437
good 25, 29, 79, 85, 100, 103, 117, 121,
    147, 156, 167, 172, 182, 204, 221, 238,
    248, 269, 278, 323, 338, 379, 402, 435,
    452, 514, 522, 530, 579, 596
goose 333, 573
gossip 208
grandmother 219
grass 46, 543, 570
grave 381, 384
grease (vb) 424
great 38, 40, 94, 175, 182, 225, 271, 353,
    506, 520, 581
greed 198
greedy 410
green 233, 445, 473
grey 478, 513
griddle 319, 574
ground 45, 286
grove 230
grow 292, 587
grown 46

hag 425, 559
hail 471

hair 375, 501, 542
half 99, 453
halter 228
hand 18, 41, 47, 64, 257, 398, 415, 519,
    575
handful 455
handsome 189, 209, 215, 236
hang 388, 540
hangman 581
hard 27, 439, 440, 516, 559, 571, 583
hare 68, 439
harm 138, 341
harrow 62, 80
harvest 2
hat 533
hatch 43
hate 263, 270, 507
haw 476
hawk 58
hay 21, 62
He that 1, 2, 3, 6, 7, 9, 22, 64, 88, 124,
    306, 311, 321, 322, 365, 388, 389, 400,
    575
head 26, 112, 188, 246, 283, 380, 421,
    433, 492, 501, 513, 599
health 265
heap 210
health 111
hear 44, 48, 128, 131, 241, 408, 489, 494
heart 298, 592
heat 469
heavy 83, 160, 188, 591, 592
hedge 575
heifer-calf 468
hell 504
help 53, 169
helper 67
hen 12, 144, 246, 250, 335, 368, 460,
    573
herb 30, 195
herd 111
hereditary 274
hermitage 508
hiccup 314
hide 400
high 186
hill 111, 233,
hip 437

twice 48
twist 27, 159, 281
two 50, 100, 139, 169, 351, 378, 401,
   417, 438, 560

ugliness 270
ugly 236, 374
Ulster 300
understand 138, 214
uninvited 312
unknown 153
unlucky 11, 366, 431
untruth 382
up 265
uppers 100
upright 266
urge 259, 426
usual 393, 397, 412
use 524
used 533
useless 434

valley 445
value 320
variable 481
vessel 443
vicissitude 554
village 181, 262, 332, 396
violent 244
Virgin Mary 499
virtue 30, 91, 121
visit 309, 447
voice 307

walk 72, 104
warm 98, 125, 186, 348, 354, 425
wash 344
waste 390
watch 579
water 17, 87, 220, 271, 297, 360, 436,
   442
way 420
wear 533
weather 312, 471, 477
wedge 546
well (adv.) 93, 97

well 'fountain' 120
west 469, 482, 484
wet 12, 78, 483
whistle 430, 446
white 64, 243, 250, 379, 564
wide 52, 174, 363
widow 570
wife 338, 343, 349, 350
wilderness 508
willing 597
wind 33, 87, 93, 130, 272, 469, 484
window 565
wine 14
winter 481
wise 138, 364, 509; see *intelligence,*
   prudence
wisp 538
wither 27
without 59, 96, 99, 157, 163, 199, 249,
   382, 393, 394, 397, 401, 412, 413, 428,
   432, 504, 507, 508, 596
witness 193
wo 16, 562
woman 333, 334, 335, 336, 337, 339,
   340, 342, 347, 353, 377
wonder 508
wonderful 555
wood 209, 362, 468, 521
wooden 566
wool 227, 441, 556, 591
word 130, 139
work 40, 61, 105, 510
world 121, 554
worm 60
worse 113
worst 515
worth 378
wound 224, 409
write 497
wrong 204

yard 269
year 166, 476, 488, 494, 513
yellow 243, 341, 410
yet 166, 168
young 280, 362, 407

Bibliography

Adams, G B 1964: 'The Last Language Census in Northern Ireland' pp 111-46 *Ulster Dialects: An Introductory Symposium* ed G B Adams (Ulster Folk and Transport Museum, Holywood, Co Down).

Agnew, J 1996: *Belfast Merchant Families in the Seventeenth Centuries* (Four Courts Press, Dublin).

Anderson, C 1830: *Historical Sketches of the Native Irish* (Oliver and Boyd, Edinburgh).

Anderson, J 1888: *History of the Belfast Library and Society for Promoting Knowledge commonly known as The Linen Hall Library* (Linen Hall Library, Belfast).

Andrews, J H 1974: *History in the Ordnance Survey Map: An Illustrated History* (The Blackstaff Press, Belfast).

Bardon, J 1982: A *History of Ulster* (The Blackstaff Press, Belfast).

Beckett, C 1967: *Fealsúnacht Aodha Mhic Dhomhnaill* (An Clóchomhar, Baile Átha Cliath).

— 1987: *Aodh Mac Domhnaill. Dánta* (Éigse Oirghialla, Baile Átha Cliath).

— 1995: A study of Robert S. McAdam's Manuscript English-Irish Dictionary, unpublished PhD thesis, Faculty of Arts, the Queen's University of Belfast.

Benn, G 1877: A *History of the Town of Belfast* (Marcus Ward, London).

Blaney, R (1996): *Presbyterians and the Irish Language* (Ulster Historical Foundation and Ultach Trust, Belfast).

Boyne, P 1987: *John O'Donovan. A Biography* (Boethius, Kilkenny).

Brady, A M and Cleeve, B 1985: *A Biographical Dictionary of Irish Writers* (Lilliput Press, Dublin).

Brett, C E B 1985: *Buildings of Belfast 1700–1914* (revised edition Friar's Bush Press, Belfast).

Campbell, F 1991: *The Dissenting Voice. Protestant Democracy from Plantation to Partition* (The Blackstaff Press, Belfast).

Carroll, D 1995: *The Man from God Knows Where* (Gartan, Dublin).

Cen. Ire 1659 A Census of Ireland 1659 ed S Pender (Stationery Office, Dublin 1939).

Chart, D A 1931: *The Drennan Letters* (HMSO Belfast).

Chichester, Sir A P B 1871: *History of the Family of Chichester* (London).

Chitham, E 1986: *The Brontës Irish Background* (MacMillan, London).

Corkery, D 1925: *The Hidden Ireland* (McGill and Son, Dublin).

Dawson, C 1992: *Peadar Ó Gealacáin. Scríobhaí* (Éigse Oirghialla, Baile Átha Cliath).

Day, A 1986: 'Computer-based Index to Irish Ordnance Survey Memoirs', *Donegal Annual* 38, 78–80.

— and McWilliams, P 1990–8: *Ordnance Survey Memoirs of Ireland,* 40 vols (Institute of Irish Studies, the Queen's University of Belfast).

Deane, A (ed) 1924: *Belfast Natural History and Philosophical Society Centenary Volume, 1821–1921* (Belfast).

de Brún, P 1987: 'The Irish Society's Bible Teachers', *Éigse* 22, 54–106.

de hÓir, É 1961: *Royal Irish Academy Centenary Exhibtion John O'Donovan (1806–61) and Eugene O'Curry (1794–1862)* (Royal Irish Academy, Dublin).

de Paor, P 1990: 'Roibeard Mac Ádhaimh agus Uiscí Fuinniúla na hÉireann Ceannródaí Gaeilge agus Teicneolaíochta', *Comhar* (Eanáir) 20–5.

Dinneen, Rev P 1927: *Irish-English Dictionary* (Irish Texts Society, Dublin and London).

Dunleavy, J E and Dunleavy, G W 1991: *Douglas Hyde. A Maker of Modern Ireland* (Berkeley, Oxford University of California Press).

Edwards, R D 1979: *Patrick Pearse, the Triumph of Failure* (Faber, London).

Elliot, M 1989: *Wolfe Tone: Prophet of Irish Independence* (Yale University Press, New Haven, CT).

Farmer, H 1987: *The Oxford Dictionary of Saints* (new edition, OUP, Oxford).

Ferguson, Lady 1896: *Sir Samuel Ferguson and the Ireland of his Day* (London and Edinburgh).

FGB: Foclóir Gaeilge-Béarla: Irish-English Dictionary N Ó Dónaill (Oifig an tSoláthair, Baile Átha Cliath/Dublin, 1977).

Fisher, J R and Robb, J H 1913: *Book of the Royal Belfast Academical Institution: The Centenary Volume 1810–1910* (RBN, Belfast).

Fitzgerald, G 1984: 'Estimates for baronies of minumum level of Irish-speaking among successive decennial cohorts 1771–1781, to 1861–1871', *Proceedings of the Royal Irish Academy* vol 84, sect C, 117–55.

Flanagan, D 1978: 'Seventeenth-century salmon fishing in Co. Down: River-Name Documentation', *Bulletin of the Ulster Place-Names Society* series 2, vol 1, 22–6.

Flower, R 1947: *The Irish Tradition* (Oxford).

Fortescue, Sir F 1858: *An Account of the Rt Hon. Sir Arthur Chichester* (London).

Froggatt, P 1981: 'Dr James MacDonnell, MD (1763–1845)', *The Glynns* 9, 17–31.

— 1984: 'MacDonnell, father and son: James (1763–1845); John (1796–1892), Surgeon of Dublin', *Journal of the Colleges of Physicians and Surgeons* 13, 198–206.

Gregory, Lady Augusta 1914: *Our Irish Theatre* (Putnam).

Greville-Nugent, Hon Mrs 1979: 'The Place of Seven Wonders', *The Midlands* vol 1 (Spring) 16–9 (reprinted from the *Capuchin Annual* 1948).

Hamilton, J N 1974: *The Irish of Tory Island* (Institute of Irish Studies, The Queen's University of Belfast).

Harbison, J 1989: 'The Belfast Harpers' Meeting, 1792: The Legacy', *Ulster Folklife* 35, 113–28.

Hayward, R 1952: *Belfast through the Ages* (Dundalk).

Hempton, D and Hill, M 1992: *Evangelical Protestantism in Ulster Society 1740–1890.* (Routledge, London and New York).

Hindley, R 1990: *The Death of the Irish Language. A Qualified Obituary* (Routledge, London).

Holmer, N M 1965: *The Dialects of Clare. Part II* (Royal Irish Academy, Dublin).

Hughes, A J 1987: 'Anecdotes relating to Peadar Ó Doirnín and Cormac na gCeann', *Seanchas Ard Mhacha* vol 12, no 2, 128–37.

— and McDaniel, E 'A nineteenth-century translation of the Deirdre story', *Emania* 5 (Autumn 1988) 41–7; 6 (Spring 1989) 41–7.

— 1989–90: 'Old Irish *Cnogba* modern townland *Crewbane:* Conclusive evidence for a Sound Change in Meath Irish', *Ainm* 4, 224–6.

— 1991: 'Irish place-names: some perspectives, pitfalls, procedures and potential', *Seanchas Ard Mhacha vol* 14, no 2, 116–48.

— 1991b: 'Ulster Scots *Gowk storm,* Ulster Gaelic *Sgairbhshíon na Cuaiche'*, *Ulster Folklife* 37, 107–8.

— 1991–3: 'On the Ulster Place-Names: *Glynn, Glenavy, Carrickfergus* and *Forkill' Ainm, Bulletin of the Ulster Place-Name Society* 5, 92–107.

— 1992: 'Deirdre Flanagan's "Belfast and the Place-Names Therein" in Translation', *Ulster Folklife* 38, 79–97.

— and Hannan, R J 1992: *Place-Names of Northern Ireland. Volume 2*

County Down II. The Ards (Institute of Irish Studies, Queen's University of Belfast).

— 1994: 'Gaeilge Uladh' Chapter 8, pp 610–60 of *Stair na Gaeilge* ed K McCone *et al* (An Sagart, Maigh Nuad/Maynooth).

— 1994b: 'A phonetic glossary of Tyrone Irish', *Zeitschrift für Celtische Philologie* 46, 119–63.

— 1997: 'Ulster Irish **char** as a reflex of Old Irish **níconro** rather than a Scottish import', *Studia Celtica in Memoriam Heinrich Wagner* 225–58 ed S Mac Mathúna and A Ó Corráin (Uppsala).

— forthcoming: 'The Virgin St Duinseach and her three Ulster Churches near Strangford Lough', *Celtica: James Carney Memorial Volume*.

Jamieson, J 1959: *History of the Royal Belfast Academical Institution 1810–1960* (RBAI, Belfast).

Killen, J 1990: *A History of the Linen Hall Library 1788–1988* (Linen Hall Library, Belfast).

MacLysaght, E 1972: *The Surnames of Ireland* (Irish Academic Press, Dublin).

Madden, R R 1843: *The United Irishmen, Their Lives and Times* vols 1–3, 3rd series (James Duffy, Dublin).

Magee, J 1988: 'The Neilsons of Rademon and Down: Educators and Gaelic Scholars', *Familia – Ulster Genealogical Review* vol 2, no 4, 64ff.

Maguire, W A 1993: *Belfast* (Keele University Press).

McCall, H 1881: *The House of Downshire* (Mullan, Belfast).

McCavitt, J 1998: *Sir Arthur Chichester, Lord Deputy of Ireland 1605–16* (Institute of Irish Studies, the Queen's University of Belfast).

Mac Gabhann, F 1993: 'The evil eye tradition in North-East Ireland', *Sinsear* 8, 89–100.

McGimpsey, C D 1994: A paper in *The Irish Language and the Unionist Tradition* ed P Mistéil, pp 7–16 (Ulster People's College/Ultach Trust, Belfast).

Mac Giolla Domhnaigh, G and Stockman, G 1991: *Athchló Uladh* (Comhaltas Uladh, Béal Feirste).

Mac Lochlainn, A 1995: 'The Famine in the Gaelic Tradition', *Irish Review* 17/18, 90–108.

McManus, D 1991: *A Guide to Ogham* (Maynooth Monographs, Maynooth).

McNeill, M 1960: *The Life and Times of Mary Ann McCracken* (Allen Figgis, Dublin).

Martin, F X and Byrne, F J (eds) 1973: *The Scholar Revolutionary. Eoin*

Mac Neill and the Making of Modern Ireland (Irish University Press, Dublin).

Moody, T W and Beckett, J C 1959: *Queen's University Belfast 1845–1949. The History of a University* vols 1 and 2 (Faber, London).

Morris, H 1921: 'Two Belfast Gaels [Samuel Bryson and Robert MacAdam]', *The Irish Book Lover* 13 (Aug–Sept) 1–6.

Neilson, Rev W 1808: *An Introduction to the Irish Language in three parts. I An original and comprehensive grammar II familiar phrases and dialogues III extracts from Irish books manuscripts, in the original character with copious tables of the contractions* (Dublin, reprinted by Iontaobhas Ultach, Belfast 1990).

Newmann, K 1993: *Dictionary of Ulster Biography* (Institute of Irish Studies, Queen's University of Belfast).

Ó Buachalla 1962: *Clár na Láimhscríbhinní Gaeilge i Leabharlann Phoiblí Bhéal Feirste* (An Clóchomhar, Baile Átha Cliath).

— 1963: 'An Bíobla i gContae Aontroma', *Feasta* (Deireadh Fómhair, Samhain, Nollaig).

— 1968: *I mBéal Feirste Cois Cuain* (An Clóchomhar, Baile Atha Cliath).

O'Byrne, C 1946: *As I Roved Out* (Irish News Ltd, Belfast).

Ó Casaide, S 1930: *The Irish Language in Belfast and County Down A.D. 1601–1850* (Dublin).

Ó Conluain, P 1989: 'The Last Native Irish-speakers of Tyrone', *Dúiche Néill* 4, 101–18.

Ó Corráin, A 1989: *A Concordance of Idiomatic Expressions in the Writings of Séamus Ó Grianna* (Institute of Irish Studies, the Queen's University of Belfast).

Ó Cróinín, S 1980: *Seanchas Amhlaoibh Í Luínse* S Ó Cróinín a thóg síos. D Ó Cróinín a chuir in eagar (Comhairle Bhéa-loideas Éireann, Baile Átha Cliath).

Ó Cuív, B 1989–90: 'Dinnshenchas – The Literary Exploitation of Irish PlaceNames', *Ainm* 4, 90–106.

Ó Dochartaigh, C 1987: *Dialects of Ulster Irish* (Institute of Irish Studies, Queen's University of Belfast).

Ó Duibhín, C 1991: *The Irish language in Co. Down since 1750* (Cumann Gaelach Leath Cathail).

— forthcoming: booklet plus cassette of the Irish texts recorded by Dögen.

Ó Fiaich, T and Ó Caithnia, L 1979: *Art Mac Bionaid: Dánta* (Éigse Oirghialla, Baile Átha Cliath).

Ó hAilín, T 1969: 'Irish Revival Movements' pp 81–100 of B Ó Cuív (ed) A *View of the Irish Language* (Stationery Office, Dublin).

Ó hEochaidh, S, Ní Néill, M and Ó Catháin, S 1977: *Síscéalta ó Thír Chonaill: Fairy Legends from Donegal* (Irish Folklore Commission, Dublin).

Ó hOgáin, D 1990: *Myth, Legend and Romance: An Encyclopaedia of the Irish Folk Tradition* (Ryan, London).

O'Laverty, Rev J 1878–95: *An Historical Account of the Diocese of Down and Connor Ancient and Modern* vols 1–5 (James Duffy, Dublin).

Ó Máille, T S 1948 and 1952: *Sean-Fhocla Chonnacht I & II* (Oifig and tSoláthair, Baile Átha Cliath).

Ó Mainnín, M 1992: *The Place–Names of Northern Ireland, Volume 3, County Down III: The Mournes* (Institute of Irish Studies, Queen's University of Belfast).

Ó Maolfabhail, A 1989: 'An tSuirbhéireacht Ordanáis agus Logainmneacha na hÉireann 1824–34' *Proceedings of the Royal Irish Academy* vol 89, sect C, 3–66.

Ó Muirgheasa, É 1907: *Seanfhocla Uladh,* an chéad eagrán (Conradh na Gaedhilge, Baile Átha Cliath).

— 1931: *Seanfhocla Uladh,* an dara heagrán (Oifig and tSoláthair, Baile Átha Cliath).

— 1969: *Dhá Chéad de Cheoltaibh Uladh,* an dara heagrán in eagar ag T.F. Beausang (Comhaltas Uladh, Béal Feirste).

— 1976: *Seanfhocail Uladh,* an tríú heagrán leasuithe le Nollaig Ó hUrmoltaigh (Oifig and tSoláthair, Baile Átha Cliath).

Ó Muirí, R 1994: *Láimhscríbhinn Staire an Bhionadaigh. Comhrac na nGael agus na nGall le Chéile* (Éigse Oirghialla, Muineachán).

Ó Murchú, M 1989: *East Perthshire Gaelic* (Dublin Institute for Advanced Studies, Dublin).

Ó Néill, S 1966: 'The Hidden Ulster: Gaelic Pioneers in the North', *Studies* 55, 60–6.

O'Rahilly, T F 1932: *Irish Dialects Past and Present* (Browne and Nolan, Dublin).

— 1946: *Early Irish History and Mythology* (Dublin Institute for Advanced Studies, Dublin).

O'Reilly, C C 1993: 'The Development of the Irish Language in Belfast: A Brief Historical Background', *Ulster Local Studies* vol 15, no 1 (Summer) 72–79.

Ó Siochfhradha, P (nom de plume An Seabhac) 1926: *Seanfhocail na Muimhneach* (Cló Seandána, Corcaigh).

— (nom de plume An Seabhac) 1984: *Seanfhocail na Mumhan* 2 heagrán in eagar ag P. Ua Maoileoin (An Gúm, Baile Átha Cliath).

OSL Derry John O'Donovan's Letters from County Londonderry (1834) ed G Mawhinney (Ballinascreen Historical Society 1992).

OSL Down 'Letters containing information relative to the antiquities of the County of Down collected during the progress of the Ordnance Survey in 1834'. Supplement to *Leabharlann* iii (1909).

OSM: Ordnance Survery Memoirs of Ireland, ed A Day and P McWilliams (Institute of Irish Studies, the Queen's University of Belfast, 1990–8).

Ó Snodaigh, P 1995: *Hidden Ulster: Protestants and the Irish Language* (Lagan Press, Belfast).

Ó Tuama, S 1972: *The Gaelic League Idea* (Mercier Press, Cork).

Ó Tuathail, É 1933: *Sgéalta Mhuintir Luinigh: Munterloney Folk-Tales* (Irish Folklore Commission, Dublin).

Paczolay, G 1997: *European Proverbs in 55 Languages* (Vesprém, Hungary).

Pedersen, H 1984: *Scéalta Mháirtín Neile. Bailiúchán Scéalta ó Árainn* H Pedersen a thóg síos sa bhliain 1895, Ole Munch-Pedersen a chóirigh agus a chuir in eagar (Comhairle Bhéaloideas Éireann, Baile Átha Cliath).

Plummer, C 1910: *Vitae Sanctorum Hiberniae* (Tomus Secundus) (Oxford).

Quiggin, E C 1906: *A Dialect of Donegal* (University of Cambridge, Cambridge).

Robb, J 1946: 'A Famous Irish Grammar', *Irish News* 9 January 1946.

Robinson, M 1985: *The Concise Scots Dictionary* (Aberdeen University Press, Aberdeen).

Robinson, P 1986: *Carrickfergus: Irish Historical Towns Atlas No. 2* (Royal Irish Academy, Dublin).

Shearman, H 1935: *Belfast Royal Academy 1785–1935* (H M Strain & Sons, Belfast).

Smith, G 1902: *Belfast Literary Society 1801–1901* (Belfast).

Smyth, J 1993: 'Freemasonry and the United Irishmen', pp 167–75 of *The United Irishmen: Republicanism, Radicalism and Rebellion* ed D Dickson, D Keogh and K Whelan (Lilliput Press, Dublin).

Stockman, G 1974: *The Irish of Achill, Co. Mayo* (Institute of Irish Studies, Queen's University of Belfast).

Stokes, W (ed) 1905: *Félire Óengusso Céli Dé. The Martyrology of Óengus the Culdee* (H Bradshaw Society, London).

Strauss, E 1995: *Dictionary of European Proverbs* 3 vols (Routledge, London).

Toner, G and Ó Mainnín, M 1992: *The Place-Names of Northern Ireland, Volume 1, County Down 1: Newry and South-West Down* (Institute of Irish Studies, Queen's University of Belfast).

Ua Súilleabháin, S 1994: 'Gaeilge na Mumhan' Chapter 6, pp 479–538 of *Stair na Gaeilge* ed K McCone *et al* (An Sagart, Maigh Nuad/Maynooth).

von Wartburg, W 1971: *Évolution et Strucure de la Langue Française,* 10ème édition (Francke, Bern).

Wagner, H 1958 *Linguistic Atlas and Survey of Irish Dialects* vol 1, maps (Dublin Institute for Advanced Studies, Dublin).

— and Ó Baoill, C 1969: *Linguistic Atlas and Survey of Irish Dialects* vol 4, Ulster, with appendices for the Isle of Man and Scotland (Dublin Institute for Advanced Studies, Dublin).

— and Mac Congáil, N 1983: *Oral Literature from Dunquin* (Belfast).

Walker, B M and McCreary, A 1994: *Degrees of Excellence: The Story of Queen's, Belfast 1845–1995* (Institute of Irish Studies, Queen's University of Belfast).

Walsh, Rev L 1844: *The Home Mission Unmasked* ... (Belfast).

Watson, S 1984: 'Séamus Ó Duilearga's Antrim Notebooks – I Texts', *Zeitschrift für Celtische Philologie* 40, 74–117.

—1987 'Séamus Ó Duilearga's Antrim Notebooks – II Language', *Zeitschrift für Celtische Philologie* 42, 138–218.

Welch, R (ed) 1996: *The Oxford Companion to Irish Literature* (OUP, Oxford).

Whitaker, T K 1982: 'James Hamilton Delargy', *The Glynns* 10, 20–5.

Williams, F 1986: Review of *Seanfhocail na Muimhneach* by An Seabhac, *Proverbium* 3, 407–9

—1995: ' Six Hundred Gaelic Proverbs Collected in Ulster by Robert MacAdam', *Proverbium* 12, 343–55.

Young, R 1894–5: 'The Irish Harpers in Belfast in 1792', *Ulster Journal of Archaeology* series 2, vol 1, 120–7.

General Index